ITALIAN AMERICANS

AND

THEIR PUBLIC AND PRIVATE LIFE

Proceedings of the 24th Annual Conference of the
American Italian Historical Association,
New Haven, CT,
November 14-16, 1991

Co-sponsored by the
New England Chapter of NIAF
and the
Italian American Historical Society of Greater New Haven

Edited by

Frank J. Cavaioli

Angela Danzi

Salvatore J. LaGumina

The American Italian Historical Association
c 1993

Founded in 1966, the American Italian Historical Association is an interdisciplinary group of scholars and lay people who seek to promote the understanding of the Italian experience in America. The Association promotes research through regional and national activities, including the annual conference and the publication of its proceedings.

Library of Congress Catalog Card Number: 92: 56143

IBSN: 0-934675-30-9 (soft)
IBSN: 0-934675-29-5 (hard)
IBSN: 0743-474X

Published in the United States of America by
The American Italian Historical Association, Inc.
209 Flagg Place
Staten Island, NY 10304

Printed on Recycled Paper
by Harbinger Publications

CONTENTS

PART III. RELIGION

PART IV. COMMUNITY

PART V. TRANSITION

PRESIDENT'S MESSAGE

As the momentum continued to gather for the celebration of the Columbian Quincentennial in the latter months of 1991, the American Italian Historical Association also moved toward its Annual conference held on November 14-16 of the same year. In contrast to much of the planning for the events related to Columbus by other organizations, the AIHA once again reflected its own sense of what the Italian American experience has truly been. The site of the conference was New Haven, one of the major centers of immigrant settlement and community development in New England. The program itself consisted of a richly diversified examination of the public and private dimensions of ethnic life.

From its founding as a scholarly association that sought to offer a more vigorous, objective and valid interpretation of Italians in North America, the Association has continued to grow in its membership as well as to evolve by the breadth of their interests. The increasingly wide range of approaches that has provided us an even more complex perspective on this subject matter was emphatically viable in the papers presented at the conference. The program sessions included papers on women and the fine arts; comedians of southern Italian origins; representations of immigrant life in theater and film; economic mobility; political leadership; creative literature; religious life; community organizations; folklore; feminism and various other topics. The participants provided papers on studies of Italian experience in a broad spectrum of geographical settings which included Texas, Wisconsin, New York and New Jersey. Papers on the more local communities of Waterbury, Bridgeport, and Ridgefield within the host state of Connecticut were also on the program. In keeping with the intention of the Association to allow a flexible format, other papers examined research questions on Italians in Canada, Argentina, and of course Italy, the country of origin. My remarks here can only provide a glimpse of the rich diversity of issues that comprised the program of the conference. The robust character of the program of the 1991 conference is also underscored by the support it received from the local Italian American community. The conference was co-sponsored by the New England chapter of the National Italian American Foundation and by the Italian American Historical Society of Greater New Haven. The officers of the Association are keenly aware of the importance of such cooperation in contributing to the success of its programs. We are equally mindful of how difficult it has been to secure this support. We deeply appreciate the willingness of local organizations to extend their material assistance and moral endorsement to our programs and activities.

Finally, it is necessary to acknowledge the contributions to the success of the conference that were made by some specific individuals. No one can possibly know, unless he or she has done it, how much effort is required to organize and stage the annual conference. Unlike larger organizations with a paid staff, the Association relies directly upon the generous service and devotion of its members. As the President of the Association, in behalf of our entire membership, I must indicate the great appreciation that we all must hold for John Arcudi, the general chairman of the conference; Salvatore J. LaGumina, the program chairman; and Frank J. Cavaioli, and Angela Danzi, the special coordinators. By their work, these individuals not only made the conference possible, but carefully steered it toward a high level of accomplishment and success.

The future of Italian American studies rests upon the persistent dedication and efforts of individual scholars who produce the research, analysis and writing that establish and maintain the field. It equally depends, however, upon the willingness of individuals to work together to provide the forums through which this material can reach the public. It also requires the continuation of an organizational vehicle to bring scholars together for the critical exchange of ideas such as the AIHA has represented so successfully over the past 25 years. The 1991 conference at New Haven provided a valuable manifestation of all these conditions. The meeting will be remembered as one that not only brought formidable personal satisfactions to the individuals who participated, but also as an event that reflected very well upon the role that the Association has played in meeting the difficult responsibility to serve as a unique agency in maintaining the field of Italian American studies.

Richard N. Juliani

INTRODUCTION

In arriving upon the theme, "Italian Americans and Their Public and Private Life," the organizers of the Twenty-Fourth Annual Conference of the American Italian Historical Association, which convened in New Haven, Connecticut, November 14-16, 1991, co-sponsored by the New England Chapter of the National Italian American Foundation and the Italian American Historical Society of Greater New Haven, noted what was fast becoming an obvious fact: Italian Americans were playing an increasingly large role in public affairs while clinging to their traditional ethnic values. The American Italian Historical Association has reflected this development by providing a forum for scholars in the social sciences and the humanities, as well as other leaders in public life, for recording and analyzing this aspect of their history.

Through systematic-scientific research the American Italian Historical Association has illuminated the true experience of Italians in North America. Simultaneously, the Association has preserved that experience though the publication of its PROCEEDINGS for all interested persons to enlarge their understanding of this important ethnic group. The Association has been engaged in this endeavor for nearly three decades. Of all the numerous Italian American organizations active in contemporary society, the American Italian Historical Association has produced the most comprehensive chronicle worthy of study and constant re-evaluation. As time goes by we have come to realize that the earlier generation of immigrants from the old world contributed significantly to the development of a successful United States of America and that, therefore, their history was vital to that success and uniquely important in itself. We continue to record and re-evaluate that history in these PROCEEDINGS.

We dedicate this volume to the first generation of Italian immigrants who left their homeland to take advantage of America's opportunities to improve their lives. They made an indelible impact on their adopted land. Their anguish and tribulations, their successes and accomplishments constitute an important lesson for future generations.

Frank J. Cavaioli
   SUNY Farmingdale, Emeritus
Angela Danzi
   SUNY Farmingdale
Salvatore J. LaGumina
   Nassau Community College, SUNY

RESUME` OF PAPERS

PART I, A PUBLIC LIFE. This opening chapter focuses on the extraordinary careers of two Italian Americans: Peter Sammartino and Ella Grasso. In his essay, Frank J. Cavaioli renders an informative retrospective of Sammartino, who passed away in 1992, as one of the most outstanding educators and civic leaders within the Italian American community in recent years. The article traces the Italian influence on the young Sammartino and how he, together with his resourceful wife Sally, founded Fairleigh Dickinson University. John Purmont, a one-time secretary to Governor Grasso, offers a personal memoir of the first woman elected to a governorship in her own right. Purmont centers on the unmistakably positive influence her ethnicity had on her life and career.

PART II, FAMILY, concentrates on papers that deal with aspects of family life. Mary Russo Demetrick demonstrates the family theme in her short but telling poem about enduring Italian roots. Mario Aste accomplishes this by examining filmic metaphors as representations of Italian American family life in the popular movie <u>Moonstruck</u>. He finds that the movie presents several stereotypes as fact, without any substantial countering observations thereby perpetuating stereotypical images. For Cindy Hahamovitch the family theme is exposed in the work experience of southern Italians, mostly women and children, who took seasonal work on New Jersey's farms. Contrary to the wishes of American Progressives who opposed child labor, these Italian immigrants sought employment as family units, not as a permanent solution to their economic problems, but rather as a temporary status so that their children would not long have to remain as field workers. Louis Keefer deals with family issues from a totally different perspective, namely by recounting an interesting episode revolving around Italian prisoners of war detained in the United States. The interaction between 50,000 World War II Italian internees and the various Italian American communities underscored the adoption of a surrogate type of familial relationship on the part of the host society. Joseph Salituro emphasizes the salience of family by an in-depth history of his family in Wisconsin.

This microscopic study emphasizes mobility and assimilation thereby confirming the John Bodnar thesis that ordinary immigrant families accommodated themselves and ultimately fashioned a way of life firmly ensconced in America's social, economic and political middle class.

PART III, RELIGION, demonstrates that the dynamics of religion explain much about the historic Italian American experience. Flora Breidenbach illustrates this by her account of life and labor of Fr. Samuel Mazzuchelli who traversed the frontier wilderness in mid-nineteenth century. Animated by a strong religious impulse, his respect of native Americans and Catholic settlers in this area as well as his ecumenical spirit won him deserved recognition. Secondo Casarotto investigated the Italian immigrant response to Protestant proselytizing in Buffalo, New York, in the late nineteenth and early twentieth centuries. Accordingly, he discusses methods used by these churches to deal with the "Italian problem" and compares them with the Catholic Church. Significantly both Protestant and Catholic institutions resorted to the language/ethnic model as the major means of integration. In her study of Our Lady of Pompei parish in New York City, Mary Elizabeth Brown utilized extant parish records to trace the role of Italian laymen in the development of parish life. Thus she presents lay activity in parish organizations such as sodalities, ushers societies, social service structures and church aid organizations, especially those involved in fund raising, as units that played a foremost role in parish life.

PART IV, COMMUNITY, considers how Italian Americans deal with the dynamics of community life. Suzanne Krase researched the little-explored realm of mental health to center on women's issues. She argues that in order to provide meaningful screening and health care for Italian American neighborhoods heavily populated by first and second generations, the ethnic background of the group must be taken into account. Her study of a Brooklyn, New York, enclave leads her to conclude that considerations of ethnicity are as important as socio-economic class issues in dealing with this population. Judith DeSena's microscopic investigation of a multi-ethnic neighborhood in Brooklyn, New York, emphasizes the social interaction that transpired between African Americans and Italian Americans in recent years. She concludes that a high level of social cohesion was achieved and that this example could well serve as a model for ethnic group interaction elsewhere. The relationship between African Americans and Italian Americans is also the subject of Jerome Krase's study which stresses a phenomenological approach to inter-group relations. Rejecting exclusive reliance on prevailing journalistic impressions, Jerome Krase resorted to extensive first person interviews to measure African American student reaction to an Italian feast celebration. He sees this as a much more useful tool for understanding sub-cultures. A failure to consider the characteristics of the ethnic community is the subject of Chris Newton's history of the Boston Italian American theater. Although the New Deal was moving in the right direction in providing financial support via the WPA for on-going theater to a depression-laden populace, the government agency was ignorant of the theatrical interests of Italian Americans. The consequence was that the WPA sponsored plays that evoked little interest in the ethnic community, while it overlooked extant theatrical vehicles that much more readily and meaningfully connected with their heritage. Finally, Robert Immordino offers a meaningful examination of the interaction between the community and the Botto House in Haledon, New Jersey. Built by an Italian immigrant, this residence became the focal point of early twentieth century labor upheavals that convulsed the region and now endures as a museum evoking the memories of the era that was so vital to Italian immigrant workers.

PART V, TRANSITION, scrutinizes aspects of ethnic transition from dissimilar perspectives. Accordingly, Valentino Belfiglio provides a historical account of northern Italian immigration to nineteenth century Mexico. Welcomed because of an apparent similarity in cultures due to the Latin and religious backgrounds, many of these immigrants and their descendants migrated to El Paso, Texas, which also manifests a strong Hispanic and therefore Latin environment. Salvatore J. LaGumina traces the role played by an Italian American politician in promoting American foreign policy. Specifically he demonstrates that President Harry S. Truman's administration relied heavily on Sicilian-born New York City Mayor Vincent Impellitteri to counter the threat of a Communist electoral victory in Italy in the post-World War II period. Anthony LaRuffa offers a theoretical and provocative paper on contemporary mythmaking in his effort to link the past with the present. Through literary criticism of Italian American fictional works, Rose DeAngelis analyzes and compares treatment of women. She concludes that the literature demonstrates a significant transition of women's role. In their welcome study of Italian American comedy, Salvatore Primeggia, Floyd Vivino and Joseph Varacalli posit the proposition that the southern Italian American comedic tradition, as exemplified by Matteo Cannizzaro, Lou Monte, Louie Prima and Dom DeLouise, underwent evolution. Although all of these comics demonstrate a familiarity with their ethnic heritage, it is most apparent in the performances of Cannizzaro and least typified by work of DeLouise. Finally, Richard Renoff has provided a study of Italian American participation in pugilism as a unique example of transition from an entry level to greater acceptance and assimilation.

PART I
A PUBLIC LIFE

Peter Sammartino

PETER SAMMARTINO

FRANK J. CAVAIOLI

The sudden deaths of Peter Sammartino and his wife Sally (the former Sylvia Scaramelli) on March 29, 1992, at their home in Rutherford, NJ, shocked those of us who knew and worked with them in the American Italian Historical Association. He was 87 years old and she was 88.

Peter represented the quintessential renaissance man of the twentieth century as educator, scholar, administrator, traveler, philanthropist, author, patron of the arts, and civic leader. Of his many achievements, the greatest was the founding of Fairleigh Dickinson University in 1942, and, up to 1967 when he retired as President, developed it into seven successful campuses with an enrollment of more than 20,000 students and an endowment of $62,000,000 consisting of stocks, bonds, and real estate. Today Fairleigh Dickinson is the largest private university in New Jersey with an enrollment of 12,000 at campuses in Rutherford, Teaneck-Hackensack, and Florham Park-Madison. There is also a branch in Wroxton, England. He combined his many talents with boundless energy to earn the distinction of becoming the most prominent Italian American educator of this century.

The concept of founding Fairleigh Dickinson University originated in 1933 when Peter was teaching at the New College, the experimental branch of Columbia University's Teachers College. In an exciting intellectual environment students took two basic seminars: the Central Seminar and the Contemporary Society Seminar. Students set their own goals, spent a year abroad, one term in an agricultural country, and then served an internship in teaching. This course of study led to a master's degree.

In 1942 Fairleigh Dickinson became a reality in the old Ivison Castle in Rutherford with 60 students. The initial decision to start a college had been made four days before the attack on Pearl Harbor. Peter's determination to succeed prevailed in spite of the Great Depression and the beginning of World War II. The college was initially financed by $15,000 from Peter, $15,000 from Sally's father, and $30,000 from Colonel Fairleigh Dickinson, for whom the college was named. Many years later, in looking back at his many accomplishments, he said, "...the thoughts that gave my wife and me the greatest glow is in our founding and building what is now Fairleigh Dickinson University, for it is in serving others that life becomes meaningful." The University celebrated its fiftieth anniversary in 1992.

Peter had stated on many occasions that Sally provided the guidance and support so necessary for success. He has said, "My life really has been inseparable from that of my wife Sally." She helped build Fairleigh Dickinson University. She received no salary for the first twelve years, and thereafter only a modest one. Sally organized the admission's and registrar's offices, eventually receiving the title of Dean of University Admissions, and she chaired many policy-making committees. She received numerous honors and served on various commissions and boards. Smith College, her alma mater, awarded her the Smith College Medal in recognition of her outstanding achievements in education. Sally also earned a master's degree in history from Columbia University. As Peter had stated, "We were an unusual duumvirate, not similar to any other in the history of higher education."

Peter's parents, Guy and Eva (Amendola), arrived in New York City through Ellis Island in 1901 as part of the mass movement of four million Italians who came in the period 1880-1920. He was born August 15, 1904, in New York City and spent his childhood in the Tompkins Square Park neighborhood, attending Public Schools 122 and 25 and Stuyvesant High School. He received a B.A. degree from City College in 1924 and M.A. and Ph.D. degrees from New York University in 1928 and 1931, respectively. While at City College he participated in Italian clubs and joined the Italian fraternity, Alpha Phi Delta. Soon after completing graduate work, he studied at the Sorbonne. Commenting on how he was able to complete his doctoral thesis while conducting other work activities, he stated, "I was embarked on a pattern that was to mark my life until I retired in 1967, that of working night and day and enjoying it." His weekly schedule consisted of working from seven in the morning to eleven at night, and on weekends from eight to five, confining his social life to Saturday and Sunday evenings.

In the meantime, he took teaching positions at public schools where he taught high school Italian and French in New York City and the Preparatory School of City College. He also found time to write language textbooks and a French language standardized test.

Fully aware of the ethnic constellation in New York City, young Peter was influenced most by his Godfather, Captain Achille Cuomo Cerulli, who taught him Italian, took him on parades with Garibaldian veterans and to Staten Island to visit the home where Garibaldi lived as a guest of Antonio

Meucci who was the first person to receive a patent for the telephone. Peter said of Cerulli:

> He came to America in 1900 and founded one of the first Italian newspapers in the United States, *LA TROMBA*. His greatest delight was to march or be with the Garibaldi veterans. Every July 4th, the anniversary of the birth of Garibaldi, at his home on First Avenue we would squeeze into an open horsedrawn carriage with three or four red-shirted and bemedaled Garibaldinians. We would proceed first to Washington Square Park, where there was a statue of Garibaldi, lay a wreath at the Great Liberator's feet, and listen to a few ardent speeches.
>
> I went to see my Godfather every afternoon and he taught me Italian. We started with the sillabario, with its phonetic exercises. There was reading, dictation, and composition and, throughout, conversation that opened up a new world. I was often there when he had visitors. I remember meeting Mother Cabrini, when she sought his help in setting up a small hospital for Italians on Spring Street in New York. I remember also meeting Anthony Caminetti, who had just been made commissioner of immigration for Ellis Island.

In 1982, upon the one-hundredth anniversary of the death of Garibaldi, Peter proudly served as the National Chairman of the Garibaldi Centennial Commemoration. He became acquainted with the great Italian hero's great-granddaughter, Anita Garibaldi Hibbert, and he arranged to have her two sons visit the Meucci-Garibaldi House in Staten Island, New York. Peter also led a delegation on a sentimental pilgrimage to Caprera, an island off the northeastern coast of Sardinia to visit the house that Garibaldi had built with his own hands.

In recent years Peter had devoted much of his time to the study and promotion of Italian contributions to the creation of America. Inspired by the pioneer Italian American historian, Giovanni Schiavo, he worked tirelessly with Dr. Margherita Marchione in the support of her research and publications on the life and writings of Philip Mazzei, a friend of Thomas Jefferson and an important influence in the American revolutionary and constitutional periods. With the assistance of Italian Americans in Providence, Rhode Island, Peter spearheaded the cataloguing project and exhibit of books and maps, written by Italians in the creation of America, at the John Carter Brown Library of Brown University in 1981. This exhibit was also shown at the Strozzi Plaza in Florence, Italy, and at the Museum of History of the Smithsonian in Washington, D.C. He stated in 1984:

> If we take the sum total of the influences, of philosophy, of government and in jurisprudence, discoveries,

exploration, the influence on literature, on music, on art, on architecture and on science, then America would not have been the country it is without the contributions of Italians, and this stretches from the thirteenth century to the nineteenth centuries.

In 1941, Peter attended an educational workshop in California to learn about that state's successful community college movement. He learned that the same Anthony Caminetti, whom he had met as a child and who had been Commissioner of Ellis Island, had played an important role in creating college opportunities for young people who lacked financial resources to go away to college. Caminetti, as a California state senator at the turn of the century, worked with other legislators to use vacant high school buildings after regular hours for two-year college student programs. A new tax on gasoline was levied and, with the increased use of the automobile, this gasoline tax generated enough revenue to allow California to establish an elaborate community college system.

Again, this time in 1974, Peter fondly remembered Caminetti when he organized the drive to restore Ellis Island, obtain congressional appropriations, and succeeded in getting the Island opened to the public.

Peter had been an active participant in Italian American affairs. His sound guidance as a long-time member of the American Italian Historical Association Executive Council produced important scholarship in the ethnic studies field. Also, as Vice President of the Upper Atlantic Region of the National Italian American Foundation, he helped in establishing an Italian American visibility in the nation's capital and a national agenda. He served as Chairman of the Board of Trustees of Corfinio College and also in that capacity of the American Institute of Italian Studies. He was a Trustee of the American Italy Society and recipient of the Order of Merit of Italy.

His contributions to education produced exemplary results. He was a delegate to the White Conference on Education. President Lyndon B. Johnson appointed him to the Advisory Board of the Peace Corps and President Richard M. Nixon selected him to serve on the Board of Foreign Scholarships. Other important positions held by him were: Chairman of the Board of Directors of Villa Walsh College; Chairman-Emeritus of St. Stephen's School in Rome; Trustee of the Rutherford Free Library; Trustee of the New Jersey Historical Society; member of New Jersey Historical Commission's Committee on Historic Preservation; Vice-Chairman of the Friends of Cuttington College; member of the Board of Directors of the Tibetan Foundation; member of the American College in Switzerland Graduate Council; and Trustee of the Black House in Ellsworth, Maine. Peter served as a consultant to universities in thirty-two countries throughout Europe, Africa, and Asia, received honors in five countries, and was honored by seven others. In the meantime, he found time to write 18 books, numerous articles, and edit journals. He founded the International Association of University Professors and became its President. New York University gave him its Distinguished Alumni Award in 1968.

Peter's record as a patron of the arts characterized his selfless service to the community. He served as President and Trustee of the New York Cultural Center, on the Board of Governors of the New Jersey State Opera Society, on the Board of Trustees of the Garden State Ballet, and was a Life Fellow in the Royal Society of Arts, England. A man of many talents, Peter led the Shakespeare Oxford Society Palm Beach, Florida, Chapter as President. He resigned this position because of his failing health five months before his death.

As Peter and Sally entered their twilight years and, having passed their fiftieth wedding anniversary, he continued to maintain an active life. Good work and nutritional habits allowed him to remain involved in travel, serving on boards, doing charitable work, writing, and corresponding with friends and colleagues. Aware of the effects of old age, Peter addressed the challenge of retirement in 1985:

> We feel young, full of spirited ideas and anxious to try out new things, and yet we know that it can't last forever. We know full well that we are not as spry as we were ten or twenty years ago. We creak with age even though, when we are alone in our house, we may dance for a few minutes to some music we like just to convince ourselves we will possess some of the old-time energy. But we know, oh yes, we know that we are getting old and that some day the light will flicker out.

The life of Peter Sammartino reveals a remarkable career that mirrored success of the son of immigrant parents. He seized the opportunity offered to America's adopted sons and daughters. His driving ambition, obsession with work, teaching and administrative success, cultural activities, keen interest in Italian civilization and Italian American studies, and civic leadership contributed significantly to enriching the life of this nation. It can easily be understood why he was the driving force as chairman of the committee to refurbish and restore Ellis Island. Those of us who knew Peter and Sally all have fond memories. Mine go back to the summer of 1985 when my wife, Lorraine, and I visited him and Sally at their East Sullivan home in Maine. This marvelous home, furnished with exquisite Shaker furniture and American paintings, had served as the summer administrative office during the growth period of Fairleigh Dickinson University. We were in Maine because my ninety-year-old uncle and aunt had just moved from Bar Harbor to a lovely senior citizen home in nearby Ellsworth. Peter and Sally were gracious hosts as we spent a congenial evening conversing over a broad range of subjects. Sally, in particular, expressed an interest in the health of my uncle and aunt and their status in their apartment. Apparently she was concerned about her old age and Peter's, how those last years would be spent, and with whom. They had no children and no immediate heirs. Peter showed concern also. Several weeks later my uncle called me to tell me about an unexpected visit from a college president and his wife who had brought a bouquet of flowers to them and what delightful company they had been.

As time passed, Peter developed a hearing problem and, ever conscious of helping others, he formed the Committee for Hearing-Impaired (CHIP). Sally often accompanied him to executive council meetings of the American Italian Historical Association. The last one he attended in 1986, which met at the Center for Migrations Study in Staten Island, she had to repeat many points he had missed during our discussions.

The last few months were very painful for them. Peter had undergone surgery for the removal of a kidney in November 1991. He had been complaining of pain. Sally had developed Alzheimer's disease. It was difficult for this dynamic husband-wife team to be in failing health. They had accomplished so much in a lifetime. Nevertheless, in the spring of 1991 Peter had suggested an idea to have the works of Giovanni Schiavo edited to be made available to scholars and the public. Unfortunately he was unable to complete this worthy project. Right to the end he remained the quintessential educator-scholar. We in the American Italian Historical Association will miss Peter and Sally Sammartino and we can thank them for enriching our lives.

Sister Margherita Marchione, a close friend of this unique couple, eulogized them in a special memorial service at Fairleigh Dickinson University on April 23, 1992. She spoke warmly of them and stated that Peter and Sally had requested that a memorial service be a celebration and that when the occasion arose she was to read a poem by Alfred Lord Tennyson which they had selected to express their sentiments:

> Sunset and evening star
> And one clear call for me!
> And may there be no moaning of the bar
> When I put out to sea.

2

ELLA GRASSO

Jon E. Purmont

I first met Ella Grasso one summer evening in 1966 at a political gathering in Wallingford, Connecticut.

I had recently returned to Connecticut after a two-year stay in Italy. I moved through the receiving line, along with hundreds of other people, meeting various Connecticut political figures and, as my parents approached Ella Grasso, my mother proudly announced that "my son just came back from living in Rome, he speaks Italian." Ella Grasso turned to me in her friendly, gregarious manner and greeted me in flawless Italian. I blurted out "Piacere sua conoscenza," in my best Italian accent. That was my first introduction to this remarkable child of twentieth century pilgrims.

That impression of Ella Grasso — gregarious, friendly, outgoing and ready fluency with her parents' native tongue — has remained with me to this day. It etched in my mind recognition of the fact that here was a lady who never lost touch with the native language of her parents' ancestral homeland and who was always happy to meet people who shared — even in a small way — knowledge of that marvelous language and culture of Europe's southern frontier.

I interacted with her more directly in the 1970s and it became evident to me that pride in her Italian ancestry was something she kept foremost in her life. In addition, her close relationship with her parents, who came to America early in the twentieth century, remained a strong bond until their deaths.

When one discusses Ella Grasso one must focus first on her parents and on Windsor Locks, Connecticut. It was the town in which both her parents settled; and it was Ella's birthplace. Her parents came from the same area of northern Italy near Tortona although they had never met until settling in

Connecticut. Her mother, Maria Oliva, was from Medassina — now called Voghera, Italy, and her father Giacomo, or James, Tambussi was born in Perleto, Italy.[1]

Windsor Locks had a sizeable number of Italian immigrants from that area of Italy and it was natural that her parents settled there. Ella Grasso often recalled her early upbringing in that northern Connecticut town in a neighborhood filled with relatives and friends. In fact, at each end of Olive Street, where the Tambussis lived, were people they had known in Italy.

The town has been described by Bernard Asbell as a "milieu of scant means and status, but rich with striving and pervading tradition."[2] It was there that Ella Grasso was planted and where she bloomed — and where her sense of community was first developed and nurtured.

She was an only child born May 10, 1919 and when she spoke of her childhood surrounded by loving parents, aunts, cousins, uncles, and neighborhood friends, she spoke of it with fondness and affection. Her roots were there and her ambitions formed there — and she returned there for the last time on February 9, 1981.

As one looks at Ella Grasso's early, formative years in Windsor Locks, there were three major influences in her life. First, her parents, especially her father; second, Windsor Locks, particularly during the Depression; third, her education and schooling.

As an only child Ella Grasso's youthful world was clearly the focus of her parents' attention. Her mother, Ella said, had a passionate "love of learning"[3] which she passed on to her daughter. Maria Tambussi worked for a time in a mill in Windsor Locks and then for General Electric next to the Windsor Locks railroad station. She made five dollars a week, "her best wages,"[4] said her admiring daughter.

I believe, however, she was the apple of her father's eye — not untypical of any father's feelings but surely an Italian father's affection poured out to her.

Her wonderful recollections of her father tell the story very well. He worked first as a paper-mill hand, next as a small machine shop worker and then as a baker in Windsor Locks. He and his brother Natale operated the Windsor Locks Bakery.[5] From all accounts, James Tambussi was an able provider for his wife and daughter even during the depths of the Depression. His influence was large in her life. This memorable remembrance of him, written by Ella appeared in 1975:

> My father was as delighted to have me for his child as I was to be his daughter. I thought he was going to live forever, and I got the shock of my life when he died two years ago — I became a pathetic, fifty year old orphan. I still think of him all the time. He was a baker, and he used to work nights. He'd come home from work about 10 o'clock

in the morning, and when I was a very little girl I would rush out to meet him so we could walk back home together. I would tell him all my secrets, and he would listen patiently and kindly. He worked long hours, six days a week, but he always had time for me, and he took me seriously. From him I learned respect for others and persistence — he would never stop trying to get a vine to grow properly, or to solve a problem until he had succeeded. By his example I learned that one does not abandon a task. Quit? We didn't quit anything. When I think of my father, I think of him in a golden glow, I loved him dearly, and I respected him. He was one of the great people in my life.[6]

The second influence on her life was the community of Windsor Locks, particularly during the Depression years of the 1930s. Her memories of those difficult times remained indelibly fixed in her mind throughout her life. She put it this way:

One day my mother and I were walking home ... it was just dusk and in our little town of Windsor Locks there was such a chill in the air that it was horrible. The lights in the houses seemed to be dimmer and the bank had closed. This was absolutely traumatic because every penny that anyone had been able to save was there. And then not long after that I watched a family being evicted from their home. I knew the kids. I had gone to school with them and suddenly they were out and everyone looked at them strangely until other families were evicted too. I watched the WPA and the food programs. You know, some of them were not well managed, but they certainly were well-intentioned. They served a very real public purpose and I think that was the first time I realized that the machinery of government can be used for the service of people.[7]

It was an enduring impression that she carried with her into the world of politics but which also carried over to her deeply compassionate feelings for people whose lives were irrevocably changed either by the loss of a job, loss of home or even the loss of a loved one.

I often heard her recall those bleak and sad times of the Depression. One particular occasion stands out: an informal news conference in her State Capitol office in the summer of 1979. She had returned from a visit to Camp David as a guest of President Jimmy Carter. The President had summoned some of the nation's leaders to the Presidential retreat in the Catoctin Mountains in Maryland. The Governor spoke of the meetings she had attended and said how important it was that the President forge a strong policy to deal with the enormous social and economic problems the country faced. She recalled, for those assembled, how in an earlier time, another

Democratic President had to undertake similar bold initiatives to move the country forward offering hope where there was so much despair.

It was vintage Ella Grasso, striking the pose of having rubbed shoulders with the high and mighty but never forgetting to focus on the fact that people were hurting: interest rates were moving higher, inflation was excessive, and the economy stagnant. Government had to be mobilized to help people — just as it had been in Franklin Roosevelt's time.

The next major influence in her life, in my judgment, was her education both within the confines of the classroom and that which she learned in her association with schoolmates, teachers, professors, and colleagues.

In Ella Grasso's case the most significant educational influence was a nun — Mother de Chantal whom she called the "most remarkable woman I've ever met."[8] It must have been a special relationship because when interviewed in 1980 and asked to name five women she most admired, Ella Grasso listed Mother de Chantal on that list.[9] The others included Madame Curie, Mother Teresa, Margaret Mead, and her own mother. It seems ironic that in a Gallup Poll released December 25, 1980, Ella Grasso was the fourth most admired woman in America and Mother Teresa was number one.[10]

Mother de Chantal's admiring pupil remembered the special spark that lit up her life in those early grammar school years. Mother de Chantal, Ella said, would "tell all those little kids that each of them had a very special gift, and they had a special opportunity. There was one thing they could do better than anybody, and they had an obligation to develop that quality, because that's why they had been born. So that became part of my thinking."[11]

In 1932, Ella Grasso won a scholarship to the Chaffee School in Windsor, Connecticut. Chaffee, described by one writer as an "elegant place" with a "picture book campus,"[12] was considered an outstanding preparatory school for exclusive private colleges.

Her academic achievements at Chaffee were significant, leading to a scholarship to Mount Holyoke College in South Hadley, Massachusetts. Speculation in her Chaffee yearbook that she would someday be Mayor of Windsor Locks apparently "horrified her." "Politics," she said, "I mean I aspired to something eminently greater."[13]

This remarkable achiever broke new ground even then by moving into the realm of an elite educational institution by utilizing her intellectual abilities and scholarly dedication — a combination she would apply with great success in her public career.

It was during those Mount Holyoke years that she matured into a young woman with a clear vision of what she wanted to do with her life. At Mount Holyoke "I was always taken seriously," she said. "And I had many models to emulate among the faculty, administration, and speakers who came to campus. It was where I was encouraged to think of my life not as something that would happen to me but something I would shape for myself."[14]

Her academic concentration was in history and economics and she received a B.A. degree in 1940 followed two years later with an M.A. in economics and sociology. In her own words she recalled her college years with great affection:

> I did all sorts of blissful things. There were some real giants on that faculty, early leaders of thinking about the consumer movement and about world economics.[15]

Like most college students, Ella Grasso fits the pattern that Seymour Martin Lipset suggests in his marvelous monograph *Rebellion in the University*. Lipset suggests that students' personal attributes and characteristics are shaped and molded by their social and cultural backgrounds. Yet once a student enters college his persona is affected by the classes he or she attends, relationships established with faculty, the friends selected, and particularly in extra-curricular activities.[16] Mount Holyoke was where Ella Grasso's plans for the future were developed more concretely. A letter from her college roommate lends credence to that conclusion. She wrote:

> At Holyoke a long time ago I knew Ella very well and loved her very much ... nothing has taken away the memory of our intimacy in college. I remember walking with Ella through the snow on Mr. Skinner's place next to the Sycamores, and on cold New England Saturday nights walking out to Ella's church. I remember our rooms in Rocky and lying in our beds in the dark talking about all the things we meant to do in the world. Well she did them all — and then some! But even before she became great and full of grand achievements I never forgot that strong, clear spoken straight standing girl in her blouse and long wool skirt who seemed to set the air around her vibrating with purpose and life.[17]

It was there at Mount Holyoke that she set out to do all those great things many of us aim to do in life. And it was from there she moved into the world of politics believing "in a very real sense of a relationship between politics and the lives of people — that what happens to us was affected by government and I wanted to be part of that government."[18] It was to be a marvelous journey for this remarkable child of twentieth century pilgrims.

What Ella Grasso achieved in terms of education and striving was in some measure not unlike what other children of immigrant parents accomplished as well. In her case, however, her achievements loom large because she was a woman who chose a life in a political world predominantly male; a world not known for gentility. In fact, it was once described by the late Connecticut Congressman Stewart McKinney as a "world of sharks."[19] That notion, coupled with the fact that she came from an ethnic group just beginning to move into elective politics in Connecticut, made her attainments even more admirable. She achieved elective office first as a State Representative in 1952, Secretary of State in 1958, Congresswoman in 1970, and Governor in 1975.

The details of her accomplishments in Connecticut and national politics is not the account I relate here. Rather, I want to share some personal observations of this remarkable woman. Further, I want to suggest what I perceive to be attributes she possessed that led to such a successful career.

As a child of twentieth century pilgrims, her trailblazing achievements are significant because she was the first — the first of many who now enjoy the fruits of her early labors. When Ella Grasso commenced her electoral career she was one of forty-one women in Connecticut's three-hundred-fifteen member legislature. Today, forty-three women serve in a General Assembly of one-hundred fifty-one members. Many female legislators serve in major positions of leadership at the state capitol. More telling, however, is that three members of Connecticut's six member Congressional representatives is female, and two of Connecticut's largest city governments are led by women.

Nationally, there are three women governors in states as disparate as Kansas, Oregon, and Texas. These numbers give strong testimony to the legacy Ella Grasso left but it is also clear evidence of the prodigious strides this state and nation have made to develop and encourage women's participation in state and national politics.

Ella Grasso was a hard worker; she paid attention to details and was very disciplined. She has been quoted by many, including her husband Dr. Thomas Grasso, as one who worried a lot. But she never appeared undaunted and her marvelous optimism — despite some very bleak assessments of her tenure as Governor — only made her more determined to stay the course. For example, the *Wall Street Journal* in a front page story on June 26, 1976, entitled, "Madame Governor: Connecticut's Grasso Fails to Make Splash that was Anticipated," claimed that Ella Grasso "has been a disappointment to some Connecticut politicians and voters."[20] *The New York Times*, in an article headlined "Ella Grasso's Two Year Fall From Triumph" cited "one political disaster after another, turning friends into enemies and minor problems into fiascoes."[21] The press, at least, nearly gave up on her.

What kept her going? Was it Italian "ostinazione" — stubbornness? Yes, in part it was that and more. I believe it can be answered in a revealing Ella Grasso quote: "I must do well so others can have an easier chance."[22] In that simple phrase I suggest one hears the determined Ella Grasso. She was cognizant of her special place in Connecticut, and American political history and she was determined, always determined, to do well so that those who came after would find the road easier to travel — and perhaps venture a little further.

It is remarkable to ponder the breadth and depth her electoral success had on women in all walks of life. Geraldine Ferraro, in a campaign appearance in Hartford, Connecticut, on August 30, 1984, recalled how "Ella Grasso opened the door"[23] for women to be taken seriously as candidates for national office. From California, former Chief Justice Rose Bird's letter noted that "you can never know what an inspiration you were and are to women in public life. In many ways you personify what all women seek — equality and acceptance as an individual of merit."[24] Or consider also the words of television's Barbara Walters who wrote the Governor on January 5, 1981, that "you are an inspiration to us all … but you have been an inspiration to me for a very long time."[25]

One letter, dated December 15, 1980, from a doctor, a Connecticut native serving in the Peace Corps in Africa, is especially impressive:

> You will be pleased to learn, I hope, that every time there's mention made among my African friends that I am from Connecticut, ministers, judges, counsellors, and officials of all levels in Cameroon, Central Africa, and here in Gabon all want to know about my "Lady Governor" — how she got there, how she's doing — and how the people support her. You're a celebrity here — especially in Cameroon where so many women hold high posts in that progressive government, and envy your achievement.[26]

Ella Grasso's success meant a great deal to many people in many places.

Like any successful political figure, however, she had her critics. The clear chorus of opponents emerged not only from the ranks of Republican partisans but also from the sphere of the feminist movement.

Her 1978 gubernatorial opponent, Congressman Ronald Sarasin, said the public had been misled by what he characterized as the "myth of Ella Grasso."[27] Another Republican spokesman called her cabinet selections "mediocre and distinctly second rate."[28] The Republican minority leader of the House of Representatives claimed in 1975 that she "merchandized her image"[29] and one unnamed opponent questioned whether she had the "leadership vision."[30] The attacks from the feminist movement, however, saddened her. Many women's groups thought she would champion their causes. But she did not stand with them on many issues. One in particular was abortion. "A fetus is a human being,"[31] she said. And that was where the line was drawn. "I'm considered to have betrayed women," she noted. "That makes me very sad. I just have not done enough because I don't subscribe to everything they want me to subscribe to. I don't think that's fair and I don't think they are being fair to themselves."[32]

Despite that criticism her name surfaced periodically as a possible nominee for national office. While she publicly dismissed the idea of running for national office, she had an intuitive sense that putting a woman on the ticket in 1984 might help open the door someday, enabling a woman to seek the Presidency.

I believe Ella Grasso was perceived as one who could open — and did open — the door for others. She often said, "I don't think I'd be asked to be Vice President" and "It's nice to be Chief Executive of something."[33] And answering a *Wall Street Journal* reporter in 1976, she said, "Why is it they never mention me for the top office?"[34] Those remarks, off hand though they may have been, tell us a great deal. I believe her remarkable breakthrough as the nation's first female Governor elected in her own right laid the groundwork for the day when a woman could be President. She hoped, of course, it would be in her lifetime. Her wonderful description of the characteristics a female President should possess, aired in a Connecticut Public Television documentary, was revealing:

> ...a female President would have to be someone who would have a *feeling* for people, an ability to *communicate* with others, and able to hold *tight* the reigns of power with open hands.[35]

Part of her success, in my judgment, can be seen right there. It rested in her ability to articulate, communicate, and to express herself vividly and movingly with the spoken word. It is an enduring part of her legacy that her ability to inspire and motivate people, to influence and persuade them, to uplift them with the magic and majesty of words, is a noble and admirable trait that political leaders would do well to emulate.

In that revealing public television interview, she remarked about her success this way. She explained, "I'm a survivor and being a survivor is a very good thing — it makes one aware of how precious life is. Always listen to the opinion of others. Improve your universe and enlarge your relationships."[36]

While she possessed a special ability with the spoken word, she was also a gifted writer. Her marvelous capability with the written word was something she applied throughout her public life.

I would like to share with you three letters that she wrote that are revealing not only for the content but for the spirit and style she evoked in each one.

The first is a brief note she penned to a prominent union leader on February 15, 1980. The circumstances which prompted this letter was that the gentleman had resigned from a key state commission to which the Governor had appointed him. His mistake, as I recall, was that he went public with his resignation and criticism of her and the commission.

In her reply, she contained her anger, transformed it into prudent advice, with a gentle reprimand framed with literary distinction and meaning:

> May I respectfully suggest that it is possible to work with others with whom we do not agree, so as to enlarge in some measure our service to people. Tolerance is not without merit in a troubled world. Perhaps at some future time you may choose to pursue this path in making your judgments.[37]

The second letter, humorous and witty, was sent to William Buckley, editor of the *National Review.* She had read about his invitation to be the commencement speaker at Vassar College and the subsequent outpouring of student opposition that invitation provoked. The incident reminded her of her invitation in 1979 to be the commencement speaker at Wesleyan University in Middletown, Connecticut. When that respected Connecticut institution publicly announced her invitation, that campus erupted in strong student opposition and protest.

After much agonizing, however, Ella Grasso went ahead with her speech. William Buckley, whose brother James Buckley was the Connecticut Republican candidate for United States Senator at the time, chose not to speak at Vassar. His decision prompted her to write the following,

> Dear Bill,
> CHICKEN
> You should have gone. And they should have listened. I can't believe that Vassar has become so fossilized. But it would have been good for each side — for them to be captivated by the magic and majesty of words and for you to observe the foibles of human kind — especially there in the cloister of academia. (Note, since I don't teach English Composition I don't worry about sentence structure.)
>
> In truth, I had a similar experience at Wesleyan and after much anguish decided to give it a try. I never had as much fun with a speech, included a few Buckley-type bon mots and still get fan mail about my coup.
>
> Anyway, take comfort. In an election year better you should be shot down by the poison serpent in the Daisy Chain than brother James. The Connecticut voters would never understand.[38]

The final example is a very personal letter Ella Grasso wrote to the husband of a deceased Mount Holyoke classmate. The woman had been

Ella's close friend at college and they had taken one last sentimental journey together up to South Hadley, Massachusetts, a few months before the woman died. It stands out as a marvelously vivid and moving message. Ella wrote:

> We rollicked like middle-aged school girls, drank from deep cups of wisdom and Dubonnet blonde, settled the affairs of our lives and the world and looked forward to the autumn of our lives with the brilliance of the harvest.[39]

A remarkable child of twentieth century pilgrims, Ella Grasso's life was a brilliant harvest of faithful service which will never diminish even in the autumn of our lives.

Endnotes

1   Hemphill, C. "Visiting the Governor's Parents' Hometowns in Italy," *Hartford Courant Sunday Magazine*, December 19, 1976, 7.

2   Asbell, B. "In Power and Down and Out," *New York Times Magazine*, July 27, 1975, 15.

3   Tracy, N. "Ella: I Love Each and Every One of You," *Fairpress*, December 10, 1980, 1.

4   Asbell, *op. cit.*

5   Clemow, B. "A Triumph of Content Over Packaging," *West Hartford News*, October 10, 1974, 1.

6   Grasso, E. "When I Think of Him, It's In a Golden Glow," *Good Housekeeping* (July, 1975), 154.

7   Grasso, E. *Ella*, (Hartford: Privately Printed, 1981), 4.

8   Grasso, E. "A Conversation with Ella Grasso," interview with John Norton (1980), *Connecticut Public Television*, February 9, 1981.

9   *Ibid.*

10   Gallup, G. "Carter, Mother Teresa Lead List," *Hartford Courant*, December 25, 1980, 16.

11   United States Information Agency, Biographical Information on Ella Grasso, 3-4.

12   Asbell, *op. cit.*

13   *Ibid.*

14   Grasso, E. "My Name is Ella," Special Report by Peter Mobilia, *WPOP Radio*, February 9, 1981.

15   Clemow, *op. cit.*

16   Lipset, S.M. *Rebellion in the University*, (Boston: Little, Brown and Company, 1971), 101.

17   Letter, Anne Wonders Passel to Thomas A. Grasso, February 9, 1981.

18   Mobilia, *op. cit.*

19   Tracy, *op. cit.*

20   Margolies, S. "Madame Governor: Connecticut's Grasso Fails to Make Splash That Was Anticipated," *Wall Street Journal*, June 29, 1976, 1.

21   Knight, M. "Ella Grasso's Two-Year Fall From Triumph," *The New York Times*, November 21, 1976, C4.

22   CPTV interview, *op. cit.*

23   Campaign Speech of Geraldine Ferraro at The Old State House, Hartford, CT, August 30, 1984.

24   Letter, Chief Justice Rose Elizabeth Bird to Ella T. Grasso

25.   Letter, Barbara Walters to Ella T. Grasso, January 5, 1980.

26   Letter, Eugene Sillman, M.D., to Ella T. Grasso, December 15, 1980.

27   Stone, G. "Sarasin Says Public Misled by the Myth of Ella Grasso," *New London Day*, October 10, 1978, 1.

28   Auletta, K. "Mother Ella" *Connecticut Magazine*, June 1975, 35.

29   *Ibid.*, 49.

30   *Ibid.*, 50.

31   Mobilia, *op. cit.*

32   *Ibid.*

33   Ella, *op. cit.*

34   Margolies, *op. cit.*, 31.

35   CPTV interview, *op. cit.*

36   *Ibid.*

37   Letter, Ella Grasso to Lou Kiefer, February 15, 1980.

38   Letter, Ella Grasso to William Buckley.

39   Letter, Ella Grasso to Burr Maycock.

PART II
FAMILY

3

I STUDY ITALIAN

Mary Russo Demetrick

I study Italian
to understand my heritage
why I fly off the handle
at the slightest nuance
the slightest rudeness
Why tomatos and basil
simmer in my blood
Why the smell of espresso
brings back
memories too strong to ignore

I study Italian
to understand my family
why silence was understood
but never called *omerta*`
why my mother ran the house
why my father played the mandolin

I study Italian
to understand the words
my grandmother said to me
stai zitto, a chi,
piacere, stai bene

I study Italian
to understand my bond
to roll my tongue around
double consonants
to try out my new-found
Tuscan language
on my mother's Neopolitan ear

I study Italian
to understand who I am
in the world of
spongy white american bread
turkey and mayonnaise

I study Italian
to understand why I crave
pasta on Sunday at noon
the taste of good wine
with dinner
olive oil on my salad

I study Italian
to understand
to come home
to bind with past
to create a future
where my heritage will not be lost
to my children
to keep alive
all that has gone before
I study Italian

4

MOONSTRUCK: CULTURES OBSERVING AND OBSERVED

Mario Aste

Moonstruck is a representation of Italian-American life, and in its filmic metaphors deals with an ethnic group in the same manner as the American mainstream culture, that is with little knowledge of the true Italian-American experience. It presents several stereotypes as fact and there is nothing much in the film that contradicts them.

This approach of using stereotypes is a shorthand method of labelling which defines and limits those it seeks to describe. The labels are simply convenient; if a group is already "understood," their presentation eliminates the need for much attention or exploration. But however convenient they may seem to those applying them, the labels do become damaging to the people they are trying to explain. They constrict people like those in the Italian section of Brooklyn to a certain type of behavior and expression.

If an Italian-American tries to move beyond these strictures he or she would probably not find acceptance from, and might even meet the resistance of, the mainstream culture. The majority has come to prefer the stereotypes; they have now even become a source of amusement, a fact that their full use in *Moonstruck* makes clear. The film uses the whole catalogue of the labels applied to Italian-Americans for comic effect. The plot itself could not exist without the stereotypes, since the characters' enactments of the stereotypes themselves form much of the story.

The nature and importance of mass media stereotypes and their effects on society have been debated in recent years by scholars from a wide variety of disciplines. Some have analyzed the history of popular stereotypes; others have argued about the effects of these images on the viewers; while others have considered the reasons for the evolution of these stereotypes in American popular culture (Miller 1987). Films play a role in shaping images of various ethnic and racial groups. While virtually all observers agree that mass media convey social messages, behavioral scientists have been unable to identify precisely how audiences receive, distill, and believe such messages (Miller 1987). The biases projected onto the screen can assume meanings for different audiences that the filmmaker might never have anticipated or even condoned. Studies of the relationship between film and audience suggest that films can affect the attitudes, beliefs, images, and opinions of the viewers (Miller 1987). Films in general though reinforce, rather than form, images and ideas. Stereotypes of groups, in fact, are not in large invented by filmmakers, but they are derived from popular beliefs and prejudices and as such they have relevant meanings for the audience.

Moonstruck thus must be analyzed as a mode of cultural exchange in a social context and as a way to ensemble modes of interpretation. It must be seen not just as a collection of aesthetic spaces but as political ones in order to contest and naturalize the primacy of interpretation and its relevance to the understanding of a specific culture. In this light it will exert great impact especially when the spaces are coherently put togther to form the most complete details of a reality in which the audience can place itself in a position to understand a culture not yet understood and this is done by putting together the film's signifiers on a cultural grid of intelligibility (Zavarzadez 1991).

Italian images in American film are the product of popular culture and public events. Italians are often portrayed possessing passion and lack of control, bound to excessive emotionalism and affected by a lack of privacy. They like to live at home with "momma" and with extended families. They all have nicknames and their real names are rendered on the diminutive like Ronny, Johnny, Loretta or end with a vowel — Cosmo, Carmine, and so on. "They are dumb, they are bigotted. They chew garlic and play Frank Sinatra non-stop. They either work in the sub shop, dress shop, candy shop, bakery, or they shoot people" (Eagan, *Boston Herald*, July 9, 1991). Their life is continously interwoven with some sort of religious activity bordering superstition, a sincere appraisal of the spiritual and a sense of destiny understood in a classical Greek sense.

Stereotyping Italians is an easy way for the market-driven film industry to ensure the making of a profitable margin. Italians are marketable even though they seem to gravitate only "about two things in America: dance around the spaghetti pot or become mobsters" (Eagan, *Boston Herald*). These stereotypes have been formed due to misconceptions by the majority about Italians and the multifaceted Italian American culture. In *Moonstruck,* John Stanley describes, on screen, his perception of the Italian-American experience. He looks at the lives of an extended family in Brooklyn and analyzes it through comic effects by presenting it with its own twists while it reacts to a more Americanized lifestyle. He also manages, to his credit, the creation of a storyline in which the characters are not ridiculed and Italian-American culture is played with but not laughed at. The result is a romantic comedy which, besides receiving Oscar awards, became the top grossing film of 1988.

The film takes some of the Italian passion for life and presents it as it operates in a family situation where old vlaues are continuously challenged by a multicultural society and rapidly changing mores. Within the family, individuals are never alone; they can find consolation, help, advice to any problem they may encounter. The family as an institution demands respect and it is a vital part of the Italian-American experience as in it the members discover the stronghold of traditional values.

Loosely, in *Moonstruck*, the story is about Loretta, a 38-year old widow who lives with her parents and grandfather in a large house in Brooklyn. Loretta becomes engaged to Johnny, who flies to Palermo to be with his dying mother soon after their engagement. While he is gone, Loretta meets and falls in love with his brother, Ronny, to whom she becomes engaged when Johnny returns and calls off their wedding. Obviously, the plot itself is not the source of the comedy. The entertainment is the characters, Italian-Americans portrayed with all the quirks and characteristics with which the stereotypes imbue them.

Moonstruck as a romantic comedy presents the Italians as unfailing romantics. The film opens with shots of a full moon and a love song in the background. Romanticism prevails throughout, and the idea is strongly reinforced even through the minor characters. Loretta's uncle Carmine is convinced that it was a special moon which brought together her parents, and which continues to work to unite couples. Romance permeates the movie, even at the opera during a performance of *La Boheme* to which Ronny takes Loretta.

Loretta's persistent belief in her "bad luck" is a vestige of faith in the folklore of Italy, at least as perceived by the stereotypes on which the movie seems to depend. She tells an old Sicilian woman who has put a curse on Johnny's Palermo-bound plane that she does not believe in curses, but she still looks uneasily out the window. And yet she comes across in other circumstances as a very practical woman. Her decision to marry Johnny is not based on love, but on the belief that if she has lost her "one shot at happiness" in the form of her first husband, at least she can now try to take control of her life and prevent herself from being alone. She seems, in this second choice, to ascribe to the belief that a women must take a more practical approach to marriage. The first time around she held out for love but now she feels that she must marry while she is still young and the possibility for security is real.

Rose, her mother, believes that it is better when a woman does not love her husband, because she can be driven crazy by him more easily if she does. For all the romance in the film, Loretta's mother has a very practical view of marriage: it is easier if emotions are not too heavily invested. But then, Rose knows this from experience, since she really does love her husband, Cosmo. In the matter of love and marriage, the movie seems to juggle the stereotypes about an Italian-American's view towards both. Is marriage best looked at as a valuable institution in itself, with or without the involvement of emotion, or is romance the be-all and end-all? Italian-Americans (or Italians, since the movie does not seem to differentiate) are supposed to be very romantic and sentimental souls who nonetheless take a strongly entrenched, unsentimental view of the family as an almost sacred institution. The movie does not seriously raise the questions of the dichotomy of these two issues, but then again, this is not a documentary. Instead, the stereotypes are conveniently used in the appropriate places to elicit laughter.

Another contradiction presented in the film is the contrast between the images of the Italian man as the consummate lover and the man who will always be dependent on his mother. Loretta's father, Cosmo, is an example of the first type. He is seeing another woman, Mona. She is very easily impressed by him, probably because she is not particularly bright herself. But she does make Cosmo feel good about himself; he is proud of how suave he is with her. Rose knows her husband is cheating on her, and has a theory that men need more than one woman because it lessens their fear of death. Nevertheless, she asks the opinions of a couple of men she encounters. One says: it is because of nerves, and another theorizes that men need to find the missing piece of themsleves: the rib that God used to create the first woman. But it seems a foregone conclsuion that at some point in his life, man will "need" more than one woman. Cosmo himself is not exactly wracked with guilt about it.

In Cosmo's ethical world women are divided in two classes: virgin-whore. The woman's role of the first class is to become a wife and a mother and therefore the custodian and the protector of the home and family values. The father is the patriarch, the uncontested ruler, the "pater familias" of Roman times. The mother is the keeper of the flame as represented by the kitchen and the fireplace which binds the unity of the family. Her role is to keep the family clear from unnecessary trouble. As a wife the women must remember that the man is expected to be forgiven if he strays off the path: "the stability and good name of the family notoriously depends more on the wife's faithfulness than on her husband's" (Barzini 1965). Family honor is to be upheld by the women of the family, and men are there to preserve the woman's honor, yet if a man should stray it is forgiven because he is a man. Men often play the role of the "rooster" and the social game of "Gallismo." This is well represented by Cosmo, and by the fumbling professor who is rejected twice by two young women while he is trying to seduce them in a restaurant.

The protrayal of men as "roosters" chasing every available woman is misleading and contradictory. Although the idea of "Gallismo" may be acceptable to certain strata of society it would be unfair to categorize all Italian males in this way because it falsely presents those who are faithful to their wives. This must be emphatically pointed out because anybody watching the film may get the impression that cheating on the wife is not only acceptable but the norm of life for Italian men.

Though Cosmo can cheat on his wife, he can and does still have strong feelings about how his own daughter conducts her life — it should be unlike his. He can still take a moral stand on the subject of a woman's morality. The stereotype of the Italian lover very definitely applies only to men; the women are supposed to be docile and submissive. The definition of morality is not interchangeable, and this observation, too, is used for a laugh in the film. When Cosmo and Mona are discovered at the opera by Loretta, who is with Ronny during Johnny's absence in Palermo and despite her engagement, her father, with a grand gesture, says "You are my daughter — I will not have you act like a puttana!" The fact that he himself is with someone he would categorize that way is irrelevant. His daughter is of the only other class of women, the respectable kind. It is important that he continue to think of her that way, and when Loretta spends the night with Ronny, Rose lies to Cosmo to cover up for her.

Johnny is the other aspect of the Italian male. He cannot marry Loretta until his mother in Sicily is dead. Cosmo does not like him because "he's a big baby," Loretta knows that his mother "drives him crazy," and his brother, irritated, says that "she still runs his life." Johnny is an embodiment of the stereotype of the Italian son who reveres his mother, taken to the extreme for comic purposes. Johnny's ties to his mother's apron strings are reinforced when he hovers over her on her deathbed sobbing despite her annoyed gestures for him to get away. Finally she forbids him to marry Loretta and as soon as he agrees to her wishes she becomes well again. This stereotypical representation of Johnny as a momma's boy is so strong on him that he believes that his marrying Loretta or not could project the ultimate fate of his mother. These two ideas of the independent-minded lover and the foolish momma's boy are exploited to full advantage in *Moonstruck*, especially when presented side by side for best filmic effect.

Ronny, the other man in Loretta's life, is totally different from his brother Johnny. He is the stereotypical opposite. He represents the struggling Italian-American working hard in his bakery to make a living. This character is interesting because of his change and growth as the film progresses. When Ronny is first seen he appears to be a raving lunatic. He is consumed with hate and self-pity. He works in the cellar of the bakery which is his own private hell, and because his job is to shovel coal into the ovens he is in a sense keeping his own hell alive. The parallelism between the ovens and Ronny's present life is interesting. He is dealing with fire, a symbol of passion and hate, of which he is overwhelmed. His job is practically an image of Hell, and as such Ronny feels that his life is a living Hell. Though his work is hard he has time to enjoy music, espcially opera. This love of music indicates to the viewers the cultural and artistic side of the stereotypical Italian.

His apartment is suffused by background operatic music and has in a prominent place a painting portraying the doomed lover of *La Boheme*. There is in this an interesting ironic representation by the film director. The love story of *La Boheme* is paralleled here to Ronny's love story, who lost his woman because of his brother, and to Loretta's past marriage born in love but destroyed in a premature death. The correspondence between Ronny's passion for Loretta and his passion for opera must not be taken lightly. The two doomed lovers have found a way to overcome their fate: Loretta's bad luck and Ronny's brotherly interference. At this point in the film representation of the characters equates the sense of Italianess through music to the justification of their love affair (Williamson, 1988) which will be eventually channelled into the traditional mold.

Loretta, by going to the Met and by dating her fiance's brother, breaks tradition and honor code. Not only does she date him but spends an entire night at his apartment and sleeps with him. Before this grand evening Loretta goes to the hairdresser and has her hair permed, a facial and her fingernails painted. On her way home she buys a new outfit, and for once in her life she feels good about herself. She is finally doing what feels good and not what may be right. In doing all these things, she is breaking the mold of the stereotypical Italian-American woman.

The characteristics of the woman stereotype are wisdom, as the focus of the home, religion and cooking. All three are used at the appropriate moment for punchline and to establish atmosphere. Loretta emobides all of them but although she may live at home, she works out of the house by doing accounting for neighborhood businesses. Oddly, the stereotypes combine when Loretta and Ronny go to his apartment to discuss his relationship with Johnny, from whom he has been estranged for five years. Within minutes of meeting him, Loretta marches into his kitchen, finds the apron, and starts cooking him a steak. She can immediately analyze and diagnose what Ronny thinks are his most serious problems. She is aggressive and willing to take charge — but in the arena of the home and kitchen, and when she has the opportunity to take care of a man.

More signficantly the women, especially Rose, seem to have a stronger sense of self than the men. Her husband has involved himself with another woman, somewhat out of a sense of despair at discovering that his life is "based on nothing." Rose, on the other hand, will not invite another man into her home at night because "...I'm married. I know who I am." Again, the film's use of stereotypical characteristics raises a question. Is the fact that Rose is so sure of her place a good or bad thing? Does the movie approve? Has she given anything up for that security? She and her daughter are shown as competent and confident, but mostly in the context of their home, or taking care of men, who still feel free to dictate to them. The issue is not explored or even recognized as an issue, but it is used for a laugh and more than a few points.

Rose's behavior raises several sets of questions which remain unresolved in the film. She goes alone to the restaurant, drinks in public with another man who is not her husband and she is seen walking home with him. These actions need to be explored in a much deeper fashion than the simple manner in which *Moonstruck* analyzes them. If the purpose of the director was to tease the audience without looking for a questioning response or intellectual challenge certainly it was successful. If the purpose was to challenge the audience in a discussion about values and acculturation the director fails miserably.

In this context of new mores and changing values we must also analyze the encounter of Loretta and her father during the intermission at the performance of *La Boheme*. We can see and almost touch the shock on Cosmo's face when he is confronted by his daughter's life as paralleling his own when they meet and they are both with the "wrong" people. The question for both is "What are you doing here?" They are guilty and ashamed of the other for the same crime. One might see their infidelity on different levels. The father's behavior might be analyzed as a fear of death. He must maintain his masculine image in order to find meaning in life. He is supposed to be with more than one woman so that he can feel worthwhile. Loretta on the other hand is a woman who is finding romance and fun in love. She will not accept it at first; she denies her feelings and acts as if the decision to sleep with her fiancé's brother is all Ronny's idea. Her words, however, do not match her actions and we see in these filmic images humorous contradictions.

Moonstruck also uses to great advantage the stereotype of large families, with generations of Italian-Americans living together or close by. Loretta's grandfather lives with his son's family, her mother assumes that Loretta and her new husband will live with them after her marriage, or at least, like Loretta's aunt and uncle, live nearby. Whether or not this is any longer a realistic picture of the Italian-American family is not considered. The structure of the Italian-American family is the subject of yet another stereotype employed in the film. The man is the head of the household, figuratively at least. The men have control over the women, who define their lives in relationship to some man. Even the rather simpering Johnny giggles at a man who has publicly quarreled with his female companion: "A man who cannot control his woman is funny!" When Cosmo's father tells his son that he should pay for the wedding of his only daughter, he gives the advice with tact, since it is important for his son to hold a sense of authority over the women of the family.

This can be taken as an example of the respect due to the elderly man from whom Cosmo's authority flows. The patriarchal authority is confirmed and reaffirmed in the relationship between Cosmo and his father, but there are in this film several scenes and sequences where the character of the old man puzzles the audiences. He is often seen taking the dogs for a walk and concerting with them in howling at the moon. This image is surely symptomatic of the kind of knowledge of Italian-American culture and its values by other ethnic groups. These actions which border on the lunatic certainly leave us with a perplexed mind. Does the director have a meaning? Or is he just easing the viewers by lulling them into believing that the role of this old man is lost in the structure of the film without any specific purpose other than the one to reinforce the role of the extended family.

The church, as a stereotype, also plays a role in the Italian-American lifestyle. In the film Loretta goes to confession after having left Ronny's apartment and having made love to him. The full moon was perhaps the reason, as the uncle pointed out, for her true love. There is in the representation a mixture of superstition and religious experience. The confessional is used as a superstitious instrument in case of future bad luck and not necessarily to address the sin committed. Loretta confesses making love to Ronny, quickly by mentioning it in between two minor sins. The priest does hear it and gives her a due penance and warns her of the gravity of her situation. This is overshadowed by Loretta meeting her mother Rose in church and their discussion about women's relationships with men.

Moonstruck indulges also into another stereotype: the lack of privacy. This is evident from the very start. Loretta and her boyfriend, Johnny, are having dinner in a restaurant at which they are well known. Johnny proposes to Loretta on his knees, this obviously attracts the attention of others especially when Loretta asks him for the engagement ring. Johnny does not have one and gives her his pinkie ring in lieu of a diamond. The man at the next table leans over to Johnny and says, "I would have sprung for a ring if it was me." Upon her acceptance the entire restaurant applauds. In an American context a marriage proposal is a private affair between the two partners without any choral participation of relatives and acquaintances, especially strangers.

The final scene of the film besides the lack of privacy is a further extension of the stereotype of the woman being the focus of the home. Since her place is in the kitchen, this room will become the literal center of all home life and so in *Moonstruck* Loretta and Ronny with Johnny present and all the members of the extended family, reach the climax of their whirlwind of love. When Johnny arrives at Loretta's house upon his return from Sicily and announces that he cannot marry her, since he believes this would kill his mother, Ronny immediately borrows his brother's pinkie ring, proposes to Loretta and is accepted.

The interaction among the characters and their reactions are the source of the comedy in this scene, and this would not have been possible if this were another group of people, who supposedly would have discreetly excused themselves and slipped out of the room to give the couple privacy. The new engagement is then celebrated with the omnipresent wine, and the toast "*Alla famiglia!* To the family!" Even Johnny can participate, since as the grandfather points out, "You're part of the family, don't you realize?" The film closes with the sounds of the celebration and continued toasting as the camera pans through pictures of generations of the family, ending with a 19th century photograph of an elderly couple. So the last words and shots of *Moonstruck* stress the most widely known stereotype about Italian-Americans, their dependence on family, and this is meant as a comforting and heartwarming affirmation of that idea.

This is the reason for the prevalence of stereotypes to begin with; they are comforting and dependable. They make it simple for those outside a particular group who need to know what to expect about people with whom they are not familiar. When stereotypes are negative, they're called prejudices; when they are positive or nonjudgemental (i.e., family will always be important, Italians use lots of hand gestures), they're somewhat more acceptable. They are certainly acceptable, and unquestioned enough, to be used as a source of comedy in *Moonstruck*. The film was never presented as a factual depiction of contemporary Italian-American lifestyles, but it was intended as a comedy, and goes to the extreme in its use of popular stereotypes about this group.

The makers of *Moonstruck* clearly opted for a stereotypical representation without reflecting about the "Americanization" process of acculturation and the accompanying conflicts which confront the three generations under the same roof or in the same neighborhood. Loretta does not seem that far removed from the lifestyle and the attitudes of her grandfather. What there is of an "Americanization" is reflected only half-heartedly. Loretta clearly does not ascribe to the traditional and patriarchal either/or - virgin/whore picture of womanhood. She can have an affair with her fiancé's brother, her only worry afterward being not the immorality of her action but the fear that it may have jinxed her hope of good luck for the future.

Loretta, a widow, has moved back home to live with her parents. While the film does not state the reason specifically, the fact is that Loretta has not chosen to live independently, apart from a man. In this case, she is regressed back to living under the roof of her father. But this is more of a regression in general, since it seems a remnant of an old world belief that independent women are bad women. In this choice, Loretta does not seem very "Americanized," despite the fact that she works outside the home.

The film does not talk about the old man's life much and the next generation in the person Cosmo could be said to be "Americanized" if the definition of that term is limited to financial standing. He is a wealthy plumber, and if his father had come to this country for financial security, the second generation has quickly earned it. But Cosmo is not "Americanized" in outlook of values. If the stereotypes are true definition of Italian men, an issue this light-hearted comedy does not explore, then Cosmo is still very much his father's son. Having chosen to live and work in his father's world, and apparently proud of the success he has earned there, he does not seem to have struggled with any conflict between the values of his father's generation and American ones. The only "American value" hinted at is financial success, and Cosmo has taken care of that one.

Based on the above considerations *Moonstruck* falls into the category of one which tries to show the rich tradition of the Italian family and the Italian-American culture, but it comes across as a collection of prejudices. The Italian-American family is shown outside any context of acculturation while at the same time Loretta's behavior implies a certain amount of integration which reflects several levels of intellectual resolution to conflicts that the individual faces on the road to define what is best of the old and the new. The evolution of the characters is the one element that brings liberation, and hopefully the media will try to keep this liberating aspect in mind in the future. Unfortunately the director and the scriptwriter of *Moonstruck* opted to base their plot on the stereotypes and as in many other films about Italian-Americans, have failed to represent correctly all the nuances of the Italian-American experience.

ENDNOTES

Ansen, L. "Moonstruck," *Newsweek,* December 21, 1987, p. 69.

Barzini, L. *The Italians,* New York: Athenaum, 1965.

Coyle, M. "Theatrical Releases" *Video September* 1988, p. 119.

Denby, D. "Movies," *New York,* January 4, 1988: p.44.

Eagan, M. "Stereotyping Italians," *The Boston Herald,* July 9, 1991, p. 10.

Fugue, L. "The Current Cinema," *New Yorker,* January 25, 1988, pp. 99-100.

Gross, J. "Moonstruck," *New York Times,* February 14, 1988, pp. 11.

Kael, P. "The Current Cinema," *New Yorker,* January 25, 1988, pp. 99-100.

Kauffman, S. "A Clutch of Comedies," *The New Republic,* February 8, 1988, p. 26.

Miller, R. and Woll, A. *Ethnic and Racial Images in American Film and Television,* New York, Garland Publishing, 1987.

Tomasi, L.F. *The Italian American Family,* New York: Center for Migration Studies, 1972.

Williamson Jr., C. "Moonstruck in Review," *National Review*, March 4, 1988, pp. 53-54.

Zavarzadeh, M. *Seeing Films Politically*, Albany: State University of New York Press, 1991.

5

ITALIAN MIGRANT WORKERS IN TURN-OF-THE-CENTURY NEW JERSEY

Cindy Hahamovitch

A lot is known about New Immigration and about Italian immigration in particular. So, let me begin by explaining how this paper relates to that literature. Immigration patterns changed in the late 19th century, which is why historians refer to "new immigration." Immigrants to the United States came increasingly from southern and eastern Europe rather than from northern and western Europe, and they headed for urban and industrial destinations, rather than for farms. Italians, who formed the largest single national group among the "new immigrants," fit this pattern. They headed straight for the nation's largest cities and for industrial jobs. The people I'm going to discuss now were exceptions to that rule: they are southern Italians, mostly women and children, who took seasonal work on New Jersey's farms.

The obvious question then, is why study Italian migrant farm workers, if their experience was out of the ordinary? The answer is the usual one — that their historical import is far greater than their numbers. Italian migrant farm workers were a cause célèbre around the turn-of-the-century. For the migrants themselves farm work was a temporary solution to a private problem. But they found themselves working in New Jersey fields in the midst of the Progressive Reform movement.

Fresh from a victorious fight to restrict child labor in industrial workplaces in New York and New Jersey, progressive reformers were appalled to find immigrant children at work alongside their parents on the large and lucrative cranberry bogs of southern New Jersey. They were affronted by the living quarters provided by growers for immigrant families and by the fact that migrant children lost weeks of schooling while they labored in the fields.

For reformers the problem was child labor and the padrone system, or as they put it, the "Sacrifice of Golden Boys and Girls" to the profits of berry growers and brutal padroni. It was the padroni who brought Italian families to the berry field, who bossed them while they were at work, and who housed them in chicken coops and barns. The employment of families in New Jersey agriculture not only subjected children to long hours of work and unsanitary conditions, according to reformers, it threatened to produce a generation of unassimilated, uneducated and uncontrollable immigrant children. Progressives demanded no less then a legal prohibition against child labor in agriculture and the enforcement of this prohibition by state agencies.[1]

Thus when Italian families disembarked from the trains that transported them to New Jersey's berry region, they brought more than food, pillows, mattresses and baby carriages. They were followed by an entourage of progressive reformers, photographers, state immigration authorities and federal investigators. The private lives of Italian farmworkers had become a public affair. And even though Italian farm workers were few in number and they were an exception to the rules of "new immigration" history, their experience raises issues central to the concerns of labor history, immigration history and the history of progressive reform.

Progressives believed that children should be banned from the fields and the padrone system eliminated. However, they didn't necessarily appreciate or understand the people they sought to protect, although they considered themselves advocates of immigrant farmworkers. What I would like to do in this paper is reconstruct the lives of the private individuals who found themselves in the public limelight. I'd like to do what progressive reformers never attempted: to understand Italian berry pickers not as victims or as objects but agents, as subjects of their own lives.

To do this I must explain why there were jobs for immigrants on farms in New Jersey in the first place. As cities became more and more congested in the second half of the 19th century, as buildings took the place of urban gardens, city dwellers became totally dependent on markets for their food. This meant that farmers who could get perishable vegetables and fruits to market quickly had a ready market, so truck farms, or market gardens as they were euphemistically called, grew up in the shadow of the nation's largest cities. Because of its proximity to New York, Philadelphia, Newark and several smaller industrial cities, South Jersey became a crucial truck farming region. That is why New Jersey is known as the Garden State.

Although truck farmers benefitted from growing urban markets, the

19th century shift in the nation's population from the countryside to cities left farmers short of labor during peak harvest seasons. They could mechanize some aspects of the production process — plowing, fertilizing and cultivation — but most berries and vegetables could not be harvested by machine (and still can't). So, growers sought workers who would appear when they were needed and move on when the harvest was over; they sought migrant workers.

In particular, they coveted the Italian workers who rode the vast wave of migration to North American shores in the late nineteenth century. In fact, they would regularly see Italian men passing by their farms on their way to work on roads and rails. But few Italian men came seeking agricultural jobs. Most of the Italian men who streamed into New Jersey in the 1880s and '90s had worked on the land in Italy and many intended to do so again, but they came to the United States for industrial work and industrial wages.

It's not hard to understand why Italian men shunned agriculture work upon their arrival in the United States. As Dino Cinel and others have shown, migration to the U.S. was generally meant as a temporary solution to economic problems at home, particularly the difficulties of buying land. Emigrants who left southern Italy in the hands of padroni came to the U.S. in search of high paying work that would allow them to return to Italy and buy or rent land.[2] Intent on quick earnings and a speedy return home, few Italians sought agricultural work in the United States. Only five percent of New Jersey's Italian population worked in agriculture at the turn of the century.[3]

For those who worked furiously toward the goal of landownership in Italy, the disadvantages of farm work in the U.S. were obvious. Why take six weeks of work in a cranberry bog and face certain unemployment at the end of the harvest season when coal mines and railroads operated virtually year-round?[4] So, the people whom Michael Piore and contempories called "birds of passage" were indifferent to offers of temporary farm work.

The Italians who ultimately provided New Jersey's truck farmers with the workers they so desperately wanted were members of established families — the families of men who stayed and settled in the U.S. Why would settled families be interested in migrant farm work? The answer is fairly obvious; the going wages for unskilled work were rarely enough to support a family.[5] Unable to feed their families on the wages earned by their husbands, women had to find ways to combine their roles as mothers and workers. Italian women dominated New York's artificial flower industry which permitted them to work at home. Women in Buffalo took their children with them when they worked in the canneries of the Niagara farm belt.[6] And Italian women in Philadelphia and New York took their children to work on South Jersey's berry and vegetable farms during the long days of summer.

Thus the needs of Italian families in nearby Philadelphia and New York complemented the labor demands of South Jersey's growers. Still, farmers lacked contacts in immigrant communities and the time to recruit and transport large, temporary workforces. This is where the padroni came in. Upon receiving orders from growers, the padroni would begin canvassing Italian neighborhoods door-to-door, until they had sealed bargains with enough workers. Once the season began, they would arrange the transportation of their crews, receiving a fee for every worker secured for a grower and another, the bossatura, from every worker for whom they located a job. Each time a padrone's crew moved to a new crop, he would exact additional dues. Growers relinquished the problems of supervising, housing and even paying workers to the padroni and their underlings, who were known as "row-bosses," often allowing them to operate commissaries and to charge workers for sleeping in barns, sheds and stables.

The exodus of Italian families from Philadelphia would begin in May when strawberries started to ripen in Delaware and South Jersey. As fields were picked out, the padroni would move their gangs northward to Gloucester and Atlantic counties to pick blackberries and raspberries. When the blackberry season ended in late July most pickers would return to the city, with a minority remaining to gather blueberries. Because blueberries grew wild, the formally organized gangs would become "veritable gypsies" (in the words of reformers), picking the berries for themselves and selling them directly to freight agents for as much as three dollars a day. Others would find work in tomato, pepper and cucumber fields. Some would move on to Cape May County to skin tomatoes and peel sweet potatoes and pumpkins or canning.[7] Finally, in September, the pickers still scattered throughout the state would be brought by the padroni to the desolate cranberry bogs of South Jersey, where they would be joined by "a great many families" brought directly from Philadelphia for a period of three to seven weeks, according to the crop.[8]

"[T]here are women and children in swarms," the U.S. Immigration Commission reported in 1911. "Old, young and middle-aged are found in every field." "[Y]oung men can not profitably leave a living wage for berry earnings," the Commission observed, "It is the family that makes money." Wives whose husbands had work in Philadelphia, widows, their young children made up the bulk of South Jersey's harvest labor force.[9] The men and adult children who sometimes joined their families in the fields were either casual laborers who had little to lose by abandoning the city for harvest wages for several months out of the year, or workers laid off as a result of the extreme irregularity of industrial work. For example, the garment industry, which employed many Italians in both Philadelphia and New York, had two slack seasons and two busy seasons.[10] When slack seasons corresponded to harvest seasons, berry picking provided an opportunity to earn the extra money that might tide a family through winter, the most devastating season of unemployment. "Italians rank with the most frugal people of the world," declared a Charity Association worker in 1909, "but even their economy cannot make up for the loss of four or five months' wages.[11] Given the seasonality of industrial work and the inadequacy of men's wages, berry picking was an essential component of the Italian family's annual wage. The Dillingham Report was quite clear on this point: the amount earned in the fields by "the whole force, from grandmother to the 7 or 8 year old child" went "to fill in the chasm between earnings and cost of living during the remainder of the year."

All who could pick did so: of the seventeen bogs visited by the National Child Labor Committee, 32 percent of the pickers were under the age of fourteen, 18 percent were under the age of ten, and on twelve bogs even children under five worked.[12] How long children worked steadily is impossible to determine. The Consumers' League reported that children above seven worked "as diligently as their parents and the boss can force them to do." However, state investigators countered that they found as many children playing as picking. Growers' complaints about the destructiveness of playful children would seem to support this conclusion.[13] Children too young to work were left to themselves or to the care of "little mothers," and infants could be found trundled in baby carriages at the end of the berry rows.

Whether at work, play or at rest, the pickers would spend as little time as possible in the shelters made available to them on the berry farms. Although some of the larger cranberry bogs offered barrack-like rows of wooden slabs and straw tick for beds. A wooden shack forty by thirty-six foot in length might shelter 130 people and enough rice, macaroni, sardines and tomato paste to last the summer. Conditions were "unspeakable," according to the National Child Labor Committee: "Families of five, six and even eight were found living in one room measuring six by eight feet, without any sanitary provisions whatever." "The congestion outslums the city," the report noted.[14]

From growers' perspective, these conditions were unavoidable. Child labor was a necessity so long as families were the only source of labor available to them. As long as they had to hire women, they would also have to employ children. They also argued that they could not afford to build better housing. They needed workers every harvest season, but since they did not need them for long, they had little incentive to devote their profits to migrant housing and toilets in the fields. Indeed, they had every incentive to cut harvest costs to the bare bone. In truck farming, perhaps more than in any other industry, growers' ability to accumulate profits turned upon the extent to which they could control the costs of labor, because virtually all their other expenses were beyond their control. They could not influence the cost of machinery, property taxes, seed prices, fertilizer costs or freight rates. Thus, as the harvest arrived, bringing with it a sudden demand for labor, growers' driving concern was to press downward on wage rates and provisions for workers. The lower market prices were at harvest, the more urgent the need to cut costs.

Progressive reformers acknowledged without appreciating the economic necessity of child labor. The National Child Labor Committee allowed, for example, that "from the standpoint of the parents, the more children one has at this time, the greater the income." But the Committee resolved that child labor could not be tolerated, despite the parents' necessity, because of the price children paid in lost schooling during their months in the fields. They calculated that Italian children who worked in New Jersey's fields lost three to four months of school. "They necessarily fall behind their classes," the Committee reported, "and there are always some who degenerate into chronic truants..." Teachers and principals in Philadelphia "say the little berry pickers are generally the most depraved children in the schools," and the loss of so much schooling ruined the chances of their "Americanization along [the] right lines."

Child labor opponents refused to face that fact that children couldn't be banned from the fields without depriving growers of their only labor source and without depriving Italian families of essential income. Not fully appreciating either the needs of workers (whom they never consulted) nor the needs of growers (who saw no alternative sources of labor) the National Child Labor Committee concluded that South Jersey's system of "sporadic family labor" was "inherently bad" and "intolerable." Children had to be banned from farm work and forced to go to school. Neither New Jersey nor Pennsylvania's compulsory school laws should be set aside, they argued, "for the benefit of cranberry growers whose profits are already large, however willing the parents may be to profit by the labor of the children."

For progressives, the padrone system was the underlying problem. The padrone system gave growers access to the cheapest of urban workers: married women, widows, children, casual laborers and members of the unemployed. It passed transportation costs on to the workers themselves and, finally, it absolved growers of responsibility for housing conditions and the use of child labor on their farms.

To progressives the padroni were "brutal," "parasitic" and "un-American" taskmasters who revelled in their power over defenseless workers, workers "who seldom know English speech or American customs." By using the padroni, growers absolved themselves of responsibility for conditions that bred disease and promiscuity. They turned a blind eye to the problem of child labor, which produced "depravation of mind and morals" and "the perversion of family life."[15] "The growers do not actually make these conditions; they merely condone them," one progressive author argued, "they pay the parsimonious padrone, and ease their conscience by letting him be responsible for the evil herding and harrying of the pickers."[16] Italian paid, housed and disciplined Italian; growers merely provided jobs.

Until quite recently, historians have tended to join progressives in attacking the padrone system as parasitic and oppressive. More recently, however, historians have begun to revamp the padroni's image by arguing that they eased immigrants' transition into urban living and industrial employment. I think the experience of berry-pickers demonstrates that the truth lay somewhere in between.

Let me first point out that, whatever their view of the padrone's role, historians have described the padrone system as a peculiarity of Italian immigration.[17] In fact, crew leaders or labor contractors are an established feature of labor migations. Whenever poor workers travel over great distances, the person who can advance their fares and secure them work wields considerable power over them. What stands out about the padrone system in turn-of-the-century agriculture is less the bosses' power over workers than the power padroni's wielded over the growers.

Because they could rarely communicate with Italians, New Jersey's American-born growers had to rely on the padroni to supervise as well as supply workers.[18] "Few of the Italian growers employ these overseers," the Dillingham investigators ovserved: "They can give directions in their own tongue, and going along from row to row are able to keep in touch with the pickers continually."

The American is handicapped in this respect. He does not know the language and frequently can not get gangs unless he agrees to pay a row boss, whose family is among the pickers. No matter how small the gang, one boss is required.[19]

"A good many complain of the Italian as a laborer for others," the Dillingham Commission reported. "He is said to be a time server, not indolent but tricky, needs constant watching, and grumbles a good deal about his work and wages."

The Director of the State Board of Agriculture painted a more flattering portrait of the Italian worker, but here too the problem of supervision remained an underlying theme. "An Italian won't do as good work as a native, nor as much," he argued:

> But most of them are willing workers and they eventually learn to do the work ... I have been very much pleased with the class I had tried last season. They have been very willing and worked very hard, especially if someone was watching.

The person watching was, of course, the padroni or his underling, the "row boss." For their services most were paid wages and some received a commission on each bushel picked.[20]

Growers' depended on padroni as foremen left them, including Director Rider, perpetually dissatisfied with labor relations on their farms. "In a good many instances," the Dillingham investigators concluded, "the row boss is a real advantage":

> He knows the members of the gang, can talk to them in their own tongue, exercise more authority than an American employer can, and becomes a real go-between to protect the interests of his proteges.[21]

But in many cases, the report observed, the padrone was "worth nothing" either to the employer or the gang: "his only desire is to earn his $1.50 per diem, and carry a big stick with some dignity."

The root of growers' frustration lay in the ambivalent role of the padrone. That growers used padroni to discipline workers is indisputable (progressives frequently published photographs of row bosses in suits and bowlers, standing watch with heavy sticks over stooping workers). Still, the coercive power of the padroni was limited. Although the bonds between padroni and workers could be exploited by employers to discipline workers from afar, workers could also pull the strings of kith and kin. Padroni were paid both by growers and workers and they were members of the Italian communities from which they recruited their crews: if they expected to compete for labor among other labor contractors, they could not risk gaining a reputation as brutal or exploitive row bosses.[22]

The Italian contract workers brought overseas by padroni might well have felt like indentured servants. Separated by an ocean from their homes and families and indebted for food and fare, they had little control over their daily lives. But the berry pickers of the early twentieth century were not so helpless. They had relatives, friends, a community to direct and advise them. In this environment, a padrone's behavior was regulated by unwritten rules, rules that were enforced by the gossip of tenement stoops and sweatshops.

How effective this community regulation of the padroni's excesses was, we may never know, but it does appear that by the first decade of the current century, some padroni were behaving more like shop stewards than row bosses. The U.S. Immigration Commission reported an incident, for example, in which a padrone refused to allow a grower to hire an additional gang, though he had brought fewer workers than promised. "The first gang refused to go out until late in the day, refusing to pick if the grower persisted in employing a larger force." Though the commission interpreted this as simple stubbornness on the padrone's part, it is quite possible that this row boss was either conceding to the gang's demand or protecting them from the loss they would incur by picking a field with too many workers. Ultimately, the grower discussed the second gang but, according to his testimony, the remaining crew was too small to bring in the entire crop and one third of it was lost. "Many instances of like sort might be cited," the Commision added.[23]

The padroni's role was thus ambigious and dynamic. A padroni might play the role of taskmaster, shop steward or indifferent mediator, depending on his interests of the moment. Thus, although the padroni secured and supervised workers and allowed growers to deny responsibility for conditions in and out of the fields, growers paid the price of dependence on an uncertain ally.

The padroni's authority over the berry pickers was never unlimited and it didn't last very long either. Although reformers thought that the same individuals were dragged back to the fields year after year, there is little evidence of this. Italian families worked in New Jersey's fields only until they could secure an adequate wage by other means. Some bought small farms of their own and settled there permanently.[24] Most returned to city jobs and were replaced by new emigrants from Italy. When New Jersey's Department of Labor surveyed the berry picking population in 1930, they found 567 Italian families on 214 farms. They were not the children of Italians who had entered the country in the later nineteenth century; all but two of the men and one of the women were themselves born in Southern Italy.[25]

Though Italian family members withdrew themselves from berry picking and from the limelight of public controversy as soon as they could, reformers kept up their campaign to ban child labor well into the present century. In 1927 they finally succeeded in bringing a bill to the state assembly designed to prohibit the employment of out-of-state children in agriculture during the school year. Upon its defeat, the Pennsylvania Bureau of Women and Children made in investigation of Philadelphia children working on New Jersey farms, which resulted in a new bill before the New Jersey Assembly. This bill too was defeated.[26] Angry at being blamed for a problem they considered beyond their control, the American Cranberry Growers' Association asked New Jersey's Department of Labor in 1930 to begin a new study that would reveal "Why New Jersey Farmers Employ Italian Family Labor." The report, submitted to the Governor in 1931, revealed that little had changed in New Jersey agriculture in fifty years. The perishability of vegetables and fruit crops required "steady, reliable and experienced forces" to pick the crops the day they were ready, the report concluded, and according to 101 farmers interviewed, local help was insufficient.[27] Alongside the hundreds of Italian men and women at work in the fields, the Department of Labor found 1342 children between the ages of six and fifteen. New Jersey finally passed a law restricting children from working in the fields during school hours at the height of the depression in 1937, only to repeal it when growers complained of labor scarcity during the Second World War.

If you focus only on the level of public debate, the controversy over child labor in New Jersey's berry fields would appear to be a conflict between growers, on the one hand, and progressive reformers on the other. But between them, going quietly about their business, were immigrant families who endured the indignities of migrant life and worked in the fields alongside their children, so that their children would not have to remain in those fields throughout their lives.

ENDNOTES

1   In 1905, the Philadelphia and New Jersey Consumer's Leagues commissioned an investigation of working and living conditions on New Jersey's cranberry bogs, and published the results in the national progressive magazine, *Charities and the Commons*. Five years later, the National Child Labor Committee reinvestigated the industry, and their report, reprinted in *The Survey*, brought a storm of outrage from New Jersey growers. The Child Labor Committee undertook a more thorough investigation in 1911 in light of growers' charges of libel and exaggeration only to uncover the same conditions reported the year before. In response to their renewed charges, the State of New Jersey created a commission of its own in 1911, and this Commission of Immigration investigated sixteen bogs and held hearings at which both growers and representatives of the Child Labor Committee testified. And in the same year, a federal Commission on Immigration, known as the Dillingham Commission, sent investigators to New Jersey's berry fields and bogs as part of its massive study to inform Congress on the question of immigration restriction. Together these commissions and inquiries provide the main sources of information on migrant farmworkers in turn-of-the century New Jersey.

2   Of those who arrived between 1887 and 1907, 43 percent returned home. Cinel, D. "The Seasonal Emigrations of Italians in the Nineteenth Century: From Internal to International Destinations." *The Journal of Ethnic Studies* 10, 1 (Spring, 1982): 43.

3   Starr, D.J. *The Italian of New Jersey: A Historical Introduction and Bibliography*, Newark: New Jersey Historical Society, 1985) 11-12. See also *Report of the New Jersey Commission of Immigration, Trenton*, 1914, pg. 33.

4   Schuyler, E. "Italian Immigration in the United States," *Political Science Quarterly*, 4 (1899): 481, cited in Cinel, pg. 43.

5   John Bodnar has shown, for example, that a family of five living in Buffalo, New York between 1890 and 1916 needed an income of $650 to $752 a year simply to subsist, but the average Italian laborer earned only $364 to $624. *The Transplanted*, pg. 76.

6   Bodnar, pg. 76-83.

7   *Ibid.*, pg. 166-167.

8   *Report of the New Jersey Immigration Commission*, Trenton, New Jersey, 1914, pg. 36-37.

9   One widow earned $112 last season, aided only by one child, the report notes. "A family of 3 women earned $70 in six weeks on strawberries." "A widow and a small daughter, 10 to 12 years old, earned $44 in less than four weeks, strawberry picking." "Three women picked strawberries for seventeen days and earned $64." Dillingham Commission, pg. 522-523.

10   Italians made up 75 percent of the women working in the men's and boy's clothing industry and 93 percent of the women doing hand embroidery in New York City. Bodnar, pg. 64.

11   Among the young women interviewed by the Dillingham Commission's investigators were many who made artificial flowers or worked in shirt, overalls and women's clothing factories. In one gang of fifty berry pickers interviewed, all the women did "tailer work" in their homes. Factories located in rural districts such as those in Millville and Vineland, New Jersey, even timed their slack seasons to correspond to the berry harvest. Vineland's shoe factory freed 150 Italians for harvest work. Dillingham Commission, pp. 523 and 71.

12   Dillingham Commission, pg. 528; Chute, "The Cost of the Cranberry Sauce," *The Survey*, pg. 1283.

13   Ginger, "In Berry Field and Bog," pg. 166; NJ Commission on Immigration, Trenton, 1914, pg. 38.

14   Chute, pg. 1283.

15   Markham, E., Lindsey, B.B. and Creel, G.. *Children in Bondage: A Complete and Careful Presentation of the Anxious Problem of Child Labor — its Causes, its Crimes, and its Cure* (New York: Hearst International Library Co., 1914. Reprint ed., NY: Arno and the New York Times, 1969): 202-204.

16   Ibid., pg. 202.

17   Vecoli, R.J. "Italian American Workers, 1880-1920: Padrone Slaves or Primitive Rebels?" in S.M. Tomasi, ed. *Perspectives in Italian Immigration and Ethnicity*, New York: Center for Migration Studies, 1977 and Marie Lipari, "The Padrone System: An Aspect of American Economic History," in Francesco Cordasco and Eugene Bucchioni, eds. *The Italians: Social Background of an American Group*, Clifton, NJ: Augustus M. Kelley Publishers, 1974.

18   The Italian berry growers of Vineland and Hammonton tended to keep their farms small (their average acreage was 15) so as to avoid the need for outside labor. It is estimated that berry farms under 25 acres could be managed without hired help.

19   Dillingham Commission, pg. 524.

20   Chute, "The Cost of the Cranberry Sauce," pg. 1281-1284; *32nd Annual Report of the State Board of Agriculture*, Trenton, New Jersey, 1904, pg. 112.

21   *Ibid.*, pg. 525.

22   Jacqueline Hall *et al.*, *Like A Family*.

23   *2nd Annual Report of the State Board of Agriculture*, Trenton, New Jersey, 1904, pg. 112-113.

24   Dillingham Commission investigators found upon interviewing fifty male "representative heads of farm families" in Hammonton that only ten had purchased their land upon their arrival in the United States. Of the 72 percent who had worked for wages before buying berry farms, half had worked as farm laborers. And, after they bought land, most of these men continued to work on neighboring farms for a period of one to ten years. Dillingham Commission, pg. 101.

25   New Jersey Department of Labor, *Why New Jersey Farmers Employ Italian Family Labor,* Trenton, NJ, 1931.

26   New Jersey Assembly No. 182, Feb. 7, 1927; Assembly No. 32, Jan. 16, 1928. See the *Report of the Commission to Investigate the Employment of Migratory Children in the State of New Jersey* (Trenton: State Printers, 1931): pg. 3; "Employment of Philadelphia Children at Farm Labor," *Monthly Labor Review* v, 28 (1929):82-83.

27   *Ibid.,* pg. 12-33.

6

ITALIAN POW'S AND THE ITALIAN-AMERICAN COMMUNITY, 1943-1945: AN OVERVIEW

Louis Keefer

Fifty thousand Italian prisoners of war were held in the United States during World War II. Under what circumstances did these men interact with the Italian-American community, and what resulted from such interaction?

First, some background information. The 1940 U.S. census counted 4.6 million Italian-Americans and, early in Benito Mussolini's drive to make Italy a recognized world power, many strongly supported his efforts. John P. Diggins, in his book *Mussolini and Fascism: The View from America*, wrote:

> Tens of thousands turned out for rallies in New York, Chicago, Philadelphia, Boston and elsewhere. Here women contributed their gold wedding rings, receiving in turn steel rings from Mussolini which were blessed by a parish priest. At a Brooklyn rally the Italian Red Cross passed trays to collect gold watches, cigarette lighters, crucifixes, and other metallic mementoes needed to finance the war effort — two hundred tons of copper postcards, it was estimated, were sent to the home country when the United States government halted copper shipments to Italy[1]

Gradually, this support base was eroded, and immediately after the Japanese attack at Pearl Harbor and Mussolini's declaration of war on the U.S., his approval rating fell precipitously. A *Fortune* magazine article may have said it best: "Four and a half million first and second generation

48

Italians are longing for a miracle: American victory without Italian defeat."[2]

Later, when the full implications of the war became apparent, an overwhelming majority of Italian-Americans supported the U.S. war effort without reservation. When Italy declared war on Germany in October, 1943, there were sighs of relief throughout the Italian-American community. At least 500,000 Americans of Italian descent served in the U.S. military.[3]

As Italian prisoners of war began to arrive in this country, a few in late 1942, most of them in early- and mid-1943, the Army tried to minimize any publicity concerning them and the southern and southwestern camps to which they were initially sent. This proved difficult for the simple reason that local populaces often watched them arrive, not only at ocean ports but at the inland prisoner of war stockades as well.

In short order, newspapers such as the *New York Times* and family magazines such as the *Saturday Evening Post* began to provide emotional "human interest" stories in which — quite consistent with the war's developments in Sicily and Italy — most Italian prisoners were depicted pretty much as "nice guys" who never wanted anything to do with the war anyway.

Approximately 4% of the 50,000 Italian prisoners were noncommissioned officers and 7% were officers. Most of these men were well-educated but not necessarily English-speaking. The average soldier was neither.

Having suffered severe sleep and food deprivation over long periods of fighting (mainly in North Africa), the prisoners needed time to recover physical strength. Gradually, many were able to see that most of what they had been told about America and about the war was false (including Il Duce's claim that New York City had been bombed to rubble).

Many men were deeply disappointed to be sent to camps in the southwestern deserts — sprawling, bleak, semi-uninhabitable layouts such as found in Hereford, Texas, Florence, Arizona, and Lordsburg, New Mexico. The blowing sand and tumbleweeds, the snakes and scorpions, and the temperature extremes were much too reminiscent of their recent Saharan experience. Others, assigned to more hospitable camps near towns such as Como, Mississippi, Monticello, Arkansas, or Weingarten, Missouri, were altogether more pleased.

When permitted to do so, large numbers of prisoners worked outside the camps in order to earn extra money and to escape the awful boredom of confinement. Some picked corn, cotton, beets, peanuts, and other crops. Others learned to rope and brand cattle, became loggers, and worked in small industrial shops. Theoretically, such pursuits would not be considered "war work," as that would have been prohibited by the rules of the Geneva Convention.

At all camps, the men quickly found special activities and sport opportunities inside the barbed wire. Their favorite game was soccer, but they also played volleyball, and even softball (some thinking it was Joe DiMaggio's game). The less athletic produced camp newsletters, read the Italian-language books provided by local well-wishers, listened to music on the radio, saw American movies, and often staged their own musicals and operas.

Up to this point, the Italian prisoners had not been exposed to many Americans. But then a unique situation developed. In September, 1943, Marshal Pietro Badoglio's Italian government surrendered to the Allies, and in a matter of weeks declared war on Germany. How would the reversal change the status of the Italian POW?

In early 1944, the U.S. announced the formation of the "Italian Service Units" (ISUs). POWs could pledge loyalty to Allied war aims and work beside U.S. Army personnel in non-combat roles. While technically still POWs, the volunteers would receive certain freedoms, and would wear regular army uniforms with special ISU identification patches.

The Army screened out 2,000 POWs as "Fascists" and ruled them ineligible for ISU membership. The remaining men were given the freedom of choice. In round numbers, 35,000 POWs became ISU "cooperators," while 13,000 refused, feeling that switching sides in the middle of the war was either immoral or wrong-headed. Those who said "no" — the "non-cooperators" — remained behind barbed wire, essentially sequestered from the Italian-American community for the war's duration.

What a different situation for most of the 35,000 Italians formed into 195 company-sized units and assigned to various Army posts throughout the United States!

A high proportion of these posts were located along the east and west coasts, and were near concentrated Italian-American populations. Although the men could only visit nearby towns and go to museums, zoos, and other public places on escorted group sight-seeing tours, they could entertain friends and families on their own posts. Large numbers of Italian-Americans came to teas, dances, picnics, and theatrical presentations.

For example, between 3,000 and 4,000 civilian guests crowded Camp Knight (Oakland, California) every Sunday. Traffic jams were so bad the base commander, Col. Louis B. Rapp, set up a system of advance written approvals for visitors. He limited visits to adult family members, who would only see men known to them.[4]

This rule was intended to eliminate the practice of coming to search at random for a cousin or other relative thought to be a POW somewhere in the U.S. Such searches were taking place at ISU installations all over the country.

Agnes Piva met her husband-to-be, Bruno Piva, while seeking relatives at San Francisco's Presidio. Later, he was sent to Camp Knight, where she saw him frequently. During these visits, she says, "Bruno and I would sit on benches in front of the barracks and do a little smooching, only interrupted now and then by this mean American sergeant who patrolled in a jeep and screamed at us and all the other smoochers to cut it out. We would stop when he went by, but we resumed the second he was out of sight. Trying to stop us was like trying to stop the dawn."

Though the Army made no official attempts to "advertise" the presence of ISU detachments near any particular communities, here and there a kindly commandant might hint that visitors would be welcomed. In fact, visitors were crucial to morale.

Italian-American families in the Baltimore, Maryland, area first learned of the ISU men at Fort Meade from an Italian-speaking radio broadcaster, Guy Sardella, who was eventually honored by the men for working to arrange Saturday afternoon dances. The dances were so popular that special buses were needed to carry all the eager young women and their families and friends from Baltimore's "Little Italy." Giovanni Ribero met his wife Rose at a Fort Meade dance, just as Bruno Brotto would meet his wife Gabriella.

Just imagine the many, many variations of such activity taking place wherever there were Italian Service Units! And, do not assume that ISU men in more remote areas were ignored. On weekends, Italian-Americans from Philadelphia drove a 200-mile round trip to visit ISU men stationed near Chambersburg, Pennsylvania. That's how Ennio Calabresi met his wife Sarah, and they did little more exciting than talk and stroll along post pathways.

Before the end of 1944 the Army was allowing small groups of ISU men to visit individual families. Commonly, six to ten ISU men, escorted by an Italian-American NCO from the same unit, would go to someone's home for dinner. The meal might be followed by singing and dancing. The host family sometimes invited neighbors and friends to join the party.

In time, the system of group passes was widely abused — men stayed AWOL overnight with their hosts, and got into trouble with MPs and local police when they tried to sneak back into camp undetected. The prisoners committed no crimes greater than stealing someone's car and perhaps running a red light, but public opinion did not approve of former enemies having, as some critics put it, "the keys to the city."

Outraged citizens soon were accusing the Army of "coddling" its POWs, and for a time some of the prisoners' hard-earned freedoms were sharply curtailed. Among the well-known media personalities abetting the controversy were Walter Winchell and Drew Pearson. Almost all of the alleged "abuses" with which the Italians were charged — such as a Winchell item saying they threw empty beer bottles from the windows of a New York City bus — were proved false in meticulous Army investigations.

But in early 1945 when the war seemed won, the Army's control over

ISU activities eased. Those in charge of the ISU men began to say, "Hey, what does it matter, let them have fun." In some camps, prisoners even slipped out at night alone, with tacit approval and no one officially any the wiser. Only the men's fear that they might ruin their chances for early repatriation kept the situation in hand.

The Italian prisoners serving in ISU detachments and large numbers of Italian-Americans became so close they resembled an extended family: the prisoners worked all week for Uncle Sam — during which time they made valuable contributions to the war effort — then went "home" each weekend to relax and enjoy themselves. After all, most had the same language and the same culture, the same religion, and the same dreams of the peace to come. Closeness came naturally.

Being exposed to a democratic way of life, and having the concept of democracy explained to them by trusted Italian-American friends, must have had quite an influence on some of these young men. Considering that the youngest had never lived in a democracy, never read a free paper, or voted in a free election, their American tutors had a difficult task.

In some cases, relationships between ISU men and young American women developed into much more than friendships. Couples "went steady," became engaged, and occasionally began unscheduled families. A few managed to marry against Army rules. If the marriage was discovered, the offending ISU man was returned to a regular POW camp.

Giuseppe Pagliarulo "eloped" for one day from his ISU company to marry a Yuma, Arizona, girl. He was caught, sent back to the Monticello, Arkansas, POW camp and did not see his wife Ellen for two years (until March 2, 1947) when he returned from Italy and she met him at a dock in New York.

Francesco Tarasco was lucky. He and his wife Elsa were wed in a Catholic Church by a Baltimore priest without the U.S. Army ever finding out. Subsequently, Tarasco returned to America more quickly than the other hundreds of POWs who had to wait for their future wives to come to Italy, there to marry and bring them back as spouses of American citizens.

Based on my interviews with more than two dozen of these couples, it appears that the marriages have been largely happy and successful. They certainly have produced for America a wealth of fine, well-educated young people.

My interviews were always unstructured, and ranged widely. All of the men spoke English reasonably well (unluckily, I do not speak Italian), though all seemed also to have kept full fluency in Italian or in their own dialect. Many of their Italian-American wives are no longer fluent, and the children of these couples seldom speak Italian at all.

Most of the men return to Italy periodically, often taking their wives along. They have by no means given up on their roots, and seem to love Italy and the United States more or less equally. They are, of course, mostly now in their 70s, or even older, but still have sisters and brothers, nieces and nephews, and multitudinous cousins still living in the old country.

In my book, *Italian Prisoners of War in America, 1942-1946: Captives or Allies?*[5] I present dozens of instances where the POWs interacted with Italian-Americans in both social and in work contexts. Generally speaking, there was full understanding and affection running in both directions. I made no attempt to quantify how much either group influenced the other.

In general, I should report, the book relies largely on the spoken and written words of these former prisoners to make whatever points seem valid and pertinent. I deliberately refrained from "interpretations" and "conclusions," feeling, rather, that the men's words speak for themselves. I make no case for this approach, but simply say that's how I worked.

By way of concluding, it is sufficient for me to say that a relatively small number of Italian war prisoners held in America influenced a much, much larger Italian-American community just by being almost a part of it for a time.

The influence of the Italian-American community, and of the United States itself, on the war prisoners was far greater — as evidenced by the hundreds and probably even thousands of prisoners returning to America to become part of it forever.

ENDNOTES

1   Diggins, J.P., *Mussolini and Fascism: The View from America* (Princeton: Princeton University Press, 1972), 302.

2   "Steam from the Melting Pot," *Fortune*, Sept. 1942, 75.

3   LaGumina, S.J., *An Album of the Italian-American* (New York: Franklin Watts, Inc., 1972), 39-40.

4   Col. Rapp's policy was reprinted in *Il Corriere del Popolo*, San Francisco, CA, 23 June 1944.

5   Keefer, L.E., *Italian Prisoners of War in America, 1942-1946: Captives or Allies?* (New York: Praeger, 1992).

7

THE ITALIANS IN KENOSHA, WISCONSIN

JOSEPH SALITURO

> After thirty days in the steamship
> We got to America;
> We slept on the bare earth,
> We ate bread and sausages ...
>
> ... We ate bread and sausages,
> But the industry of us Italians
> Founded the towns and cities ... [1]
> (old immigrant song)

Although Italians had been coming to America since colonial times, they did not come in great numbers until after the unification of Italy in the 1870's.[2] Unlike the earlier Italian immigrants who came here in small numbers, were better educated and mainly from northern Italy, these later immigrants came in great numbers, were less educated and came mainly from southern Italy and Sicily.[3] From the time of Italian unification to the start of World War I, some 3,500,000 Italians came to the United States, a little over 2,000,000 coming in one decade alone, 1900 to 1910.[4] This large scale Italian immigration continued, though in decreasing numbers until the National Origins Quota Laws of the 1920's severely limited further Italian immigration to the United States. Those who came after this time did so mainly to join family members who were already here.

Most of these Italian immigrants settled in the large industrialized urban centers of the Northeast and the Midwest, including Chicago. From these centers, they made their way throughout the entire country. Italian immigrants in Chicago eventually moved north to the small Wisconsin city of Kenosha.

This paper will focus on the Italian settlement of Kenosha and the development of the Italian community in that city. Who were these settlers, why did they come, how did they get here, and where did they settle? Life in the Italian community will be looked at, as will the relation of this community with the outside "American" community. Particular emphasis will be put on the Calabresi immigrants, as they make up the largest segment of the Kenosha Italians. The adjustment of the Italians to Kenosha and their rise up the social, economic and political ladders will be covered.

Woven into this will be the history of the Salituro family, as a microcosm of the larger Italian community. This paper will show how the process of chain migration brought the Salituros to Kenosha and how they adjusted to life in America.

The period covered is from the arrival of the first Italian immigrants to Kenosha to the election of the first Italian American Mayor, approximately 1890 to 1980. Though coverage of some of the period between these dates will be minimal, the inclusion of the latter is to show the acceptance of the Italians to full participation in the Kenosha community.[5]

Kenosha is located in the southeast corner of Wisconsin, about half way between the metropolitan areas of Chicago, Illinois, and Milwaukee, Wisconsin. Although located in Wisconsin, Kenosha has identified strongly with Chicago, especially so have the Kenosha Italians who have family and cultural ties with that city. Originally founded in the 1830's by New England and New York Yankees, Kenosha is today a city of many diverse ethnic groups. Both new and old immigrants found a place in Kenosha. Immigrants from Northern and Western Europe started coming to Kenosha soon after its founding. These were mainly German, but also included were Danes, Norwegians, Irish, English, Welsh and Czechs. Then just before the turn of the century and continuing into the 20th century, Southern and Eastern Europeans came. These included Hungarians, Lithuanians, Slovaks, Serbians, Croatians, Armenians, Russians, Eastern European Jews and Italians.[6]

It was during the time of the arrival of these later immigrants that Kenosha went through a rapid economic and demographic growth. The city moved from agriculturally related light industry to heavy industry, and the population increased from 6,532 inhabitants in 1890 to 50,262 to 1930. Much of this growth was provided by immigrants, in particular those from Southern and Eastern Europe.[7]

Sometime in the late 1880's or early 1890's, Italians from Chicago "discovered" Kenosha. They came here as railroad construction crews or "section gangs" of the Chicago and Northwestern Railroad. Once here, they found that Kenosha had jobs for immigrants and that it was a nice place to live. Many left the railroad gangs, got jobs in Kenosha and moved there. They also sent word to their relatives and paisani both in Chicago and Italy that there was work in Kenosha.[8] This began the chain migration of Italians to Kenosha. From this small trickle, Italians then started flooding Kenosha. These early Italian settlers were primarily from the Calabria region of Italy. A few were northern Italians from the Lucca province of Tuscany. They may have come at the same time as the Calabresi or followed them and came to cater to them. They were merchants and operated such enterprises as fruit stands and grocery stores.[9]

Eventually, immigrants from virtually every part of Italy came to Kenosha; however, the Calabresi make up by far the largest group with estimates as high as 70%, followed, a distant second and third, by immigrants from the Marche region and those from Tuscany. Kenosha has more Italians in relation to population than any other of the larger Wisconsin cities.[10]

By 1900, these were 102 foreign-born Italians living in Kenosha County, most all of them in the city of Kenosha.[11] Mrs. Rose Gennacaro Scalzo, who is now 94 years old, was the first girl of Italian descent to graduate from high school. She came to Kenosha with her mother in 1900. Her father, Francesco, had come two years earlier. She knew of two Italian families who were in Kenosha before her father came.[12] Rosemary Giorno Brunner, now in her fifties, states that her grandfather, Santo Giorno, came to Kenosha about 1892 when there were other Italian families already there. Her grandfather for awhile went by the name of Sam Williams, as it was easier for him to get jobs this way.[13] Other Italian names were changed for a variety of reasons. One Italian, Antonio Molinaro, went by the name of Tony Miller.[14] A number of elderly Italians were interviewed by the author of *Peoples of Wisconsin*, who stated they had come from Italy in the late 1880's and early 1890's.[15] These early settlers were from the village of Platania in the province of Catanzaro and the village of Marano in the province of Cosenza, both in the region of Calabria.

These early settlers lived in an area just to the Northwest of the downtown area. Later, they established two other neighborhoods. First, largest and the most cohesive was on the west side near the Geoffry-Nash Motor Plant, the Allen A. Underwear Company and Black Cat Hosiery Company, the second and somewhat smaller was on the south side in the area of the American Brass Works. These early Italians wanted to live close enough to their work to be able to walk there.[16] As the Calabresi residents moved to the west and south sides of town, the downtown area was taken over by Italian immigrants from the Piedmont region of Italy. These had first worked in the copper mines of the Upper Michigan-Northern Wisconsin area of the coal mines in Pennsylvania.[17] By 1905, there were a number of grocery stores, barber shops, and an ice cream parlor operated by Italians. An Italian, Charles Pacini, owned and operated the first silent movie theater in Kenosha, the Majestic Theater, which charged five cents admission. The west side neighborhood boasted an Italian doctor, Dr. Guisseppe Germano, and a mid-wife known as Dona Luisa.[18]

Once the Italian community in Kenosha became large enough, it began to develop a social structure that provided for the needs of the community. Italians immediately started fraternal or benevolent societies to help the members and their families in case of illness and to defray funeral expenses, as well as provide some of their social needs. These were usually small and the members were from the same village of Italy. Among the more important were the Giusseppe Garibaldi Society founded in 1904, the San Francesco di Paola Society founded in 1907, the Santa Maria Santissima della Schiava Society founded in 1910 and the San Michele Arcangelo Society founded in 1911. In the early 1920's, the leaders of these societies thought it better to merge into one large society and the Italian American Society was born.[19] This was a major step in making "Italians" as well as Americans out of the various regional groups.

In Kenosha, as in other cities, the Italian immigrants first worshipped in churches where they were a minority. These were primarily German or Irish Catholic Parishes.[20] The first Italian settlers in Kenosha worshipped at St. James Catholic Church which was a parish made up primarily of Irish immigrants and their descendants. In 1904, Archbishop Sebastian Messmer of Milwaukee sent Italian-born Father Joseph Angelletti to Kenosha with directions to organize a parish for the Italians. Forty-three families enrolled as members and the church was built on the west side. It was called Our Lady of the Holy Rosary Catholic Church. The corner stone was laid on November 14, 1904. On August 13, 1905, the church was dedicated. A commemorative church booklet describes this event

> ...a procession from St. James Church to the new church was held. Numerous societies of the parish were present as well as societies from other parishes and groups. At the head of this line marched a group of musicians, the Holy Rosary Band, this was the first appearance for this group... The religious service, speeches, and festivities lasted throughout the day, to the pleasure of all concerned. It was a gala event, a memorial one indeed.[21]

English language classes were given to the parishioners, and, in 1913, a small chapel to serve the Italians of the south side was opened. This was known as the St. Joseph's Chapel and was later sold to a Russian Evangelical

Congregation when a new Catholic Parish, St. Mark's, was built on the south side. By 1929, the membership of Holy Rosary outgrew the parish facilities. A wealthy Kenosha family, the Alfords, donated land on the north end of the city and a new church was built which retained the original name of Holy Rosary. The intent was to sell or tear down the old church, but parishioners who did not want to move objected and that church was kept, first as a mission of the new church and later as a separate parish. It was given the name "Our Lady of Mount Carmel." Both parishes served primarily Italian members. Those that remained at Mount Carmel were mainly the Calabresi with the Italians from other regions of Italy going to the new church.[22]

Church festivals provided the main social attraction for the Kenosha Italians. These were to celebrate the feast day of the saint for which the church was named, as well as other saints. These celebrations started with a devotional service in the church, then men of the parish carried a large statue of the Madonna in a parade around the neighborhood. They would stop every so often so that people could pin money on the clothing of the Madonna. A band usually led the procession followed by the clergy and the various church societies. Later in the evening, there would be celebrations on the parish grounds. These celebrations even continued into the parish-ioners' homes. Nicholas Margaro, a school principal, who, along with his father, Raffaele, was interviewed for the series, *The Peoples of Wisconsin,* recalls that after the festival there was dancing at people's homes.

> ... as a child, I can remember these folks coming over to Uncle Tommie's granddad's place. He had his basement all fixed up so that they could have dances down there or in the backyard. And granddad just loved to play the bagpipes and the folks would come and dance and they'd dance their tarantella and those other dances that were native that they had learned.[23]

Though not among the very first settlers, the Salituro family replicates the pattern of the Italian immigrants who came to Kenosha. The Giovanni Salituro and Carmine DeRose family from Rende, province of Cosenza in Calabria, sent one of their five sons, Santo, to Kenosha in 1911. He was followed two years later by an older brother, Francesco. Santo joined the American Army in World War I, while two other brothers, Luigi and Pasquale, fought in the Italian Army. Francesco returned to Italy in 1920 and came back in 1922 bringing with him a younger brother, Settino. Meanwhile in 1921, brothers Luigi and Pasquale had come to America to join brother Santo. Luigi and Pasquale had already married in Italy, but Settino was still single.

The Salituros lived together in various boarding houses run by other

Italian immigrants. What historian Michael LaSorte says about how the young Italian boarders treated the boarding house owner and his family with great respect held true for the Salituros. They called the owners "padrono" and "padrona," and "boss" and "bossa," and looked on them as substitute parents and family.[24] When Santo married, however, the brothers insisted on living with him. Pasquale is quoted as saying he would be happy, "to live in a closet" as long as he could live with his brother.[25]

The brothers obtained work in the industrial plants in Kenosha, three of them at the American Brass Company and two at the Simmons Bedding Company, though at times they also worked in Chicago when they were out of work in Kenosha, staying with distant relatives or other "paisani" there. Pasquale also worked as a barber while holding down a full-time job in a factory and all the brothers had various part time jobs in addition to their full time ones. The brothers that still had families in Italy sent remittance money and also bought land and homes there.

In 1930, Settino returned to Italy to marry a village girl, Concetta, and she joined him in Kenosha in 1934, bringing with her a young son, Cesare. Along with them came Giovanni, the eldest son of Francesco to join his father. Giovanni soon bought an old truck and went house to house in the Italian neighborhoods selling fruit and vegetables.[26] In 1928, the wife of Pasquale (another Concetta) and her young son Armando came to join him, though the whole family along with Yolanda, a girl born in Kenosha, went back to live in Italy, returning to Kenosha in 1936. In 1938, others of Francesco's family joined him in Kenosha. These were his wife Angela, son Antonio, and daughter Rosina. Another daughter, Carmela, who had married in Italy, joined the family in the 1950's, moving to Chicago, where relatives of her husband lived. Luigi's family, consisting of wife Rosina, daughters Ida and Elena, and sons Guisseppe and Eugenio, also came in 1938 to join him.

All the brothers, except Santo, went back and forth to Italy, as did other Italian "birds of passage;" however, even Santo sent money home so that his father could purchase land for him, evidently hoping some day to return to Italy. However, in 1923 he married sixteen year old Clara Missurelli in Kenosha and started to raise a family there, never to return to Italy. Also somewhere along the way, a spelling change took place in his name replacing the final vowel o with an e, as someone thought this sounded more "American."[27] Brothers Luigi, Pasquale, Settino, and Francesco purchased properties in Italy and their families lived on these properties until coming to Kenosha.

The Italian colony in Kenosha in many ways was like the ethnic neighborhoods described by historians John Bodnar, Rudolph Vecoli and others. Vecoli says that the Italian neighborhoods were made up of people who came from the same village in Italy. This was known as "campanalismo" (within the shadow of the village church bell).[28] To a certain extent, this was true in Kenosha especially in the more cohesive West side neighborhood and the downtown Piamontese neighborhood. Bodnar says that immigrant settlements included peoples of various nationalities.[29] This was definitely true in the Kenosha south side Italian neighborhood where the Salituro family lived. Though this neighborhood consisted of a large number of Italians, there was a good number of Germans and other Southern and Eastern Europeans. Several stores in the area were owned by East European Jews. The son of one of these (a dry goods merchant) became a good friend of the Salituro children. Even as far back as 1938, there were three Black families in the neighborhood and the Italian children played with the children of these families. Italian parents, however, encouraged their children to associate only with Italians and to keep away from the "Americani," who were all the non-Italians, and marriage to non-Italians was discouraged.

All the Italians had large vegetable gardens, many fruit trees, and the ubiquitous grape arbor. The households consisted of many children with a significant number of families taking in boarders. Families with five, six or more children lived in what were essentially two bedroom homes. Young Italians addressed the elderly with the titles Zio or Zia (Uncle and Aunt) and were taught to have considerable respect for them.

New Calabresi immigrants were accepted immediately by other Southern Italian families, but not always so by the non-Italians or the Northern Italians. Many non-Italians would refer to them as "Dagoes," and some Northern Italians acted as if they were better than the Calabresi. Mrs. Rose Scalzo describes her early school years, where she was the only Italian, as being very sad because the other children would not play with her. She also mentions the aloofness of Northern Italians towards Calabresi which she noticed as she grew older.[30]

> My mother was especially welcomed in the Italian neighborhood since she met a traditional need, that of a folk healer. Her power to nullify the evil eye, or "mal occhio," was very strong and consequently everyone immediately accepted and respected her. She also knew much about practical medical healing and people sought her for setting sprained arms, massaging sore muscles, and curing other maladies.[31]

Like Vecoli's contadini, she did not leave this art behind in Italy. Life in the ethnic neighborhood was pleasant. Everyone knew each other and there was music and laughter in people's homes. It seems every family had someone who sang or played the accordion. Events such as baptisms, first communions, confirmations, weddings, and even funerals were celebrated with much vigor.

The immigrants soon came in contact with America, the men at work, the children at school, and the wives to a lesser extent, with social workers and non-Italian neighbors and merchants. The Protestant churches in the area also tried to influence the immigrants by inviting them to social events. There developed two Italian Protestant churches in Kenosha, almost as early as the Italian Catholic parishes, one was Evangelical and the other Baptist. The Evangelical church had an Italian convert as its minister.[32]

Italian immigrants to Kenosha, like others before them, rose up the economic, social, and political ladders. Coming at a time of rapid industrilization and unionization, Italians were able to get involved in the labor movement on an equal footing with others. Many became labor leaders and headed a number of the larger Kenosha unions.[33] My father was a member of the United Furniture Workers at Simmons Company where he worked and was very faithful in attendance at, and participation in, union meetings. He also took great pride in marching with his union in the annual Labor Day parade.

As they began to dominate certain wards, Italians got involved in politics. First as ward bosses, delivering votes for some "America" politicians in return for jobs and other favors, then running for office themselves. As early as 1904, an Italian, Frank Guardiola, was elected to the school board, and in 1912 Nicholas Conforti became not only the first Italian, but the first of the new immigrants elected to the City Council.[34] Fearing the growing power of the new immigrants in the ethnic wards, the old immigrants and Yankees in 1922 succeeded in creating a City Manager form of government with aldermen elected at large rather than by wards. In spite of this, the Italians in 1932 were able to elect the first new immigrant alderman at large, Jasper Gentile. This was due to the efforts of the Italian Non-Partisan League formed in the late 1920's.[35] Finally in 1957, the City Manager form of government was abolished and Kenosha returned to a Mayor and Councilman elected by wards. This did not help the Italians and other ethnics that much, as by then the old ethnic wards had been broken up; however, in 1980, Kenosha elected its first Italian American Mayor John Biolitti, a grandson of Calabresi immigrants. In the meantime in 1946, the first Italian American from Kenosha was elected to the Wisconsin Legislature. This was Assemblyman George Molinaro, the son of Calabresi immigrants.[36]

Going to college was a quick way of advancing economically and socially, and the Salituro family encouraged its members to do this. Cousin Armando was the first of the Salituros to get a college degree. He joined the Merchant Marines during World War II and was sent to their academy where he obtained his bachelor degree in Engineering along with a commission as an officer. After World War II, cousin Tony, taking advantage of the GI Bill as did many other Italian Americans, went on to college and received a bachelor degree in Business Administration. He went to work for

Simmons Bedding Company and is now plant manager at the Janesville, Wisconsin, plant. In the mid-1950's, Joe, Gene, and cousin Santo received bachelor degrees. In 1959, Joe graduated from law school and went to work for Kenosha County where he soon became head of the Civil Legal Department. Santo went to work for Northwestern Life Insurance Company in the public relations section. Gene went to work for the sales department of Western Printing Company. The third generation has so far produced a sports editor, a teacher, a dentist, a real estate salesman, a building contractor, a nurse, an insurance salesman, and a medical doctor. A number of others have received bachelor degrees.

As late comers and mostly without money or skills, the Italians, like other late immigrant groups had to settle in the industrialized urban areas of America where unskilled work was readily available. They lived in their own colonies for protection and sociability, and their churches and self-help organizations played an important part in their adjustment to America, as well as helping them maintain old world ties and traditions. They started businesses, got involved in unions and politics, and rose up the social and economic ladders. In Kenosha, they found jobs and a place where they could settle down and bring up their children.

As Bodnar put it, "...on the level of everyday life, where ordinary people could inject themselves into the dynamic of history, immigrants acquiesced, resisted, hoped, despaired, and ultimately fashioned a life as best they could."

The history of the Italians in Kenosha, including the Salituro family, validates Bodnar's insight. Pushed by forces beyond their control into a new setting, they had to work very hard to achieve their dream of a better life. Slowly but surely, they adapted to the new environment and they began to reshape it in their favor. By the second generation, the third for sure, they had worked their way from the lowest rungs of society to a solid position in America's social, economic and political middle class.

ENDNOTES

1   Alexanader DeConde, *Half Bitter, Half Sweet* (New York: Charles Scribner's Sons, 1971), 181.
2   Luciano Iorizzo and Salvatore Mondello, *The Italian Americans* (Boston: Twayne Publishers, 1980), Chapters II and III. Nelli, Humbert S., "Italians," *Harvard Encyclopedia of American Ethnic Groups* (Cambridge: Harvard University Press, 1980), 547-548.
3   Betty Boyd Caroli, *The Italian Repatriation from the U.S.* (New York: Center for Migration Studies, 1973), 26-29. Robert Harney, "The Italian Experience in the United States," *Italians in North America* (Canada: Multicultural Society of Ontario, Toronto), 2-3.

4   U.S. Immigration and Naturalization Service, *Annual Report* (Washington, D.C.: U.S. Government Printing Office, 1977), Table 13.

5   On the Italians in Kenosha and my own family, I have made use of citizenship records in the Area Research Center at the University of Wisconsin-Parkside, census reports, city directories, interviews, personal recollection, and materials available in local newspapers and institutions.

6   John D. Buenker, "Immigration and Ethnic Groups"*Kenosha County in the 20th Century* (John A. Neuenschwander, editor, 1976), 1-4. Carrie Cropely, *Kenosha from Pioneer Village to Modern City: 1835-1935* (Kenosha County Historical Society, 1958).

7   Buenker, 3-7.

8   Domenick Romano Interviews (Kenosha, Wisconsin) May 17, October 20, and November 16, 1989. William J. Scherick, *The Peoples of Wisconsin* (Madison, Wisconsin: State Historical Society of Wisconsin, 1955), 24-26.

9   Romano Interviews, Kenosha City Directories, Naturalization Records (Area Research Center, University of Wisconsin-Parkside).

10   Sample taken by students of John Buenker, University of Wisconsin-Parkside, 1988. Scherick, 23. Scherick gave Italian population of Kenosha in 1955 at 10,000.

11   Buenker, Table III, page 4.

12   Rose Scalzo Interview (Kenosha, Wisconsin), September 24, 1989.

13   Rosemary Brunner Interview (Kenosha, Wisconsin), September 25, 1989.

14   Naturalization Records (University of Wisconsin-Parkside: Area Research Center).

15   Scherick, 24-25.

16   Romano Interview.

17   Rinaldo Tovo Interview (Kenosha, Wisconsin), April 6, 1989.

18   Romano Interview.

19   *Kenosha News Special Edition*, "Italian American Society Golden Anniversary" (September 7, 1973), 2. *Italian American Society Membership Manual*, 1-2.

20   Iorizzo and Mondello, 219.

21   Father Thomas Suriano, Editor, *Our Lady of Mount Carmel Parish Commemorative Booklet* (1965), 1.

22   *Kenosha News* (November 18, 1949). Steven M. Avella "For the Welfare of My Italian Children: Samuel Strich, Angelo Simeone and Religious Ethnic Conflicts in Kenosha" unpublished paper delivered at University of Wisconsin-Parkside (May 21, 1988).

23   Scherick, 26.

24   Michael LaSorte, *La Merica* (Philadelphia: Temple University Press, 1985), 122. Clara Salituro Interview (Kenosha, Wisconsin), September 20, 1989.

25   Clara Salituro Interview.

26   John Salituro Interview (Kenosha, Wisconsin), September 21, 1989.

27   Somewhere in the process, all of our names got changed. Giuseppe became Joseph or Joe, Eugenio became Eugene or Gene, Ida became Edith, and Elena became Helen, without any of us really having anything to say about it.

28   Rudolph Vecoli, "Contadini in Chicago: A Critique of the Uprooted," *Journal of American History* (June 1964), 406.

29   John Bodnar, *The Transplanted* (Bloomington: Indiana University Press, 1987), 177-178.

30   Scalzo Interview.
31   Vecoli, 416.
32   Buenker, 18-19.
33   Ibid, 30.
34   Ibid, 33.
35   Ibid, 33-34.
36   John D. Buenker "George Molinaro: Labor-Ethnic Politician," *Kenosha Retrospective*, Nicholas C. Burchel and John A. Neuenschwander, Editors, (Kenosha County Bicentennial Commission, 1981), 252.
37   Bodnar, 215.

PART III
RELIGION

8

SAMUEL CHARLES MAZZUCHELLI: GIFTED PIONEER OF THE MIDWEST

Flora Breidenbach

In 1843, a statue of Mary, the mother of Jesus, was shipped from Paris, France, addressed simply to "M. Mazzuchelli, United States of America."[1] Though the population of the United States was about sixteen million people and its territory vast, it found its way to the correct person, Father Samuel Charles Mazzuchelli in Galena, Illinois. In the mid-nineteenth century, Mazzuchelli was well-known in the United States, yet today very few people in the Midwest, and even fewer elsewhere, know who he was.

The purpose of this paper is to bring to the attention of others the magnitude of the work of Father Mazzuchelli, thereby contributing to the cultural history of the Midwest and of Italians in America.

Carlo Gaetano Samuele Mazzuchelli was born in Milan, Italy, on November 4, 1806, to a family famous in banking, business, and the arts. Given a private education by tutors as was befitting the child of a well-to-do family, Samuel was later sent to Switzerland to continue his studies when the political situation changed as the movement for independence and unification began.

Hoping Samuel would eventually enter politics, his family was disappointed when, at the age of seventeen, he asked for his father's permission to enter the Dominican Order to study for the priesthood. Opposed at first, his father eventually consented, and the young man went to Rome to begin his studies. Five years later, Samuel Mazzuchelli left Italy. He spent several months in France improving his French, then emigrated to the United States. After a long voyage by ship, stagecoach, and steamboat, he arrived in Cincinnati. Shortly thereafter, he was sent to Kentucky to study English.

67

The trip from Cincinnati to Kentucky was a rugged introduction to life on the American frontier. After a long train ride, the cultured young man from Italy mounted a horse; he had never been on a horse before, and, after an exhausting thirty-eight mile non-stop trip, which put him to bed for two days, Mazzuchelli "prayed earnestly that he would never see a horse again."[2] Little did he know at the time that horseback would become his primary means of transportation!

After an intensive study of English, Mazzuchelli was able to continue his theological studies, and in September, 1830, he was ordained a priest. A month later, at the age of twenty-four, the tolerant, gentle, mild-mannered young priest set out for his first assignment, Machinac Island. There were no other priests in the area at the time and his parish covered 200,000 square miles. It was removed by thousands of miles and hundreds of years from the refined culture of Milan which he had known.

Years before Mazzuchelli's arrival in Mackinac, French Jesuit priests, including Father Marquette, had built a church there. It was the only place where Mazzuchelli ever found a church "already built and waiting for him."[3]

After some time, Mazzuchelli moved on to northeastern Wisconsin. There he ministered to fur trappers, traders, and several tribes of Native Americans: the Winnebago, Menominee, Ottawa, and Chippewa. Mazzuchelli was well-liked by the Native Americans. In 1833, Whirling Thunder, representing the Winnebago tribe, presented a petition to the United States government agent for Indian Affairs. It stated, "We wish to know more of our great Father above. We want Mr. Mazzuchelli to remain with us...."[4] Mazzuchelli remained with the Native Americans of Wisconsin until 1835 when he was requested to minister to the people of the lead-mining area around Galena, Illinois, and Dubuque, Iowa, because he was the only available priest who could preach well in English. Though not the first priest in the area, he was the first to remain there. Those who had preceded him had either died in one of the frequent cholera epidemics, or had left, "unable to stomach the ugliness of the hard-drinking mining area."[5] Deeply moved by the number of orphans left by the cholera epidemics, Mazzuchelli became the foster parent of two of them, John Cavanaugh and Frank Mealiff.

The Irish had an especially difficult time with the name of Mazzuchelli and, because of this, he was known variously as Father Samuel, Father Mathew Kelly, Father Kelly, and Father Massy Kelly. As a result, it is believed that many of his accomplishments have been lost; it has made it difficult to trace them.[6]

By 1839, Mazzuchelli's parish of 3500 Catholics spanned an area that extended two hundred miles long by thirty to fifty miles wide. In an area without developed roads or bridges, many of his parishioners lived in cabins without windows or floors, though an occasionally wealthy soul had a piano.

Mazzuchelli revealed an open-minded attitude. His ideas were modern for his time, and he was criticized by those more conservative than he. For example, he said Mass wherever it was possible to do so, not hesitating to use a table, a dresser, or even a piano for an altar. When ministering to the Native Americans he used the vernacular in the liturgy rather than Latin as was the custom, or he said one verse in Latin and one in the Native American language. He won respect from the Protestants in the area because of his strong and simple life-style. They admired him so much that they did not hesitate to contribute money for the construction of Catholic churches. On the other hand, when a Protestant church was destroyed by an arsonist's fire, Mazzuchelli donated money to help rebuild it. He did not object to non-Catholics attending Catholic religious services; he did not care whether they attended out of mere curiosity or out of a real desire to learn about Catholicism. In fact, he always welcomed them, even allowing for a non-Catholic Native American chief to carry the cross at the funeral of a woman of his tribe. Today this act would be called "ecumenical."

In 1847, Mazzuchelli made a long-lasting contribution to the Church in the New World. This was the year in which, under his direction, four women became the first Dominican Sisters of Sinsinawa, Wisconsin, a congregation which today numbers over one thousand members who minister in a variety of fields throughout the United States, Trinidad, and Bolivia. Mattias Hannon, a contemporary of his, described Mazzuchelli as a missionary "in the order of Marquette... He was the grand missionary of the Northwest."[7]

This apostle of midwestern America was more than a simple missionary, however. He possessed an astonishingly wide range of interests and abilities, and he generously shared his talents with others.

One of his salient talents was that of educator, coupled with a strong sense of social justice. A modernist in his approach to learning, he believed that education was necessary for women as well as men, for minorities, in this case Native Americans, as well as whites, and for adults as well as children.

Mazzuchelli developed a plan to educate adults and children of the Menominee nation. He wanted to: 1) establish a school located in the center of the village so it would be easily accessible; 2) hold classes in the Menominee language in order to preserve the native culture; 3) introduce a broad curriculum that included arithmetic, spelling, singing, musical instruments, geography, history of the United States, patriotism, carpentry, agriculture, and needlework; and 4) establish lodging for those students who lived far from the village. The Indian agent in Green Bay, Colonel Stambaugh, a non-Catholic, approved Mazzuchelli's plan and recommended it to the Secretary of War. However, the government granted only two hundred dollars to Mazzuchelli. Distressed over the paucity of funds, he nevertheless continued his work to achieve his goals.

Proficient in the languages of the Native Americans among whom he worked, Mazzuchelli, while visiting Detroit, had an eighteen-page book printed in the Winnebago language, one of the Sioux dialects. The book, *Ocangra Aramee Wawakakara*, containing a pronunciation key according to the English language, the Ten Commandants, and various prayers, is the first known publication in one of the Sioux dialects. The following year, Mazzuchelli published a Chippewa almanac at Green Bay, the first known printing job done in Wisconsin. The only known copy of the almanac is in the rare book room collection of the Library of Congress.

Mazzuchelli never lost sight of the needs of Native Americans and he never tired of making them known to government officials. He continued to be their advocate after leaving the Native American missions. He lobbied hard to procure funds to establish schools for Native Americans, though he met with little success in this endeavor. Depressed, he later wrote prophetically in his *Memoirs*:

> the education of the tribes, even to a moderate degree, is practically impossible under the present conditions and these appear to be so permanent as to foretell the future destiny of the Indians who will have to continue in their … roving … state until the day when the … population of European origin will have filled the entire continent. Then the Indian will have left scarcely a trace of his existence in the land.[8]

In the Galena-Dubuque area, Mazzuchelli met George Wallace Jones, the congressional delegate from Prairie du Chien. In 1844, for $6,500.00 Mazzuchelli purchased eight hundred acres in southwest Wisconsin from Jones to establish a college for the young people of the area. The following year, a school for boys and young men, from eight to twenty years of age, opened at the site known as Sinsinawa Mound. At the beginning, the students lived in a log cabin, but in 1846 the cornerstone was laid for a large stone building for the school. That stone building still stands and remains in use to this day. In March, 1848, the college was incorporated by one of the first acts of the new Wisconsin state legislature. By the fall of that year, the school, which charged twelve dollars per month for tuition, advertised in the Eastern and Southern press in the promotional language of the day:

> The system of education embraces the various arts and sciences usually taught in colleges. A complete knowledge of the Greek and Latin languages and literatures, of Mathematics, Natural Philosophy, Geography, Rhetoric, His-

tory, and English Composition is indispensable for graduation.[9]

Father Mazzuchelli headed the college as its president and also served as one of its instructors.

At about the same time that the college was being developed, Mazzuchelli had established his community of Dominican Sisters. He personally prepared them, teaching them to be intellectually objective but at the same time sensitive. He always "respected their intelligence and treated them as men's equals," a concept not popular historically.[10]

Eventually the college at Sinsinawa Mound became a girls' school, St. Clara. Mazzuchelli loved teaching and he gained the reputation of being an excellent teacher. The curriculum at the girls' school included Moral Theology, Sacred History, Latin, French, German, Rhetoric, English Literature, Mathematics, Bookkeeping, Geography, Astronomy, and Physics. Mazzuchelli purchased pianos and encouraged singing. He directed plays and designed costumes for the students. He himself taught "Human Affairs" using newspapers and magazines as textbooks. He became the first teacher of Physics, then called Natural Philosophy, in the state of Wisconsin. He introduced the laboratory method in Wisconsin and is considered to be "the father of science" in that state.[11] The scientific instruments he used were considered to be superior to what the University of Wisconsin had. Among other equipment, Mazzuchelli had a galvanic battery, a mini Morse telegraph, revolving globes of both the earth and the heavens, Magdeburg spheres, an electric motor, apparatus to show the center of gravity, and a gadget which was a precursor of the neon light.

Mazzuchelli was also the Astronomy instructor at the school. On clear nights he took students out to look through the telescope, even in midwinter. He had slides which he projected by using a miner's lantern. Some of the slides which he used came from a company in New York, but others were apparently made by Mazzuchelli because they were made of materials differing from those used in commercial slides of the day, albeit of equal quality. Many of his slides are displayed at Sinsinawa Mound, to this day the motherhouse of the congregation of Dominican women which he founded.

When Samuel Mazzuchelli first began his ministry among Native Americans, he used temporary churches constructed of Indian mats that could easily be dismantled, but he soon realized that makeshift churches were not enough and that permanent church buildings were needed. Having an accurate vision of the future development of the United States, Mazzuchelli purchased land for churches, schools, and cemeteries. He believed in the security of what is today called "real estate." In a letter dated January 1, 1863, he wrote: "Gold pays no interest and greenbacks are doubtful stuff. Land and minerals never fail."[12]

On the land he purchased, Mazzuchelli began to organize parishes, often serving as architect, master craftsman, and builder of the church. He cut timber, quarried stone, and carved the oranamentation. In 1831, he acquired land for the first Catholic church in Green Bay. Between then and 1852, he built more than thirty churches in Wisconsin, Illinois, and Iowa. He designed and supervised the construction of St. Augustine's in New Diggings, Wisconsin, in 1844, probably the only church which has survived unaltered. It is listed in the National Register of Historic Places. This church has an elegance of grace which is surprising in a frontier church. Much of the charm of the church is due to its altar which Mazzuchelli carved with a pocket knife, modeling it after an altar in Rome sculpted by Bramante. Mazzuchelli also chiseled groves in the wood siding of the building to make it look like blocks of stone. St. Michael's in Galena, Illinois, is another important church built by Mazzuchelli. It features a trussed roof, a type of construction which eliminated the need for pillars, thereby creating a large, magnificent open space on the inside. Mazzuchelli was the architect of many other Galena buildings, including the old market-house, various private homes, and the stone portion of the County Courthouse.

As Mazzuchelli's fame as a builder grew, he was asked to design buildings for pay. The new Iowa Territory Legislature decided to lay out a new capitol and call it Iowa City. Mazzuchelli has been credited with planning the entire community. The *Iowa Historical Record*, among other publications of the time, listed Mazzuchelli as designer of the state capitol itself, a building 120 feet long and 60 feet wide. Built of stone, consisting of three stories, it is an example of classic architecture, containing a hanging stairway that features a two-story-high spiral that appears to be without support. The work Mazzuchelli accomplished in Iowa City and the churches he built make him worthy of the title given to him, "Builder of the West."[13]

Mazzuchelli's labors as priest, educator, and builder should be sufficient for him to be important in the history of the United States, as well as Italian American ethnicity. But this dynamic individual accomplished even more. He started Temperance Societies, directed the Galena Town Choir, belonged to the Shakespeare Coffee Club of Dubuque, and organized the festivities conducted in Dubuque on July 4, 1836, to celebrate the nation's birthday, creation of the Wisconsin territory, and inauguration of Henry Dodge as the Territory's first governor. Aware of Mazzuchelli's interest in government, the members of the legislature elected him to address them at the first session on October 25, 1836. In a learned, instructive, and humorous speech Mazzuchelli spoke to the legislators about the responsibilities of their fiduciary mandate and gave them a brief history of the forms of governments from absolute monarchy to modern democracy. He remained as chaplain to the legislature. Humbly awed at having been chosen chaplain, he wrote in his *Memoirs*: "It would be difficult to find in the history of any country whatsoever a legislative assembly where Protestants outnumbering Catholics eighteen to one have nevertheless conferred the office of chaplain on a priest."[14]

In a ceremony in Burlington, Iowa, 1841, Mazzuchelli made official his love for his adopted country: he became a United States citizen.

Traveling through the vast area where he ministered, occasionally accompanied by Native American guides, but often alone, Mazzuchelli further distinguished himself as a trail blazer. More important, however, is the fact that as he traveled he recorded his findings in little drawings with comments and names in both English and Italian. Out of his drawings he created maps. Indeed, he was one of the first map-makers to detail the central region of the United States. In the introduction to the 1915 edition of Mazzuchelli's *Memoirs*, Archbishop Ireland of St. Paul wrote:

> Mazzuchelli understood with singular clearness the principles of American law and life, and conformed himself to them in heartfelt loyalty. There lay one of the chief causes of the influence allowed him by his fellow-citizens of all classes, and of the remarkable success with which his ministry was rewarded. He was a foreigner by birth and education; situations in his native Italy were much the antipodes of those in the country of his adoption. Yet he was American to the core of his heart, to the tip of his finger. He understood America. He loved America.[15]

Mazzuchelli's *Memoirs* were written precisely out of his love for America and out of his desire to acquaint the Italians of his time with the New World. They provide a vivid picture of the era in which he worked in the Midwest.

Mazzuchelli formulated a topic of keen interest about the Native Americans' culture and their exploitation at the hands of whites. In his *Memoirs*, he compared and contrasted various tribes. Upset, he described how Native Americans lost their lands and how they were forced to move to new areas. He commented that this moving is "always accompanied by dissipation, by disease, and by various calamities which ... lessen the numbers of the Indians."[16] Always interested in the causes of events, Mazzuchelli described how lands taken from Native Americans were settled, how the land was divided among the settlers, the order in which merchants established their businesses, and how cities came to be.

The variety of topics which he presented in his *Memoirs* illustrated his keen powers of observation and the broad spectrum of his interests. He provided accurate descriptions of nature, means of transportation, differences between a territory and a state, making of syrup, construction of log and frame houses, various religious denominations, electoral system, principles of American democracy, and many other elements of significance on the frontier. Mazzuchelli's understanding of the times in which he lived is evident from a remark he made the night after John Brown's attack at Harper's Ferry in 1859: "This is the beginning of the end of human slavery in the United States. It is but a premonition of the approaching storm that is destined to break over this happy land with a violence that will shock the world."[17] Indeed, slavery was the one thing that Mazzuchelli disliked about the United States.

Mazzuchelli's comments are valuable for the light they shed on many aspects of early life in the Midwest. Archbishop Ireland reflected on Mazzuchelli's *Memoirs*:

> As a historical document the *Memoirs* is of exceptional value. It tells of a wide region of territory — from the waters of Huron to those of the Mississippi and to Des Moines — exactly as it was in the days of its wilderness and its first entrance into civilization. The populations that tenanted its forests and prairies — the Ottawa, the Menominee, and the Winnebago, the fur-gatherer and the trader, the incoming land seeker and the town builder — rise from its pages in full native vividness. The reader is brought into immediate touch with them, made to mingle in their daily doings and manners of life. It is precise and exact in descriptions … The writer was a keen observer of incidents of every nature, and a faithful narrator of what he saw and heard … No fervent student of American history will be without a copy of the *Memoirs* on the shelves of his library room.[18]

One of Mazzuchelli's duties as priest was to anoint the sick. Riding his faithful horse, Napoleon, he would leave his house at any time of day or night in good or bad weather to minister to a person's spiritual need. On February 15, 1864, during a blizzard, he was called to minister to a dying person. In haste, Mazzuchelli left without putting on his overcoat. He became ill with double pneumonia and died on February 23, 1864. After a funeral attended by hundreds of people, both Catholic and Protestant, some of whom traveled great distances, Father Mazzuchelli was buried in Benton, Wisconsin, close to St. Patrick's church which contains a painting thought to be his work. Mazzuchelli's obituary appeared in many newspapers throughout the country, including the *San Francisco Monitor* and the *Metropolitan Record of New York*. The latter newspaper commented:

> There he is high up on the scaffold of the church, with coat off and sleeves tucked up, industriously at work in brick and mortar. In the evening you see him in the pulpit discoursing on some abstruse questions of Christian philosophy and tomorrow he lectures before the governor, judges and legislators on the science of political economy but he is always and everywhere present when the sacred duties of the ministry require.[19]

At the time of his death, Mazzuchelli was known from New York to California. Why is it, then, that so few Americans today are aware of the man and his achievements? At one point, he had written to the bishop of Dubuque: "To live retired not known to the world is great happiness ... If the Lord is not very much displeased with me He will permit me to sink into oblivion before the world."[20] This wish of his seems to have been fulfilled, but it is a "shame that America, who honors her heroes so magnanimously, should have overlooked this man who brought to our New World the finest gifts of the old."[21] Samuel Charles Mazzuchelli, O.P., was indeed a pioneer of the Midwest and the fact that he was born in Italy and became an Italian American attests to the rich ethnic tapestry of American civilization. His story is central to the development of the American Midwest.

ENDNOTES

1   Archives of Sinsinawa Mound.
2   Dorcy, S.M.J. *Saint Dominic's Family* (Washington, D.C.: Dominicana Publications, 1983), p. 522.
3   Bartels, J. and Alderson, J.M. *The Man Mazzuchelli: Pioneer Priest* (Madison: Wisconsin House, Ltd., 1974), Chapter 2, n.p.
4   Mazzuchelli, S.C. *The Memoirs of Father Samuel Mazzuchelli*, O.P. (Chicago: Priory Press, 1967), p. 84.
5   Alderson, *The Man Mazzuchelli: Pioneer Priest*, Chapter 7.
6   Alderson, *The Man Mazzuchelli: Pioneer Priest*, Chapter 16.
7   Alderson, *The Man Mazzuchelli: Pioneer Priest*, Chapter 16.
8   Alderson, *The Man Mazzuchelli: Pioneer Priest*, Chapter 5.
9   S. Mary Nona McGreal, *Samuel Mazzuchelli, O.P.: A Kaleidoscope of Scenes From His Life* (n.p., n.d.), p. 44.
10   Alderson, *The Man Mazzuchelli: Pioneer Priest*, Chapter 13.
11   Archives of Sinsinawa Mound.
12   Archives of Sinsinawa Mound.
13   Dorcy, *Saint Dominic's Family*, p. 524.
14   Mazzuchelli, *The Memoirs of Father Samuel Mazzuchelli*, O.P., p. 166.
15   Mazzuchelli, *The Memoirs of Father Samuel Mazzuchelli*, O.P., p. 327.
16   Mazzuchelli, *The Memoirs of Father Samuel Mazzuchelli*, O.P., p. 205.
17   Alderson, *The Man Mazzuchelli: Pioneer Priest*, Chapter 14.
18   Mazzuchelli, *The Memoirs of Father Samuel Mazzuchelli*, O.P., p. 329.
19   McGreal, *Samuel Mazzuchelli, O.P.: A Kaleidoscope of Scenes From His Life*, p. 38.
20   John G. Piquette, *Providence Did Provide* (Galena, 1989), Tape.
21   Dorcy, *Saint Dominic's Family*, p. 524.

9

ITALIAN PROTESTANTS AND THE CATHOLIC CHURCH IN BUFFALO, NY

SECONDO CASAROTTO

Introduction

The fourth largest port in the world and the gateway to the West, Buffalo could, in 1887, boast of being also one of the most industrialized cities in the United States and a powerful magnet for cheap European labor. Grain, lumber, cattle, and iron ore were brought in by the Great Lakes trade, the Erie Canal and the new railway extensions. The New York State Census of 1892, the year Ellis Island opened, put the number of Italians living in Buffalo at about 2,500. Eighteen years later, the Italian-American population in the city had grown to 11,399 and by 1920 Italian-Americans had become the 3rd largest ethnic group, surpassed in numbers only by the Germans and the Polish. By 1940 the Italians had overtaken the Germans to become the city's second largest ethnic group.

Many Italian regions provided a contingent of immigrants, beginning with Liguria, Tuscany, Lombardy, Emilia-Romagna, and later Abruzzo, Basilicata, Campania, and eventually Sicily. After World War II a number of displaced persons arrived also from the Istria region while southern Italians continued to trickle into Western New York. In 1990, the Italian-American community in Buffalo's metropolitan area could be estimated to number about 300,000.[1]

This paper will focus on the role of the "Italian church" both in the Catholic and Protestant affiliation by offering a comparative analysis of the establishment, methods and development of their response to the "Italian Problem" as experienced in Western New York during the past century.

Catholics of Another Kind

As masses of Italian immigrants settled in the United States in the latter part of the 19th century, they faced not only a different political, cultural, and social environment, but also a new religious world which was equally foreign and troublesome.[2] Italian Catholic exuberance in religious practices, accentuated by the need to affirm one's identity in a threatening and hostile world, were bound to challenge Puritanical Anglo-Saxon Americans, both Catholic and Non-Catholic. Lacking often formal education, including religious, lost in a new world and struggling for survival, many Italians became lapsed in their Catholic faith and also abandoned it. Although defections of Italian Catholics did not reach the open confrontations and proportions of other ethnic communities, such as the Polish National Church, efforts were made to organize the "Italian International Independent Catholic Church" in the United States by Rev. Paolo Gullotti Miraglia, and the "Italian Problem" became one of the most burning issues for the American Church at the turn of the century.

Antonio Mangano, a veteran in Protestant work among Italian immigrants, appraised the situation prevailing in most major cities in the United States in the early 1900s: "Wherever the foreigner moves in, the Protestant Church moves out." More optimistic was Professor Steiner who wrote at the same time: "Without the immigrant, Protestantism will languish and die; with him alone she has a future."

Even though in 1881 the Baptist Home Mission Society had characterized Italians as "not a generally desirable accession to our population, nor an inviting or hopeful field for evangelical effort,"[3] "Christianization" of Italian immigrants to this country became one of the greatest challenges of Protestant churches since Reformation. In addition, Protestants often regarded the Catholic Church as "foreigner" and "un-American" (if not anti-American), a church which had come to Maryland in 1634 and even earlier in Florida and the Far West. Consequently, religious and ethnic relations soon became a three-way struggle between Americans, Protestants and Catholics.

Evangelization of the newcomer was considered also a means of social stability. When in September, 1896, labor unrest developed in Buffalo's Italian quarters with several arrests and one woman shot, a local minister bellowed: "Which is a better way to Americanize the immigrant, with a policeman or a missionary? with a chapel or a cell? with a Bible or a club? which is cheaper and on the whole more effective?"[4] Evangelical settlement houses, schools and churches became centers for "bringing Italians from the lowest stage of social life into the maturity of Christian gentlemen and true American citizens." Should this effort fail, these institutions could be used to influence Italians by "directing them to the West, to the great fields where a new life would be open to them."[5]

When Italians began to appear in Buffalo, they were considered "dregs of society," "swarthy, dirty and lazy."[6] Even though many social and charitable institutions were then established to alleviate the needs of Italian immigrants, such as Rescue Mission (1884), Trinity Settlement House (1895), and Protestant Home for Unprotected Children (1896?), Protestant reformers concentrated on changing the Italian immigrant more than his living conditions. Consequently, the enlightenment of Catholic masses through the American educational system was also considered a great gift to Italian immigrant children. In fact, "the public school is the greatest digestive organ of the body politic which assimilates the foreigner and transforms the children of immigrants into Americans," it was argued.[7] So clear was the vision of a new world order by the Protestant nativist movement that "[the Italians] will be compelled to use the English language in their daily conversation. Even their palatal taste will be trained to enjoy American food... [with] a single standard of morals..."[8]

Clinging to their religious and cultural roots, in 1891 Italian immigrants in Buffalo established the first Italian bilingual Catholic school in the United States with St. Anthony's Italian church. When given the opportunity, they overwhelmingly, at least in the beginning, opted for an Italian Catholic school for the children. However, it was not until 1906 that the second Italian Catholic school and church were built in the city. The direct and indirect exposure of Italians to social, educational, political, and religious Protestant institutions by osmosis had to initiate a process also for religious assimilation. Specific evangelical work among Italians, however, is to be singled out as the most important cause of their conversion to the Protestant faith in Buffalo as well as in the rest of the country. By 1918 Protestant work among Italian-Americans in the United States could count for 376 churches and missions, 13,777 members, 42 schools, 13,927 Italian pupils in Sunday schools, 202 Italian pastors, and a total expenditure of $225,309, not including the contribution of $31,571 by Italian Protestants.[9] Antonio Mangano was very optimistic in assessing the potential organization of Protestant missionary work among the Italians when he reported in 1917:

> In the field of Italian evangelization, the Presbyterians are setting the standards for all other denominations. They are doing a most thorough and aggressive work with the most far-reaching plans for future development. The Immigrant Work Office of the Board of the Home Mission is busy making a thorough survey of Italian colonies in many States. They aim to build a system of parishes which shall lead and minister to the entire [Italian] community life.[10]

Italian Protestant Churches in Buffalo, New York
Italian Protestantism in Buffalo may be traced to the founder of the city:

Paolo Busti, the Milan-born General Director of the Holland Land Company, who in 1803 commissioned plans for the "Village of Buffalo," was an Italian Protestant. However, it is only in the latter part of the 19th century that we find the first organized Italian Protestant congregations in the Queen's City. Protestant work among Italians was preceded by similar work in the Kingdom of Italy immediately after the 1870 unification of the country through the spread of a nucleus of pre-Protestants: the Waldensians. After the capture of Rome, the Southern Baptist Convention also established an active ministry in Italy, especially in Rome.

Although some Italian Protestants migrated from Italy, the vast majority of them were converted upon arrival in this country. Small groups of Italians embraced Protestantism while living in Barre, Vermont, or in the coalfields in Pennsylvania, and eventually settled in Buffalo. Similarly, Italian Protestants from Buffalo followed the migration flow to Louisiana, Pennsylvania, and even back to Italy. From Buffalo, for example, where in 1891 he had been the president of the "Società Industriosa Siciliana, Umberto I," Antonio D'Andrea moved to Chicago and established the "Chiesa di Sant'Antonio di Padova" with the help of the Polish National Church.

Italian Protestant congregations in Western New York were usually established in fringe or neglected areas by the local Catholic parishes. They always started with services and full organization in Italian and seldom after an open confrontation with the official church. These congregations also kept a somewhat loose relationship with their own mainstream denomination, they were generally small and very mobile like the immigrants they were serving. The documentation of these churches is therefore sketchy. In 1917 there were 5 Italian Protestant churches in Buffalo: 3 Baptist (First, Second, and Cedar St.), 1 Methodist/Episcopal, and 1 Congregational.[11] The continuous proliferation of Protestant congregations in the predominantly Catholic Italian population of Western New York during the past century raises legitimate questions on the needs, pastoral response and identity of Italian Catholics in the local church.

Welcome Hall and the Remington House

In 1882 Buffalo's Women's Circle of the First Presbyterian Church decided to embark on a relief program to alleviate a current economic crisis. After consultation with Buffalo's Charity Organization Society, it extended an invitation to a woman who was to become one of Buffalo's most important settlement missionaries: Mary Remington. A social reformer with interest in evangelical religion and temperance, Miss Remington had been conducting a successful immigrant settlement program in New Haven, Connecticut. In 1884 she established a "Welcome Hall" in Buffalo's Little Italy, the first civic center of its kind in this industrial city. Here she introduced a range of activities which were later adopted by other settlement and neighborhood houses in Buffalo. They included: diet kitchen, sewing classes, a Sunday school, mothers' meeting, a nursery and kinder-garten (first day nursery in North America, modeled on British institutions), vocational and educational classes, as well as recreational activities for women and children.

Social conditions in Buffalo's Italian quarters were poor and unhealthy. In 1893 the Buffalo Christian Homestead Association counted "75 houses of ill fame and about 100 saloons" in the Canal Street area of the city where most Italians lived. It was this open field of human squalor that drew the attention of Miss Remington. In 1897 Miss Remington, who believed that a moral problem existed with the Italian immigrants, established a new Welcome Hall under the aegis of the First Presbyterian Church and with the help of philanthropists like Sidney Shephard and J.J. Albright. She sought also the influence of Italian socialists and anarchists who had rejected Catholicism, and eventually initiated another Sunday School and an evening Gospel Service for the Italians. Realizing their associational needs, Miss Remington organized an Italian social club and a society for the natives of Miselmeri. In 1913 Welcome Hall could count on the support of some prominent Italians such as Dr. John Ragona and Dr. Francis DiBartolo, a member of the LaFayette Presbyterian Church and the son of a Waldensian minister who had come from Sicily as an extended church worker. By the 1920s, Welcome Hall had added a reading room, gymnasium, health clinic and the popular "Fresh Air Camps" for children. The work of evangelization through social services by Welcome Hall continued until 1932. Although Miss Remington's activities clearly betrayed middle class Anglo-Saxon values, ill-fitting Southern European social and economic conditions, by caring for some of their immediate needs and living among them, the result of her missionary efforts soon became visible.

First Italian Baptist Church In the United States

"The Italians are ripe for religious missionary efforts", wrote the Buffalo Baptist Record in July 1894.

> These Italians have only one Roman Catholic Church (St. Anthony of Padua) and there is no missionary among them who speaks their language. There are missions on Canal Street and Main Street that do a little toward the salvation of these people, but this is only incidental and not by specific mission work.[12]

An earlier article had pointed out that among Italians there were people who "refuse monarchical and repressive influence of Romanism" and that "many of them never attend Roman Catholic services."[13]

Italian Protestant work in Buffalo is recorded as early as the 1850 US

Census which cited a certain L. Giustiniani, a clergyman, among a handful of Italian immigrants. However, it was in 1882 that the Rev. M.A. Churchill had a small Sunday school and mission on Ohio St. for the Italians.

The great Italian Protestant missionary in Buffalo was Ariel B. Bellondi, son of an Italian minister in Florence, who had come to the United States in the summer of 1894 to further his education. The young Colgate University student began services at the Ohio Street church, but he soon realized that "the Irish were averse to this and the Italian work had to be transferred to Lloyd Street." Bellondi also realized that although the Baptist Union favoured reaching out to Italian immigrants, "this ministry was not to lay any financial burden on the treasury."[14] Bellondi left a description of the budding Italian Protestant mission.

> On Sunday I go there at 10 o'clock and until half past eleven I teach the Gospel and songs to twenty-five to thirty children. From twelve to one thirty I preach and teach songs in the church, and we have a Bible study for half an hour. At half past four I go to a second church at 92 Lloyd Street and hold services before no less than 125 people. There is manifested the true enthusiasm for the Gospel. After 7 o'clock I go elsewhere to preach and at ten or eleven I go to repose almost exhausted. On Monday I return to my studies and during the week many Italians work for me, especially Salvatore Potarno and Salvatore Genco....[15]

We may note here that timely intervention and extraordinary dedication of Italian ministers and laity, including women, will be determining factors in the establishment of both Protestant and Catholic churches in Western New York. (A Catholic church for Italians will be established on Buffalo's East Side 15 years after the Italian Protestant mission and four or five Italian Protestant chapels existed in the city before a second Italian Catholic church opened in 1906.)

Bellondi also realized the importance of regional ties in his congregation, of which the first nucleus had migrated to Buffalo from Pescasseroli, a small town in the Abruzzo region, north-east of Rome, where some of them had converted to Protestantism after listening to an evangelical minister. The Abruzzesi had settled in the Kensington area in 1887 as stone cutters and masons. The first meetings of these Italian Protestants were held in the home of Filippo D'Arcangelo at 31 Hickam Street (now Roma Street) until the Baptist Union built a wooden hut for the small congregation of which Rev. Bellondi took charge. In 1895 the missionary work was extended through Angelina Mai, a seamstress, and Salvatore Genco to missions at Erie/Seneca Streets and also at Humbolt Park. On September 3, 1896, with the help of the Baptist Union, a new chapel was dedicated on Buffalo's East

Side, in the heart of the Abruzzese community. Thus Ariel Bellondi became the founder of the "First Italian Baptist Church in the United States." He continued with zeal his missionary work, particularly with the young element of the Italian community. Rev. Bellondi's success was soon recognized and in 1898 he was appointed Superintendent of the "Baptist Home Association of America." In 1898 Baptist missionary work among Italians in Buffalo was extended to missions on Prospect Street, Cedar Street, and the Terrace, through the efforts of Rev. Angelo Peruzzi. Further progress will be made by Rev. Luigi Scelfo, a former priest from Arezzo, Tuscany, who took also a degree in pharmacology in order to provide a free medical dispensary to the West Side Italian immigrants. Baptist work among Italians continued to grow rapidly in Buffalo and elsewhere in the country. "From the beginning our work had extended until now it includes 17 missionary pastors, occupying 30 stations in six States with a church membership over 400," wrote the Baptist Home Mission in 1905.[16]

St. Paul's Italian Methodist Episcopal Church — Buffalo, NY

In 1887 a small group of Italian Methodists from Abruzzo attended Grace Methodist Church on Swan Street. They were living in a tenement at 97 Commercial Street. While through the combined efforts of Baptists and Methodists the first preaching in Italian had occurred in 1893, the first Italian Methodist mission was established in November, 1896, located at 122 Erie Street. It was only in 1900, however, that the congregation officially organized with elected officers: F.P. Strozzi, N. Capozzi, F. DeForte and P. Gerace. In 1904, under the leadership of Rev. William Burt, Superintendent of the Foreign Missions in Italy and later Methodist Bishop of Buffalo, the Italian mission was revamped with Rev. Giuseppe Paciarelli, a graduate from the University of Rome. Rev. Paciarelli opened a chapel at 61 Lower Terrace with Italian classes and patriotic and anti-papal celebrations. Through the financial support of the Methodist Union, in 1905 "St. Paul's Italian Methodist Episcopal Church" opened at 243 Court Street. The growing congregation moved in 1909 to a larger new church on Wilkinson Street, built with contributions by Italian immigrants. On the occasion of the Centennial of Methodism in Buffalo (May 1917), St. Paul's Italian M.E. Church gave the following report: Professed Conversions (Dec. 1914-Apr. 1917) 124; Present Membership 113; Epworth (Youth) League with 24 members; Sunday School with 70 pupils; Sewing School with 24 students; Girls Club with 12 members; Night English and Italian School, Citizenship classes, and Intelligence Bureau for Italian immigrants.

Sacred Heart of Mary Church — North Collins, NY
(also known as the "Christian Apostolic Independent Catholic Church")

In 1924 Catholic church officials in Buffalo became concerned about a self-styled "monk" called "Gesu', il Monaco" (Jesus, the Monk). Jesus John Alvarez claimed Spanish origin and had worked in the West Indies. He spoke fluent Italian, had come to the United States in 1913 and attended for a few months the Franciscan St. Anthony's College, Catskill, New York. In the early 1920s Alvarez began preaching in Niagara Falls, Lackawanna (where some "miracles" were reported), North Collins, and eventually Fredonia, drawing considerable following. The Monk was visiting scattered Italian farming communities throughout Chautaqua County in an unconventional fashion. In June, 1913, the "Oratorio di Maria Santissima" (Chapel of the Most Holy Mary) was established on Brant St. in North Collins. In his "oratorio," beside the altar with tabernacle, there were candles, statues of St. Michael, Our Lady of Sorrows, a large Crucifix and an Italian bible. Plans were also drawn for another chapel in Fredonia. In 1934 the small wooden chapel was replaced by the beautiful church which now stands across from St. John's Catholic church in North Collins. It was dedicated on August 25, 1935, with great participation of Italian farmers. This was to be the Mother Church of an organization which by 1941 had two more churches, one in Niagara Falls and the other in Philadelphia.

The chapel offered the warmth of a colorful Mediterranean culture. The Monk celebrated a vernacular, paraphrased version of the mass, held impressive processions with singing of litanies at festivals (like that in honor of Our Lady of Mt. Carmel) and celebrated with grand solemnity Palm Sunday and the "Agony" of Our Lord on Good Friday, in clear contrast with the austere Anglo-Saxon rituals of the local German-American Catholic church. Pilgrimages to the North Collins chapel were organized also from all of Western New York and as far away as Philadelphia and Vineland, New Jersey.

At a time when financial contributions were perceived to be exacted by the American church from poor Italian immigrants, Sacred Heart of Mary Church was paid for in a very short time by free contributions by Italian farmers. Sunday services were often followed by family style dinners with hundreds of participants. In 1919 the Monk "ordained" two women, the first members of the "Ordine del Sacro Sangue di Gesú." (Order of the Most Holy Blood of Jesus). In a unique and charismatic way, Jesus John Alvarez had understood certain traits of the Italian religious, cultural and social traditions. One contemporary said: "To the poor and ignorant people [the monk] claimed to be a Catholic; to the more intelligent, an independent or schismatic Catholic; to others, a Presbyterian...." His success story, however, bespeaks of the spirit of the people he served.

After describing three of the most representative Italian Protestant churches in Western New York, the following view of other congregations provides an insight of the widespread and ongoing Italian Protestant experience in the area.

Chiesa Cattolica Santa Maria della Salute, Buffalo, NY — formerly called "St. Mary's Mission" and opened at 163 Canal St. around 1894, this church was officially incorporated in 1898 and ministered by Rev. E. Rufane Dunkin, a former priest, under jurisdiction of Old Catholic Bishop Renat Villatte of Duval, Wisconsin. It seems to have been connected with the Polish National Church.

Chiesa Cristiana Italiana, Hulberton, NY — founded in the early 1900s by G. Berretta from Chicago, Illinois.

Italian Methodist Church, Niagara Falls, NY — connected with St. James Society in the late 1910s. The Italians built their own church a few years later. St. Luke's Methodist Church in the same city also had an Italian congregation in the 1940s.

Chiesa Cristiana Italiana, Niagara Falls, NY — an Italian Evangelical congregation worshiped on 19th St. already in the late 1920s with Pastor M. Tosetto. In 1927 the First National Convention of the "Reorganized Italian Christian Church of the United States" was held here. (An "Italian Christian Union" had been founded in 1907.) The church was publishing "Il Risveglio Italiano" (the Italian Awakening) in the early 1940s.

Chiesa Cristiana Italiana, Buffalo, NY — was incorporated in 1930 with services at 224 Hudson St. The congregation moved to several locations on the City's West Side before forming the "Calvary Full Gospel Church" in Kenmore.

Chiesa Cristiana Italiana, Batavia, NY — existed in the middle 1930s.

Italian Christian Church, Lockport, NY — established in 1934 by Rev. W. Valcarocco, this church provided services until after World War II.

Italian Methodist Church, Jamestown, NY — this congregation was established in 1942 with the publication in the local newspaper of the names of its first 45 members and had some connections with "The Monk" of North Collins.

Italian Association of Bible Students, Buffalo, NY — incorporated in 1945, the congregation "without minister and no religious affiliation" moved from South Division to the Upper West Side as "Bremmer Street Church."

Italian Evangelical Church, Buffalo, NY — was established in 1953 by Rev. Anthony Foti on Buffalo's East Side.

Christian (Italian) Congregation, Buffalo, NY — was an off-shoot of the Hudson St. congregation led by Anthony Bollea and Jack Garofalo, being incorporated in 1958.

Italian Christian Congregation of the United States, Buffalo, NY — located on Herkimer St. on Buffalo's Upper West Side, this church led by Vincent Bollea and Arno Scoccia, began serving Italians in the early 1950s. A new church was built in 1991 on Main St. and Harlem Road to serve Italian Americans who had moved to that area.

Apostolic Church of Antioch, Niagara Falls, NY — Reverend Barnardino

Santodonato (alias Joseph Kelly), a former priest, founded this church for the "unification of the Roman Catholic and Orthodox Churches" in 1938. A new church, named "Holy Saviour Catholic Church," was dedicated in 1939. The congregation eventually became affiliated with the Orthodox Church.

In addition to the above listed Italian Protestant Churches, Italian Catholics, both first and successive generations, have joined Evangelical, Pentecostal and Jehovah's Witness congregations.

The Catholic Church and the Italian Immigrants in Buffalo, NY

Among the first immigrants to Western New York were missionary priests whom Bishop John Timon recruited in Italy for his newly established diocese: Rev. J. Grimaldi, who ministered to Italians in the Albion area in the middle 1850s and the Franciscans from Rome, led by Panfilo da Magliano, who settled in Allegany in 1855.

In 1883 and 1885 efforts were made to establish an Italian Catholic church in Buffalo. The small number of immigrants and financial difficulties delayed the project. During the 3rd Plenary Council of Baltimore (1884) Bishop Stephen Ryan took up the Italian cause as Vice-Chairman of the Preparatory Committee "On Italian Immigrants." The Committee, however, met only once, and at the Council Bishop Ryan seconded a motion "to disclose to the Supreme Pontiff for the most weighty reasons" the deplorable conditions of the Italians in this country "because the Pope has authority over the Bishops of Italy." Like most other bishops, Ryan perceived the "Italian Problem" mainly as an issue with the church of origin and not of the church of arrival. On the other hand, some work among Italians in Western New York was being carried out by Hungarian Fr. X. Kofler (Black Rock) and later by Rev. Thomas Donohue (St. Patrick's Church). More regular ministry was started by Rev. James Quigley, rector of St. Joseph's Cathedral, in the late 1880s as more Italians were arriving in the Queen's City.

When in 1889 Pope Leo XIII announced to the American Bishops the institution in Italy of a missionary order for the care of Italians in America, Buffalo was among the first dioceses to respond to the appeal Fr. Antonio Gibelli, a member of the Missionaries of St. Charles, founded by Bishop Scalabrini in 1887, arrived in Buffalo in the fall of 1890 and took up residence at St. Joseph's Cathedral. On August 2, 1891 the cornerstone of the first Italian Catholic school in the United States and first Italian Catholic Church in Western New York was dedicated on Court St. to St. Anthony of Padua. Fr. Gibelli reported that there were then 3,000 Italians in Buffalo during summer and during winter, and after construction and farming work was over, they would reach over 7,000. He was happy to report in 1892 that the spiritual conditions of Buffalo's Italians were already improving, while their economic conditions were still very poor. We may ascertain their plight from the following assessment by the local Catholic newspaper on the occasion of the visit of Bishop Scalabrini to Buffalo in 1901:

> It is to be hoped that in his report to Propaganda [Fide] Monsignor [Scalabrini] will emphasize the deplorable spiritual neglect of which many of his countrymen are victims, coming from a land of priests and fount of the Catholic faith, sadly ignorant of Christian doctrine and the spiritual equipment to face the new conditions that wait for them here.[17]

Interestingly, Bishop Scalabrini gave the following appraisal of the leadership of Bishop Quigley: "In his modest amicality, [he] is a true apostolic and admirable man. If all the bishops were like him, full of esteem and loving care for the Italians, our [Italian] communities would soon rise and rank among the first...."[18]

St. Anthony's Church marked a unique experience and a leading pastoral model in the care of Italians in Western New York, particularly when seen against their defection to Italian Protestantism and the secession of the Polish National Church. The pastoral model of a fully fledged language church with a bilingual school for Italian immigrants, staffed by a missionary order of priests familiar with the language and culture of their people, was slowly accepted in Buffalo and elsewhere. Bishops Ryan, Quigley and his successor Colton repeatedly asked the Scalabrinians to establish new churches for the Italians in Buffalo, and Bishop Quigley called them to serve in Chicago (1905) soon after his appointment to that Archdiocese. The creation of a Catholic church for the Italians in Buffalo had been envisioned, however, for more practical reasons. Quigley himself had foreseen that "when taught the freedom of the Roman Catholic Church in this country and the duty of supporting their church and their priests themselves, [Italians] would become more self-reliant and American much faster than if they had to attend churches where priest foreign in race and sympathy officiated."[19] Fr. Gibelli noted that the opening of the school had to be accelerated "because trustees of St. Joseph's Cathedral did not want to have Italian children in their school.

Amidst serious difficulties, the Missionaries of St. Charles rallied the community together. "Italians here, mostly Sicilians and Neapolitans, don't give much — wrote one pastor in 1901 — Rich people don't even come to church! Italians in Buffalo need assistance... There is work for 3 priests here, but how can they make a living? Who will support them?"[20] Working hard, priests and people at St. Anthony's were able to survive and prosper, relying on natural Italian stamina and ingenuity. During difficult financial times and amidst socialist and anarchist upheavals, St. Anthony's turned its people to self-help and development. The Italian Welfare Society and the

Italian St. Vincent de Paul Society at the St. Anthony provided much needed financial aid to poor families at the turn of the century. A new Italian school and an Italian Hospital became community goals. Eventually, Columbus Italian Hospital was built in 1908 and the Italian "Scuola Scalabrini" was dedicated on the Terrace in 1912, where some 2,000 students from public schools began to receive weekly religious instruction. Priests from St. Anthony's also helped better working conditions of the Italians by siding with them in their disputes and even mediating between emplowers, Italian unions and Italian strike-breakers. Through a strong educational program, Fr. Angelo Strazzoni, for example, became known as "Father of the Italian Youth" in Buffalo, mobilizing Italians and Americans in a community project of integration of the community against the mirage of the prevailing "melting pot" public policy which he condemned.

By 1920 St. Anthony's could boast 26 societies for men and women (many of which being of mutual benefit), a Drum and Bugle Corps, a Day Nursery, vocational classes for World War veterans, an Italian Scouting program, a Drama Club, Sewing and Embroidery Classes, and State-wide acclaimed sport teams. The empowerment program developed by the Scalabrini Fathers in the Italian community helped break the barriers of diffidence toward the church, regionalism and nationalism. English, Italian, Americanization classes were offered to children and parents, many of whom had arrived illiterate in this country.

For the 1991 Centennial Year, the Italian Mother Church of St. Anthony's offered the following statistics: 25,265 baptisms; 8,992 confirmations; 6,744 marriages, and 7,430 funerals. Fr. Secondo Casarotto, CS, pastor of St. Anthony's summed up the role of the Italian Catholic church:

> In the West Side urban village, the Italian church was the heart of the community. It created a community. Here Italian popular culture exploded with the sparkle of fireworks, the laughter of families around a meager table, and the closeness of the always well informed neighborhood. In Little Italy the frustrations of the uprooted and often exploited Italian immigrant gave way to the struggle for survival and the natural zest of life. The Italian church became a bridge to heaven and to the new world.[21]

From St. Anthony's the Scalabrini Fathers reached out to other migrant communities in East and South Buffalo and Lackawanna. They cared for Italian farmers in Brant and Fredonia (where they established St. Anthony's Church and a chapel for seasonal workers in Laona). Scalabrinians followed the railroad workers and established a chapel for them in Erie, Pennsylvania, and when Italians moved to Hamilton and Toronto, Scalabrinians were the first resident priests in those cities. Many diocesan priests in Buffalo also received field-training as assistants at St. Anthony's before becoming pastors in other Italian areas of the Diocese of Buffalo, which by 1920 counted about 20 churches either established specifically for the Italians with Italian priests or with priests familiar with the Italian language and culture. Among the first Italian Catholic churches in Western New York after St. Anthony's were: St. Joseph, Niagara Falls (1903), St. Anthony, Fredonia (1905), Our Lady of Mt. Carmel and St. Lucy, Buffalo (1906). These Italian churches provided moral, material and educational support to the Italian immigrants and their American born children. It was mostly through these institutions that Italian Catholics found expression and support to their faith which ultimately helped them integrate into the religious and social American society. The Italian church was also the effective means to keep the fold in the Catholic Church in Buffalo as elsewhere. In 1898 Catholic authorities tried to establish an Italian church in the slums of Canal St. "to counteract the presence of the chapel of an Italian apostate priest."[22] In 1924 plans to establish an Italian Presbyterian church on Buffalo's West Side were thwarted when the intended building was hastily purchased by the Diocese and transformed into an Italian Catholic chapel "to forestall any possible harm to the Catholic faith of the Italians."[23]

A comparison between Italian Protestant and Catholic churches in their response to the care of Italian immigrants in Buffalo finds interesting similarities and differences. Besides offering a monolithic organization to the immigrants, the Catholic Church offered Italians comparatively a smaller but more permanent supply of Italian personnel than the Protestants. This gave a lower sense of personal contact, somehow compensated with a longer stability in the otherwise very fluctuating world of immigrants. Catholic pastors were often in office almost for life, and language parishes remained at the original place of foundation, thus preventing often an updating in ministry with changing conditions and location of immigrants. In clear contrast with Protestants, Italian Catholics in Buffalo counted on religious orders, particularly the Missionaries of St. Charles. Among others we must mention the Pallottine Sisters and the Missionary Sisters of the Divine Child, founded in 1926 on Buffalo's West Side for the care of Italian families. However, the number of Italian priests and nuns in Buffalo is clearly smaller in comparison to Polish Catholics.

Regionalism seems to have given occasional ground for confrontation more in Catholic than Protestant churches. While most of the Italian immigrants to the United States came from Southern Italy, the vast majority of priests came from Northern and Central Italy or from families native from those regions. This is true also for Buffalo where the authorities, at least in the beginning, could not find priests from southern Italy. Protestant churches seem to have drawn membership from a broad spectrum of Italians and accepted more readily ministers from different regions. This may be due to the fact that organization in Italian Catholic churches relied on "congreghe" (religious societies) which were usually based on "paesani" (natives of the same town or region). Interesting in this regard is the incident in the late 1890s in which some Italian women scuffled with the pastor of St. Anthony's in order to impose a priest from Sicily, a relative of theirs, as pastor of said church "because — the women said — we are Sicilians, only in part Italian!" Not much time later, on the other hand, two Catholic factions used regionalism in their preference between two priests, when in fact both priests in question had been born and educated in the same town!

The universal character of the church, particularly as expressed through the language parish, not only contributed to multicultural identity between Italian and non-Italians, but also between Italians from different regions. While hundreds of Italian clubs and societies with religious, social, political goals have been established in the past century in Western New York, it was mainly at the threshold of the "Italian Church" that the immigrant felt both Italian and Catholic in America.

Notwithstanding their poverty, Italian immigrants overwhelmingly opted to send their children to a Catholic school such as St. Anthony's and Our Lady of Mt. Carmel. The trend, however, reversed around 1910 when the vast majority of Buffalo's Italian children began attending public schools. This may be attributed to economic recession, insufficient number of Catholic schools and imposed monolinguism in the curriculum. Worth noting here is the fact that during the same years more than half of Buffalo's Polish children were attending a large number of Catholic schools where Polish orders of women were teaching, thus keeping the control of the language, culture, and faith within their own community. In this regard the material poverty of Italian immigrants and the lack of an organization to voice the concerns of the whole community, particularly after the 1918 Canon Law, was reflected not only in their faster cultural assimilation, but also influenced the religious practice and affiliation of Italian families.

Relationships between Protestant and Catholic in Buffalo at the turn of the century were far from the ecumenical spirit manifested by Vatican II. In the Italian community, vitriolic attacks, open proselytization and anti-papal propaganda were frequent. In Buffalo, memories of Protestant hostilities to Bishops Timon and Ryan were still vivid. The schism of the Polish National Church had Catholic Church authorities worried about the future of Italian Catholics, such as with their plans to buy property for an Italian cemetery in the late 1890s. Ethnic identity played a major part in religious confrontations when Italian was equated with Catholic and American with Protestant. In Little Italy the occupation of the Pontiff's State by the Kingdom of Savoy continued to have interreligious shockwaves for many years. Besides, the mere association of Italian Catholic clergymen with Italian converts to Protestantism was looked upon with much suspicion. "Fr. X ... goes to a

Sicilian pharmacy and mingles with renegade Catholics. The Bishop is all rattled up...," commented one observer in 1908.[24] Italian labor disputes in Buffalo also played an important part in religious relations between Italian Protestants and Catholics. Italian socialists and anarchists often frowned upon the Catholic Church, identified with the "Irish" establishment and unionism, even when it espoused their cause, and they sided with Protestants.

Italian immigrants often looked at the Catholic Church as rich and powerful, and had a special difficulty in accepting a mandated financial contribution, such as the "chair fee" and the "Sunday Envelope System." At least in the beginning, Italian Protestant churches in Buffalo received proportionately greater financial help from their mainline churches than Italian Catholics. This was in part due to the more established and affluent Protestant congregations, while the Catholic Church was relatively young and burdened with the arrival of masses of poor immigrants from different countries. Yet, in their own way and over time, Italian Catholics and Protestants made a substantial financial contribution in the establishment and development of their churches through a sense of belonging based on natural affinity and ownership, and through fundraising activities more congenial to their culture and traditions. While compelled parish membership by geographic boundaries and financial contributions were particularly opposed by Italians, the Italian church, both Catholic and Protestant, offered a free and gradual opportunity for integration while keeping their roots. Notwithstanding their poverty, through the Italian church Italians in this country were able to maintain ties with the Catholic church of their native towns, often supporting it with donations and community projects, and experiencing a sense of continuity and belonging with the people they had left behind.

Italian Protestants and Catholics showed a marked difference in the use of the media. Notwithstanding high illiteracy among Italian immigrants, Protestants made a larger use of the press than Catholics. "L'Amico del Popolo" (1897), "La Voce della Verita'" (1899), and "Il Risveglio" (1907) are among Buffalo's Italian Protestant publications which lasted several years, while the only Italian Catholic publication, "L'Italiano nella Diocesi di Buffalo" lasted only a few months in 1911. In recent years, Italian Protestants have also made use of a locally-produced weekly radio program in cooperation with the "Chiese Italiane Cristiane" of Canada.

Italian Protestant churches seem to have made some effort in coordination, while there is no record of any diocesan organization to support the needs and resources of Italian Catholics in Western New York during the past century. In fact, praiseworthy community projects for the empowerment and service of Italian Catholics, such as the Italian school, the Italian cemetery and the Italian Hospital, ran aground in the shallow waters of petty parochialism, institutionalized by the 1918 Code of Canon Law, which did not acknowledge the long standing experience of language/ethnic parishes and tied Italians to geographic boundaries. Italian Protestants were able to give an unhindered "sense of belonging" to their people beyond "parish lines," founded on natural affinity, which the Catholic church apparently did not keep. Not surprisingly, the nativist American movement eventually reached the sanctuary and in 1924 diocesan authorities forbade the teaching of Italian in all Catholic schools in Buffalo.

The advent of Fascism in Italy brought mixed reactions among religious and political leaders in Western New York, both Italian and non-Italian, Catholic and non-Catholic, many of whom saw with much sympathy the emergence of a new Italy and of Italian identity abroad. This changed suddenly with the breaking out of World War II. More than any other institution, however, St. Anthony's church continued to defend Italian Catholic identity above political lines. Even though many Italian churches, for example, existed in Western New York during World War II, ministry to Italian Prisoners of War in Medina and Oakfield was provided by the missionaries and priests from St. Anthony's.

More and before any other religious and social institution throughout this past century, St. Anthony's Italian church offered not only specific services to Italians and their families, but also fostered awareness and response to the needs of its people both within and without the Italian community. Its leading role became also an institutionalized buffer between the church of departure and the church of arrival, between Italian and American."The Italian priest was often between the gun of the Bishop and that of their people." (S. Tomasi) In this sense it gave a distinctive meaning to being Catholic.

When Protestantism began to appear among Buffalo's Italians, the local Catholic Church could only look with surprise and scorned "renegade" Catholics who turned to other pastures. More often than not, American Catholic churches, accustomed to religious pluralism and linguistically ill-equipped, failed to realize changes in religious practice and affiliation of Italian Catholics. After all, if Italians were betraying the Church, their faith must have been weak... So it happened that "(the Italians) do not seek the Church and the Church does not seek them!"[25] There is a sad irony in the triumphalistic prediction of Buffalo's Catholic newspaper at the turn of the century:

> The cold and iconoclastic, unsatisfying gospel of dissent can not find a home in the sunny-hearted sons and daughters of Italy. It is like mixing olive oil and water! Italians may become bad Catholics and even infidels, but never Protestants![26]

The challenge, however, has always been too real to be overlooked. "Our Italian colony in danger?" asked the same editor a few years later.[27] Interestingly, with the decline of the recognized role of the language/ethnic parish and the specialized missionary nature of migrant ministry, particularly with the arrival of Italians after World War II in Western New York, the issue of their defection has resurfaced.

Antonio Mangano caught the unique aspect between culture and evangelization when he wrote:

> We believe in freedom of religious life according to racial type. An Italian Protestant church will have and should have distinctive characteristics, distinguishing it from an American Protestant Church. This means the enrichment of the Protestant conception of God and of social life. There is no Italian Gospel, but there is a Gospel for the Italian, which is the secret of his highest and best development, and a rebirth of Italian character according to the mind of Christ... The use of the Italian language in worship and service is not primarily a matter of privilege, but a responsibility for winning the Italian people to Christ. (It) has demonstrated the possibility of reaching people in a larger way through the Italian language and has usually been the determining factor in the employment of Italian missionaries.[29]

The Italian Protestant and Catholic experience in Western New York confirms the validity of the role of the language/ethnic church as a means of integration into the local church. Since Italian Protestant congregations were often formed in areas already served by ethnic clergy, the issue of specific, coordinated and specialized "Italian Ministry" is evident. According to a 1988 Diocesan Survey on "Services in Languages Other Than English," St. Anthony's was still the only church offering regular services and organizational support to Italian Catholics in the Buffalo area. It should also be noted that a focus on the "Italianità" of its people did not prevent St. Anthony's church and the Scalabrini Fathers to offer similar culturally oriented services in most recent years also to Hispanic and Vietnamese people.

The teachings of Vatican II, the articulate pronouncements by Pope John Paul II, together with the 1983 Canon Law express a vision of cultural evangelization and unity through diversity in the Church which is, and must be, universal in the origin and destination of its message. The historical role of the Italian language and ethnic parish confirms the legitimacy and validity of this institution while it raises questions on some current practices of outright inclusiveness in multi-ethnic parishes.[30] Paradoxically and significantly, what Mangano had envisioned as the mèans for converting

Italian Catholics to Protestantism has been the same means which, more than anything else, has helped Italian Catholics maintain, nourish and share their faith: the Italian Church.

ENDNOTES

1   *US Census 1980* (Elaborated). According to the same source, Buffalo metropolitan area ranked 12th in the nation for Single, Multiple, and Total Italian Ancestry categories; 15th in the Italian Born category; and 9th in the Italian percentage of Total Population category.

2   Among the studies on the Italian Catholic experience in the United States, see Silvano M. Tomasi, *Piety and Power* (1975), and Rudolph Vecoli, "Prelates and Peasants: Italian Immigrants and the Catholic Church" in *Journal of Social History*, (Spring 1960).

3   Aurelio Palmieri, *Italian Immigrants in USA*, p. 131.

4   *Standard*, "A Contrast," October 3, 1896.

5   *1st Annual Report of the Montclair Italian Evangelical Missionary Society*, (1902), p.15.

6   *Express*, May 24, 1891; March 3, 1892.

7   Josiah Strong to Dr. Reed, Sept. 26, 1902, in Nancy Carter, *A Flood of Immigrants: Washington Chuuch Stays Afloat in New Century (1888-1922)*.

8   *Report of the Committee of Americanization of the Italian Baptist Missionary Association, 1906* p. 18.

9   Aurelio Palmieri, "Italian Protestantism in USA," in *Catholic World*, Vol. 107 (May 1918), p. 188.

10   *Ibid.*, p. 182

11   Antonio Mangano, *Religious Work Among the Italian in America: A Survey of the Home Mission Council, 1917*.

12   *Baptist Record* "Work Among Italians," July 1894.

13   *Ibid.*, "A Pope in America," December 1892.

14   *Ibid.*, "The New Italian Church," April 1895.

15   *Ibid.*

16   *Home Mission Monthly*, "Our Baptist Wor,k" May 1905.

17   *Catholic Union and Times*, September 17, 1901.

18   Scalabrini to Mangot, September, 1901.

19   *Express*, September 19, 1904.

20   Martinelli to Scalabrini, January 2, 1900.

21   S. Casarotto, *100th Anniversary of St. Anthony's Church, Buffalo, New York 1891-1991: Memories*.

22   *Corriere Italiano*, June 18, 1898.

23   Joseph Gambino, *History of Holy Cross Church, 1939*.

24   C. Ryan to P. Parolin, September 24, 1908.

25   Aurelio Palmieri, "Italian Protestantism in USA" in *Catholic World*, p.18.

26   *Catholic Union and Times*, May 9, 1895.

27   *Catholic Union and Times*, August 22, 1901.

28   John B. Scalabrini, *L'Emigrazione Italiana in America (1887)*, p. 11.

29   Aurelio Palmieri, "Italian Protestantism in USA" in *Catholic World*, Vol. 107 (May 1918), p. 185.

30   Pope John Paul II, "1990 World Migration Day Message," speaks of the "immigrants' right to organize among themselves" and of the unique role of the language church.

10

A CASE STUDY OF THE ITALIAN LAYMAN AND PARISH LIFE AT OUR LADY OF POMPEI, GREENWICH VILLAGE, NEW YORK CITY

MARY ELIZABETH BROWN

One fruitful trend in recent historiography is the cross pollination of ethnic and gender studies, usually women's studies. This paper focuses on a group of New York City Italian immigrant men and their experiences in Catholicism.

We know about some Italian immigrant men's alienation from Catholicism from Rudolph Vecoli.[1] New York City's calendar of ethnic celebrations, such as the San Gennaro festa, shows that other Italian men maintained their own devotional customs without much support from the institutional church. Records also indicate that some Italian men involved themselves in institutional Catholicism. An 1890 description of Saint Patrick's Old Cathedral's Italian congregation mentions a Saint Joseph Society, whose members, all family men, visited Italian families to impress upon them the importance of attending mass and enrolling their children in parochial school.[2] In 1914, men from Epiphany's basement congregation pressed John Cardinal Farley for their own church and Saint Sebastian's opened in 1915. [3] North Bronx men even knew what arguments would get them their desired church. Translated into English, they wrote Farley, "We believe it is useful to tell Your Excellency that there is here already a Protestant American mission and that another one for Italians will soon open ...."[4]

Records from Our Lady of Pompei in Greenwich Village allow us to study its men in detail. Like many "Italian" churches, Pompei's parishioners came from a specific place on the peninsula. A priest stationed there early in the twentieth century recalled Pompei was "the Genoese church," with people from Liguria's chief seacoast town.[5] The baptismal records for 1893, the first full year of operation, show a preponderance of people from Chiavari, a seaport southeast of Genoa. Other northern Italian provinces were also represented. The Michelini clan came from southern Tyrol.[6] Andrea Sabini was born in Parma.[7] (These names will recur later.)

The men of this study arrived ahead of the early twentieth century's mass migration. Luigi Fugazy came to New York in 1869.[8] Charles Baciagalupo arrived so early he left before most others came. He migrated with his family at age seven, and returned to Italy in 1905, leaving a business on Mulberry Street and taking with him the savings amassed while in New York.[9]

Most men of this study went into business for themselves. Some were sufficiently impressive to warrant inclusion in an Italian Chamber of Commerce publication. Angelo and Pietro Alpi manufactured artificial flowers. Baciagalupo was in undertaking, Fugazy in banking. Joseph Personeni was a pharmacist.

All men under study married and raised families. Charles Baciagalupo's sister Caroline married Giovanni Battista Perazzo, who worked with Charles and who in 1908 opened a funderal parlor of his own, which he later turned over to his sons and grandson.[10] Angelo and Marina Michelini had ten children, which may have contributed to their decision to make their business a boarding house.

The men joined social clubs. Angelo Michelini's sons August and Leon followed him in the Tyrol-Trentino Benevolent Society, which was formed to provide insurance, but which also met monthly for fellowship's sake.[11] Leon was also prominent in Tiro a Segno, an Italian target-shooting club founded in 1866, which ran a members-only restaurant and a charitable foundation.

In summary, these were northern Italians, slightly more acceptable to Americans than Southerners, pioneers of Italian migration, entrepreneurs, husbands, fathers, and club members. They fit Victor Greene's description of nineteenth-century, first-generation immigrant leadership.[12] These were the prominenti, and, as benefit their position, they added church involvement to their other community roles.

The prominenti didn't appear in Pompei's earliest records, probably because its founding pator didn't think in terms of developing a community to sustain a parish.[13] The Scalabrinians, the religious order which staffs Pompei to this day, sent Pietro Bandini to New York as chaplain of that city's branch of the Saint Raphael Society for the Protection of Italian Immigrants.

On 8 May 1892, he opened a chapel at the Saint Raphael house at 113 Waverly Place, thus founding Pompei. On 6 March 1895, the chapel moved to 214 Sullivan Street. In January 1896, Bandini decided against renewing his vows with the Scalabrinians.

It was at the Sullivan Street church that Bandini's successor, Francesco Zaboglio, suffered an accident which brought the laity into greater prominence at Pompei. On 14 July 1897, Zaboglio smelled gas in the church basement and, with two other men, descended to investigate. It was dark, so they struck a match. The resulting explosion killed the two men, damaged the building, and left Zaboglio permanently disabled. The next year, Pompei moved to its third home, at 210 Bleeker Street.

Perhaps the explosion destroyed some records, or perhaps it encouraged the laymen to actively enter parish life, because the first document indicating laymen's involvement is dated 20 January 1898. It is the minutes of a meeting of a nameless group. At the meeting, the group elected officers, one of whom, Michael Pepe, can be identified as a Village real estate broker. The group approved a circular letter and directed it be sent to other Italian communities to solicit donations to the church. It voted to leave to the pastor responsibility for calling a meeting at the church to inform the parishioners of the congregation's financial state. At its February 3 meeting, the group authorized a subcommittee, which included Michael Pepe and artificial flower manufacturer Pietro Alpi, to investigate insurance for the church building.[14]

That same year, on 7 March, Pompei was incorporated. In New York State, each parish has a four-member board of trustees. The ordinary and pastor are always two members, and the other two laymen. Pompei's first two trustees were Luigi Fugazy and Eduardo Bergonzi, whose family name appeared in Pompei's records for the next two generations.[15]

Zaboglio, though, relied on a laywoman more than on laymen. His financial assistance came from Annie Leary, a New York Catholic heiress whose involvement with Pompei began with an interest in the children. She also paid for repairs and decorations at the Sullivan Street church.

Pompei moved from Sullivan to Bleeker Street in May 1898. A year later, Father Zaboglio's wounds from the 1897 explosion led him to request reassignment. The new pastor was Antonio Demo. Father Bandini had followed the custom of organizing Pompei's congregation into sodalities according to age, sex and marital status. Father Demo worked more closely with the sodalites, and they took a more active role in parish life. In Italian parishes, married men were eligible to join the Saint Joseph Society, and it was through this organization that they exercised their influence on parish affairs.[16]

Pompei also had a "Church Aid Society," which had a slightly different constituency. Luigi Fugazy, who belonged to this, was apparently not a Pompeiian, for he was buried from another parish.[17] The Church Aid Society seems to have been for those with the time, money, and business experience Pompei needed, and who wanted the status of a prominent role in the local parish provided.

Both Church Aid and Saint Joseph's sponsored fund raisers. Saint Joseph held parish picnics, for which it charged a quarter admission.[18] Church Aid's First Annual Entertainment was an Ed Sullivan-like variety show. The program reference to a "Hebrew comedian" may indicate Italians were willing to laugh at other ethnic groups, but, especially in conjunction with the banjoist and the buck-and-wing dancer, it may also indicate the entertainment was designed to appeal to, and solicit funds from, a larger group than the parishioners.[19] This may be the 30 May 1990 "festival" reported in the pulpit announcements on Sunday 15 July; Demo called every fund raiser a festa, though he did not permit southern Italian-style feast day celebrations.[20] If so, it was a successful affair, netting $77.48 in profits.

Besides Church Aid and Saint Joseph, there was a third group of parish men, the collectori. The dictionary translated colletore as "collector," especially "tax collector." Leon Michelini translated the word as "usher." Michelini received his colletore badge, a pin in the shape of a Maltese cross with collectore in its center, by father Demo in 1908.[21] He was only fourteen at the time, so the collectori could be quite young.[22] Collectore membership overlapped with Church Aid and Saint Joseph; Andrea Sabini belonged to all three.[23] Pulpit announcements for 26 August 1900 thank colletrice Maria C. for gathering $35.51 at the feast of Our Lady of Guadalupe, but women ushered only at services primarily for other women.[24]

Until 1969, Pompei had a "door fee," given to the ushers upon entrance to the church.[25] The ushers passed the baskets during the offertory. When Pompei had a special need, the ushers took up a second collection. Head usher John A. Perazzo supervised the counting of all this money, most of it in changed, and readied the weekly collection for an armored truck to take to the bank.[26]

In 1905, Annie Leary dropped out of the picture. Letters between her and Demo indicate this patroness-client relationship, which inverted the usual male-female, priest-laity hierarchies, may have caused Demo some discomfort.[27] Then, on 4 April 1905, Demo saw a New York Daily News headline about "Big Start at Miss Leary's Concert," followed by a story regarding a benefit planned for Leary's charities, including Pompei. Apparently the article bothered him. Did it imply he couldn't manage his own parish? Demo wrote to Leary, who replied that she was "shocked and grieved" at "such an unkind letter." This may have adversely impacted Pompei's entire financial future. When Leary died, Pompei was not mentioned in her two-million-dollar will.

By 1911, Pompei's financial condition permitted it to expand its services beyond providing access to mass and the sacraments. Pompei launched a drive to fund a day care center for working mothers. The drive was sufficiently successful that in 1913 Pompei purchased a tenement at 8 Downing Street.[30] In 1915, Pompei opened its day care center, which functioned until 1944.

Pompei raised the initial funds for its day care center by following the New York Catholic precedent of holding a bazaar.[31] Three men composed a general supervisory committee for the bazaar: trustee and usher John A. Perazzo, A. (Angelo or perhaps his son August) Michelini and Saint Joseph Society president Giuseppe Pagliaghi.[32] Demo took the minutes at their meetings, which allowed him both to perform an act of courtesy to the laymen and to keep a careful eye on their work.

One bazaar fund raiser was a souvenir journal with advertising. The journal advertisements are interesting, because many were replaced by people whose names appeared in parish records.[33] A look at Demo's correspondence turns up other connections.[34] For some entrepreneurs, such as undertakers, the parish journal was an obvious place to advertise (to this day, funeral homes supply churches with calendars). For others, the advertising was simply an additional outlet. Pompeiians saw G.B. Fontana at the organ every Sunday, but he took out an advertisement to remind them he was available for music lessons as well. One might say some businesses had a moral obligation to advertise. Artificial flower manufacturers employed numerous Pompeiians under exploitative conditions. If they weren't going to pay their workers adequately, the least they could do was buy an advertisement and thus donate towards the day care center which, after all, was for their employees.

Among the advertisements is a photograph in memory of Andrea Sabini who died 26 May 1910 at the age of 52. In his funeral sermon, Demo credited Sabini, who arrived in New York about 1884, with guiding and advising the early Scalabrinian missionaries. Sabini's photograph is captioned zelante collectore, zealous collector of church funds.

The Saint Joseph Society was not as active as the women's societies, which brought together members for feast days and which raised money by putting on parish plays. The Saint Joseph Society men did not use their organization as a social outlet. For younger men who wanted a group, there was a string of societies. The patron of youth was Saint Aloysius, or Luigi, Gonzaga, and there are minutes from such a society dating from 1912.[35] In 1914, Demo estimated it had 200 members.[36] Pompei got a Holy Name Society in 1921. There is a list of officers dating from February of that year: Leon Michelini as president and John and Victor Podesta as vice president and financial secretary respectively.[37] These leaders recruited followers, and their group was accepted into the Holy Name structure in May 1921.[38]

Prominenti and junior-men-about-the parish involved themselves in funding Pompei's present church. In December 1924, the city unveiled maps showing 210 Bleeker Street stood directly athwart the proposed Sixth Avenue extension.[39] Lawyer and trustee Charles Zerbarini negotiated the purchase of new property, and arranged for mortgages.[40] Pepe Real Estate appraised Pompei's property so the parish knew how much to expect from condemnations proceedings.[41] The Rosotti lithography firm produced for fund raisers a thousand prints combining architectural sketches with a portrait of Pius XI.[42]

Demo sought professional assistance in developing a fund raising strategy, but parish men provided much of the labor and funds.[43] Young parish leaders took a census to determine how widely the financial burden could be distributed. August and Leon Michelini, Alfred and Charles Rosotti, and Victor Podesta were Holy Name men who became precinct captains.[44]

The census figures allowed Pompei to develop a "deferred paynment" campaign in which parishioners pledged large sums which were paid in small monthly installments.[45] The prominenti started the pledge-taking with a fund raising dinner. The business-like quality of the fund raising dinner may be suggested by the fact that invitations went to male heads of households, presumably distributors of income.

This kind of leadership was not all work and no play. The dinner was free. It was held at the Pennsylvania Hotel, across from the present Madison Square Garden and a world away, economically and socially, from a Village cafe. The feast went far beyond pasta e fagioli: antipasto, minestrone, celery, arcifiono, olives, filet of sole italienne with parsley potatoes, one-half a roast stuffed chicken per diner, butter beans, salad, ice cream, cake, coffee, cigars and cigarettes. The Honorable John J. Freschi, famed for his work in making Columbus Day a legal holiday in several states, was scheduled to speak; he had to cancel at the last minute, and Cardinal Hayes' representative, Michael Joseph Lavelle, spoke instead. Demo also said a few words.[46]

Comparing the 1927 dinner guest list with the 1911 souvenir journal indicates male parish leadership stability. One man whose name much publicity went out was Humbert J. ("Jack") Fugazy, Luigi's son. Other recurring names and businesses were: F. Avignone (optician), the Bergonzi family, M. Bievaschi (manufacturer specializing in hemstitching), M. Bosco (importer), S. Comollo (meats), Giovanni Fontana (contractor), L. Ginnocchio (wines and liquors), Vincent Pepe (real estate), G.B. Perazzo (undertaking), G.B. Podesta (artificial flowers), Leopold Porrino (real estate), Joseph A. Scarinzi (translator), and F. Valente (sparkling wine).[47]

The $42,035 raised at the dinner was a little less than 5% of what was needed to build the new parish plant. The young men did the leg work necessary to visit parishioners who had not been part of the elite invited to dinner, and raised $105,200 worth of promises, which the 1929 stock market crash rendered largely irredeemable.[48]

One could argue that once established, the tradition of laymen in leadership roles continued throughout Pompei's history. In 1956, when he wanted to improve the parochial school's finances, pator Mario Albanesi created Father's Club, which produced annual musical revues, presided over bingo, strengthened community life, and used its revenue to enhance the school and youth programs.[49] If one compares Pompei's parish council officers with its trustees, one will note some of the same names, and one reason Pompei's parish council did not last was trustees already performed much of parish council's work.[50]

One could also argue for change as well as for continuity, for the prominenti bore a relationship to the parish which no longer holds. For the undertaker, the organist-music teacher, the butcher, the baker, the latticeria and the olive oil importer, Pompei was a local charity which businesses patronized to demonstrate their neighborliness. Then, the parish remained local while the cafe became the fast food franchise, the pharmacist became the chain drug store, and the butcher, baker and grocer altogether were replaced by the supermarket - national concerns that advertised not in the souvenir journal but on television, and gave not to the local church but to the United Way.

Finally, one can argue for more local history studies. Look how much perceived wisdom these few pages have questioned. Along with the alienation already identified, we now have an example of involvement. Although Vatican II is widely perceived as the beginning of a more active role for the laity, here is a tradition of laymen's involvement (and one could write another paper on laywomen at Pompei). In a time of urban decline, we have a neighborhood which knit together families, businesses, and area institutions such as churches to form a network which sustained a vital community.

ENDNOTES

1   Rudolph J. Vecoli, "Prelates and Peasants: Italian Immigrants and the Catholic Church," *Journal of Social History II* (1969), 217-268.

2   John F. Kearney, "A Report of the Italian Work," in Stephen I. Hannigan, *Centennial, 1809-1909: Saint Patrick's Old Cathedral* (New York: Privately published 1909), unpaginated.

3   Generoso Valentino, et al., to John Cardinal Farley, New York, 9 December 1914 in Center for Migration Studies, Italian Americans and Religion Collection, Series I, box I, Italian Colony E. 18th St. to 24th St. NYC Folder.

4   Angelo Rezzano, et al., to Farley, Bronx, 17 May 1908, in *ibid.*, Italian Colony Van Nest and West Farm Folder.

5   Center for Migration Studies, Pio Parolin Papers, Box I, Autobiography Folder.

6   *The Village Bells* (Fall 1982), 4. This is Our Lady of Pompei's newsletter.

7   Center for Migration Studies, Our lady of Pompei, Series I, Box 11, Folder 134 (Italian). Hereafter CMS.

8   S.v., "Luigi Fugazy," in *Gli Italiani negli Stati Uniti* (New York: Italian Chamber of Commerce, 1906).

9   S.v., "Charles Baciagalupo," in *ibid.*

10   *The Village Bells* (Winter 1983), 3.

11   Private communication, 21 January 1985, Our Lady of Pompei Parish Papers 1908-1987, January 1985 Folder. Hereafter OLP

12   Victor R. Greene, *American Immigrant Leaders, 1800-1910: Marginality and Identity* (Baltimore: Johns Hopkins University Press, 1987).

13   Constantino Sassi, P.S.S.C., *Parrocchia della Madonna di Pompei in New York: Notizie Storiche dei Primi Cinquant' anni dalla sua Fondazione, 1892-1942* (Rome: Tipografia Santa Lucia, 1946), 32.

14   CMS, Series IV, Box 18, Folder 205 (Italian).

15   Certificate #00174-87C*, on file at 31 Chambers Street, Room 703, New York, New York.

16   In his oration at Demo's silver jubilee, Francesco Canonico Castellano claimed Demo founded the Saint Joseph Society to present laborers with a model for workers to offset the socialist and revolutionary ideologies of the the day. Although Saint Joseph has been used that way, this does not seem to have been the case at Pompei. Saint Joseph was also a model husband and father. A copy of Castellano's speech is in OLP Parish Memorabilia to 1975 Box, Before Fr. Albanesi Folder.

17   *New York Times*, 10 August 1930, 23:6.

18   Pulpit announcement for 8 July 1900, CMS Series VIII, Box 28, Folder 309 (Italian).

19   Program in CMS, Series II, Box 12, Folder 144.

20   Pulpit announcement for July 15, 1900, CMS Series VIII, Box 28, Folder 309 (Italian). Demo's attitude toward southern Italian Catholicism in Carolina Ware, *Greenwich Village 1920-1930: A Comment on American Civilization in the Post-War Years* (New York: Houghton-Mifflin, 1935; reprint, New York: Harper, 1965), 312.

21   Private communications, 15 May 1978, OLP Parish Papers 1975, 1980, near correspondence 1977 Folder.

22   Private communication, 5 July 1985, OLP Parish Papers 1980-1987, January 1985 Folder.

23   Saint Joseph Society Meeting Minutes, CMS, Series VI, Box 26, Folder 298 (Italian).

24   Pulpit announcement for 26 August 1900, CMS Series VIII, Box 28, Folder 309 (Italian). Maria's last name is illegible.

25   Weekly bulletin for 17 November 1968, OLP Sunday Bulletins I.

26   *The Village Bells* (Fall 1984), 3-4.

27   Annie Leary to Antonio Demo, 26 May and 4 August 1904, CMS Series I, Box 1, Folder 5.

28   Leary to Demo, New York, 15 April 1905, CMS Series I, Box 1, Folder 6.

29   *New York Times*, 4 May 1919, 22:5.

30   Charles Zerbarini to Demo, New York, 4 May 1929, CMS Series IV, Box 21, Folder 247.

31   Bernadette McCauley, "Philanthropy and Social Mobility: Ladies Auxiliary Societies in New York's Catholic Hospitals, 1906-1919," paper delivered at "American Catholicism in the Twentieth Century" conference, Cushwa Center for the Study of American Catholicism, University of Notre Dame, 2 November 1990.

32   Bazaar Meeting Minutes, 8 October 1911, CMS Series IV, Box 18, Folder 205 (Italian).

33   The names are Charles Baciagalupo, undertaking and embalming; the Bergonzi family; R. Michelini, wines and liquors; Raimond Michelini, wines and liquors; Serafino Michelini, trucking; Giuseppe Pagliaghi, newspaper agent; Pepe and Brother Real Estate and Insurance; G.B. Perazzo, funeral director; and G. Savro or J. Savio, artificial flower manufacturer.

34   Joseph A. Scarinzi advertised his translation service in the journal. His family corresponded with Demo. See Scarinzi letters to Demo dated 12 January 1911, CMS Series I, Box 1, Folder 12.

35   Saint Luigi Society meeting minutes, 14 April 1912, CMS Series VI, Box 26, Folder 300.

36   Demo to Joseph M. Sorrentino, S.J., 6 November 1914, CMS Series I, Box 7, Folder 80.

37   CMS Series II, Box 13, Folder 162.

38   Holy Name memorabilia in Ralph Stella Our Lady of Pompei Scrapbook, OLP Scrapbooks II.

39   *New York Sun*, 19 December 1924.

40   Zerbarini to Demo, 16 May 1925, CMS Series IV, Box 21, Folder 242.

41   Vincent Pepe to Demo, 16 January 1926, CMS Series IV, Box 21, Folder 243.

42   Charles C. Rosotti to Michael A. Cosenza, North Bergen, New Jersey, 29 May 1967, OLP Papers before 1975, Cosenza folder.

43   Contract between Demo and the McKeown System, 27 December 1926, CMS Series IV< Box 20, Folder 228.

44   Demo, Circular, 20 December 1926, CMS Series IV, Box 20, Folder 229.

45Pulpit announcement, 13 February 1926, CMS Series IV Box 20, Folder 230.

46   *Newsletter*, 24 January 1927, CMS Series IV, Box 20, Folder 231.

47   *Il Corriere d'America*, 2 February 1927, p. 17.

48   Demo to Patrick Cardinal Hayes, 3 March 1927, CMS Series IV, Box 20, Folder 231.

49   Vincent Lojacono, circular, undated, OLP Parish Papers before 1975, 1950-1959 Folder.

50   Parish Advisory board meeting minutes, 11 March 1976, OLP Parish Papers 1975-1980, Advisory Board Fr. Marino Folder.

PART IV
COMMUNITY

11

AN OUNCE OF PREVENTION: COMMUNITY HEALTH AND ITALIAN-AMERICAN WOMEN

Suzanne Krase

Introduction

During the past decade, public health initiatives have focused attention almost exclusively on disease prevention and health promotion. This strategy places the emphasis for healthy outcomes on individual responsibility for health actions. For example, in coronary artery disease, public health messages have advocated individual lifestyle changes in diet, smoking and exercise.

In reference to the second leading cause of death, cancer, the benefit from lifestyle changes in decreasing one's risk, except for smoking and lung cancer, is not so clearly understood. While low fat, high fiber diets are expected to decrease the risk of getting certain cancers and affect incidence rates, for the present, the secondary prevention techniques of early detection and treatment to decrease mortality rates need to be stressed. Among women, breast cancer is the leading form of cancer, and the incidence rate continues to increase. The reduction in mortality is highly dependent at this time on the adoption by women, of breast cancer screening practices, routine mammography, clinical examination and breast self-examination.

Unfortunately, the utilization of mammography, which is the most effective screening tool, is far from routine, according to the American Cancer Society. Reports of mammography screening practice have estimated its use by women over 50 years of age to be anywhere between 15 to 55 percent, with 20 to 57 percent of these women having had a mammography in the previous year (Owen & Long, 1989; Zapka, Stoddard, Costanza & Greene, 1989; Greenwald, 1986). The importance of reaching women with a message about the efficacy of breast cancer screening is beginning to receive some much needed attention in the media. Nevertheless, the investigation into who is, or who is not, likely to go for breast cancer screening is still limited; despite the tremendous importance of the subject.

The statistics on characteristics, such as sex, age, race and socioeconomic factors, are being collected to help describe the distribution of breast cancer at the national and local levels, and they do provide good broad, base line information on the incidence and mortality from this disease. Upon closer examination of the issue of preventive health behaviors, however, I suggest that they are not the "best" indicators of who is likely to go for routine breast cancer screening and, they do not provide the most complete information that is necessary for effective planning of health education strategies to increase mammography screening on the community level. The ethnic background of women, especially when they are residing in an ethnic collective, may be a better indicator of health behavior than the other features now examined.

However, there is a paucity of research on the impact of ethnicity on health behavior and health outcomes. Some of the problem is related to how research variables are constructed. For example, the lumping together of white ethnics, such as Irish, Jewish, Italian and Polish, etc., and black ethnics, such as African-Americans, Haitians and Jamaicans, etc., under simple racial breakdowns, most often shows disparities that are not based on genetics, as implied, but on cultural factors (Krieger, 1990). As noted by Gottlieb and Green (1987), "Specific cultural values, beliefs, and attitudes may influence lifestyle independently of enabling social and economic resources." (p. 37). Racial breakdowns ignore the many possible variations in interethnic health responses and health experiences.

In order to contribute to the seriously limited body of knowledge that exists on the role of ethnicity and health behavior, this research on Italian-American women and breast cancer screening was undertaken. The preliminary findings of a questionnaire answered by Italian-American women, living in Brooklyn, during a community mammography screening event will be presented. These findings will be discussed within the context of the existing literature on the impact of ethnicity on health care practices and how that influence might affect breast cancer screening behavior. The analysis of this data is exploratory in nature and attempts to describe the participants from their self report.

Review of the Literature

People who have been raised in an ethnic collectivity — that is, a group with common origins, a sense of identity, and shared standards for behavior — often acquire from that experience not only basic concepts and attitudes toward health and illness but also fundamental styles of interpersonal behavior and concerns about the world. The effects of this enculturation carry over into health-care situations and also become an important influence on personal activities devoted to health maintenance and disease prevention. (Harwood, 1981, p. 2)

The research that has been done on ethnicity reports that ethnicity is relevant even when it is difficult to separate out the influence of socio-economic class and acculturation. This relationship between ethnicity and health behavior can best be discussed by dividing the subject into the following areas — disease rates, illness behavior and utilization patterns. (Harwood, 1981)

Disease rates

Ethnic collectives have been observed to vary in incidence and mortality rates for different diseases and breast cancer is no exception. A comparison of the statistics on breast cancer between Italy and New York State, New York City and Brooklyn is important, considering that Italian-Americans in the areas of Brooklyn researched (concentrated in Community Planning Boards 10 and 11 — Bensonhurst/Bay Ridge), make up approximately 50 percent of the population, with over 20 percent listed as foreign-born (U.S. Census, 1980).

Applying incidence rates to communicate the breast cancer risk reveals that women in New York State had a high breast cancer incidence rate for the years 1983-1987 of 89.5 per 100,000. The New York City rate, during the same time frame, was 82.7 (New York State Department of Health County Data Book, 1990). Rates for the individual five boroughs and 60 local community planning districts, are not available because the population shifts since the 1980 census are considered too great for the use of the 1980s numbers in the compilation of health statistics and 1990 census data has not yet been made available for these purposes (Anecdotal information New York State Department of Epidemiology and New York City Department of Health).

For the same time period in Italy, the incidence rate for women in the northwest Lombardy region was 59.6; in the north central Province of Parma, 58.4; and, in eastern Sicily, the Ragusa Province, it was 46.7. (Muir & Waterhouse, 1987). While the variation in these rates within Italy, in and of themselves, merit investigation, for the purposes of this research, the most interesting fact is that they are all lower than those of both New York State and New York City and, therefore, are noteworthy in understanding Italian-American women's perceptions of their groups and their own susceptibility to breast cancer.

Italian-American women residing in Brooklyn may not, at this point in time, see themselves at particular risk for breast cancer because their previous experience, especially among the recent immigrants from southern Italy, has been different. The health education message that quickly needs to be given to these women is that studies of immigrants have consistently shown that "breast cancer rates of the migrants and their descendants move, although slowly, towards those prevailing in the new environment" (Kurihara, Aoki, Miller & Muir, 1987, p. 14) and that they are at risk. (Lilienfeld, Levin & Kessler, 1972; Staszewski & Haenzel, 1965; Buel & Dunn, 1965).

Mortality rates from breast cancer, like those of other cancers, are most affected by the stage of the disease at the time of detection. According to the results of the Breast Cancer Detection Demonstration Project (BCDDP), the mortality rate from breast cancer can be reduced up to 30 percent when the cancer is detected in the early stages (Seidman, Gelb, Silverberg, LaVerda & Lubera, 1987). In the BCDDP, mammography was positive in 91.8 percent of the cancers of women over 50 years of age and "of utmost importance, fewer than 20 percent of all patients with cancer detected in the BCDDP had positive nodes at surgery" (Winchester, Bernstein, Paige & Christ, 1988).

For women in Italy, the mortality rate (18.8) for the years 1978-79, was lower than the rates reported for most of Europe and for the United States (21.7) (Kurihara *et al.*, 1987). However, in both Italy and the United States, breast cancer deaths have been stable at approximately one-third of their respective incidences. This suggests that the inter-nation stage of detection of breast cancer is comparable and unfortunately unchanging despite advances in treatment.

The mammography screening behavior of women living in Italy was unavailable at the time of this research and, for Brooklyn, screening behavior needs to be inferred from the national data since there was no data on particular localities found. Greenwald (1986) reported a 15 to 20 percent annual mammography utilization rate for women 50 to 70 years of age while Zapka *et al.* results showed that 55 percent of their sample, ages 45 to 75 years, related that they had at least one mammography. Of these, 57 percent said that they had one in the last year (1989).

Recently published research on cancer and stage at detection reported on the incidence of cervical cancer and the stage of the disease at the time of detection for Brooklyn. The researchers communicated concern because their data showed that there was disproportionately high numbers of invasive cancers in areas with high concentrations of Italian-American women where the incidence of cervical cancer is low. They speculated on the basis of anecdotal material with Italian-American women in the Bay Ridge Health district, that the use of PAP screening for cervical cancer was low (Fruchter, Nayeri, Boyce, Feldman & Burnett, 1988).

Illness Behavior

While I found no previous studies during my literature review that focused on the relationship between health screening behavior and ethnicity, there was research that reported on the impact of ethnicity and illness behavior. Illness behavior, refers to the ways in which "symptoms are perceived, evaluated and acted upon (or not acted upon) by different kinds of people and in different social situations" (Mechanic, 1968, p.116).

Zabrowski's pioneering study on pain perception among Italians, Irish and Jews (1952) reported more emotional responses to pain by the Italian and Jewish patients. When researching beyond pain, for a range of symptoms, Baumann (1961) and Twaddle (1969) reported that "feeling state" changes, which were listed as pain and weakness, were the most important symptoms for all of the groups studied — Italian Catholics, Protestants and Jews. The Italians respondents, however, were the only ethnic group to list only feeling states as symptoms of illness.

Zola's study (1966) paid particular attention to the way Italian and Irish patients presented their complaints. The Irish denied that their symptoms had any effect on their relationships with other people while the Italians reported disruptions in interpersonal relationships as the major part of their complaint. The reliance on interpersonal relationships for Italian-Americans, also influences their use of medical consultation with a greater use of lay consultations within family and kinship networks (Harwood, 1981).

This focus among Italian-Americans on "feelings states," interruption of social relationships and reliance on lay consultations can determine when health care is sought and therefore, can greatly influence mammography screening behavior. In the case of breast cancer, waiting for "feeling states" of the disease, as cues to action, can significantly affect long-term survival. Social support can negatively or positively affect screening behavior depending on the advice given.

Utilization Patterns

Barriers to the recommended use of mammography, such as the lack of availability and accessibility of screening as they relate to ethnic populations, needs to be assessed. Harwood (1981) relates that the much-observed tendency for people to use medical services that are convenient to their residences has particular significance where there are patterns of ethnic clustering. He suggests that services, therefore, may have to be modified to accommodate ethnic epidemiological patterns and behavioral styles.

For women residing in Brooklyn, New York, mammography is available in numerous facilities in close proximity to the community researched. Is the nearness of mammography equipment sufficient impetus for its use? The figures quoted previously from national and regional data suggest that it is not.

Besides neighborhood availability of mammography, the cost of the procedure can affect its accessibility. The cost of mammography ranges from $45 to $350. New York State statutes mandate insurance coverage for women over 50 years of age (not the amount). Is having insurance coverage sufficient to expect utilization of mammography screening?

Examination of Participant Information

Based on the discussions in the literature concerning disease rates, illness behavior, the possible lack of feelings of susceptibility to breast cancer and concentration on "feeling states," there was an expectation that Italian-American women clustered in Brooklyn, would be less likely than American women in general to have mammography screening at the recommended frequency. Nevertheless, the assistance given by an ethnic community organization for breast cancer screening, especially when it would be available within the confines of their neighborhood, would give the social support necessary to reach women who needed to be screened.

In September, 1991, the American Italian Foundation for Cancer Research sponsored free mammography screening with the local aid of the National Federation of Italian Societies of Brooklyn. The breast cancer screening van from the Women's Outreach Network provided mammography, clinical breast examinations and breast self-examination instruction for three days. A review of the responses of 109 women with Italian surnames who participated in this neighborhood breast cancer screening event was accomplished by dividing the responses into two groups — those who were having a mammography for the first time and those who reported having at least one previously. Their age, physician recommendation, health insurance coverage and family history were compared to see if these variables appeared to have affected the individual's screening behavior.

According to the findings of this study, the expectation that there would be many Italian-American women who had never had a mammography proved to be true. The percentage of participants from this particular ethnic group, who had never had a mammography before, was higher than published reports for American women in general. The percentage (20 percent) of the women who reported being on schedule for mammography screening was also below the norms presented by other researchers (Zapka *et al.*, 1989; Winchester *et al.*; Greenwald, 1986).

Sixty five percent of the women (71 of them) were having a mammography for the first time. Of these first timers, 59 percent were over 50 years of age and long overdue for a mammography according to the American Cancer Society recommended guidelines (NIH Publication, 1984). Thirty five percent (38) of the women who participated in this screening reported having had a previous mammography but 2/3 of this group of women, who were over 50 years of age, related that they had not had one in the previous year.

When the two groups were compared according to age, doctor recommendation, family history and health insurance, the results were as follows:

Age: Of the 109 women in this sample, 63 were over 50 years of age. Only 33 percent of this age group reported having had a mammography before. For the 46 women under 50, 25 percent of the first timers were under 40 versus 3 percent of the previously screened group. This increase in mammography examinations for this younger age group reflects, hopefully, an increased awareness among this age group of breast cancer screening needs.

Insurance: The same percentage of women (63 percent), in each group, reported having insurance coverage. While the self report form did not question the Italian-American women on possible financial barriers, the fact that both groups had the same rate of insurance coverage appears to negate finances as a major obstacle to one group versus the other.

Doctor Recommendation: Only thirty seven percent of women in each group reported that their doctor had recommended that they have a mammography. Of those women over fifty, who would more likely to be advised to have a mammography, 20 percent (8) were in the group who had had a previous mammography and 20 percent (16) were first timers. This number was again lower than physician referral for asymptomatic women in the general population that has been reported to be as low as 50 percent (Fink, 1989). The small number of women who were there on the advice of their doctor is in keeping with Harwood's (1981) anecdotal accounts of the major influence of family and friends in seeking health care versus the weight of medical counsel.

Family History: Eighteen women reported having a family history of breast cancer. Of these women, 12 reported having a previous mammography and 6 did not. Family history therefore, appears to be the one area that made an impact on mammography behavior. Nevertheless, since family history accounts for approximately 25 percent of breast cancers, it leaves 75 percent of the women not feeling susceptible (Breast Cancer Digest, 1984).

Discussion

While the data collected did not directly address the question as to whether the local, ethnic social support for the mammography screening in the ethnic neighborhood itself was the necessary impetus for the positive response to the screening that was demonstrated by these Italian-American women, women who had never had a mammography before did take advantage of this opportunity. The similarities found between the two groups when the effects of other variables were taken into account — age, insurance coverage and doctor recommendation — places neighborhood social support in the forefront, along with family history, as the reason for this positive health behavior.

Based on the tentative findings discussed here, further investigation of the role of ethnicity is warranted to decrease mortality from breast cancer through early detection. Health professionals working with Italian-Americans in particular, and other ethnic groups in general, need to examine disease risk here in the United States and the country of origin, besides investigating illness behaviors and previous patterns of health care utilization that may be culturally determined. For the present, and at the very least, breast cancer education and screening should be made available in the ethnic neighborhood and local ethnic groups should be partners in the dissemination of information and services.

ENDNOTES

Bauman, B. (1961), "Diversities in Conceptions of Health and Physical Fitness," *Journal of Health and Human Behavior 2*, (1), 39-46.

Buel, P. & Dunn, J.E. (1965), "Cancer Mortality Among Japanese Issei and Nisei of California," *Cancer. 51* 656-663.

Fink, D. (1989), "Community Programs for Breast Cancer Awareness Detection," *Cancer 64* 2674-2681.

Fruchter, Nayeri, Boyce, Feldman & Burnett (1988), "Gynecologic Cancer in Brooklyn, New York, 1978-1982," *New York State Journal of Medicine 88*, 466-473.

Gottlieb, N. & Greene, L. (1987), "Ethnicity and Lifestyle Health Risk: Some Possible Mechanisms," *American Journal of Health Promotion 37*-45.

Greenwald, P. & Sondik, E.J. (1986), "Cancer Control: Objectives for the Nation 1985-2000," *NCI Monographs 69*.

Harwood, A. (1981) *Ethnicity and Medical Care* Cambridge, MA: Harvard University Press.

Krieger, N. (1990), "Social Class and the Black/White Crossover in the Age-Specific Incidence of Breast Cancer: A Study Linking Census-Derived Data to Population-Based Registry Records," *American Journal of Epidemiology 131* 804-814.

Kurikari, M., Kunio, A., Miller, R. & Muir, C. (1987) *Changing Cancer Patterns and Topics in Cancer Epidemiology*, New York: Plenum Press.

Lilienfeld, A.M., Levin, M.L. & Kessler, I.I. (1972) *Cancer in the United States* Cambridge, MA: Cambridge Press.

Muir, C.S. & Waterhouse, J.A.H. (eds.) (1987), *Cancer Incidence on Five Continents* Lyon: IARC.

Mechanic, D. (1968b), *Medical Sociology* New York: Free Press.

New York State Department of Health (1990), *County Data Book*.

Owen, P. & Long, P. (1989), "Facilitating Adherence to ACS and NCI Guidelines for Breast Cancer Screening," *American Association of Occupational Health Nurses, 37* 153-157.

Seidman, H., Gelb, S.K., Silverberg, E., LaVerda, N. & Lubera, J.A. (1987), "Survival Experience in the Breast Cancer Detection Demonstration Project," *Ca-A Cancer Journal for Clinicians, 37* 258-290.

Staszewski, J. & Haenzel, W. (1965), "Cancer Mortality among Polish-born in the United States," *Journal of the National Cancer Institute, 35,* 291-302.

Twaddle, A. & Hessler, R. (1987), *"A Sociology of Health,"* New York: MacMillan Publishing Company.

U.S. Bureau of Census (1982), *"Coverage of the National Population in the 1980 Census by Age, Sex, and Race: Preliminary Estimates by Demographic Analysis,"* (Current Population Reports, Series P-23, No. 115) Washington, D.C: U.S. Government Printing Office.

U.S. Department of Health & Human Services (1984), *The Breast Cancer Digest* (NIH Publication No. 84-1691) Bethesda, MD: U.S. Government Printing Office.

Winchester, D., Bernstein, J., Paige, M. & Christ, M. (1988), *The Early Detection and Diagnosis of Breast Cancer* Atlanta, GA: American Cancer Society.

Zabrowski, M. (1952), "Cultural Components of Response to Pain," *Journal of Social Issues 8,* 16-20.

Zapka, J., Stoddard, A., Costanza, M. & Greene, H. (1989), "Breast Cancer Screening by Mammography: Utilization and Associated Factors," *American Journal of Public Health 79,* 1499-1502.

Zola, I. (1966), "Culture and Symptoms — An Analysis of Patient's Presenting Complaints," *American Sociological Review 31,* 615-630.

12

COMMUNITY CO-OPERATION AND ACTIVISM: ITALIAN AND AFRICAN AMERICANS IN WILLIAMSBURG, BROOKLYN

Jᴜᴅɪᴛʜ N. DᴇSᴇɴᴀ

The study of urban neighborhoods in sociology has given little attention to community co-operation and organization. The focus of most studies
has been on competition and conflict among various ethnic, racial, and
economic groups who reside in urban neighborhoods (DeSena 1990;
Kornblum 1974; Krase 1982; Molotch 1972; Rieder 1985; Susser 1982; Suttles
1968).

This paper illustrates community co-operation. It is an analysis of a
grass roots, multi-ethnic, racially mixed community organization in Brooklyn
called the Greenpoint-Williamsburg Coalition of Community Organizations (GWCOCO). This organization operated between 1976 and 1982, a
period of fiscal austerity in New York City. The organization's focus and
purpose was neighborhood unity and activism. The Coalition involved
working class and poor residents of two different, but adjacent neighborhoods, who set aside their ethnic and racial differences, and worked
together to preserve the quality of life, and to fight for municipal services in
Brooklyn's Community Board. [1] In New York City, Community Boards are
political entities in which the City is divided into these sectors and services
are delivered within each Community Board. Community Boards are an
outcome of the decentralization of City services. Membership to the Coalition was through a local community organization, such as block, tenant, and

civic associations, as well as religious, health, and housing groups. Political clubs were not accepted as members. The Coalition was made up of approximately 100 groups.

Race and Ethnic Relations in Neighborhoods

The sociological literature on urban neighborhoods focuses primarily on the friction among various cultural, racial, and economic groups who share a neighborhood. The conflict and competition, for the most part, has been over "turf" and other limited resources, such as housing, jobs, institutions, and municipal services. The research can be discussed in terms of the behavior of these groups in which some attempt to preserve and maintain resources, while other groups attempt to obtain those same resources. The outcome is often conflict since there is a finite amount of resources available to groups.

Conflict and competition between groups in neighborhoods have taken a variety of forms, including violent attacks, restrictive covenants and zones, and informal, exclusionary strategies. Rieder's study of Canarsie, Brooklyn (1985), illustrates how local residents resist neighborhood change through violence toward newcomers. Canarsie is made up mainly of middle class Jews and Italians. However, during the 1960s Canarsie experienced both an increase in the number of black individuals and white flight. Canarsie's white residents resisted change by: fire-bombing houses owned by blacks, boycotting local schools to express their opposition to busing, and actively recruiting "other races and ethnics" to replace whites who were leaving Canarsie.

Krase's analysis of Lefferts Manor in Brooklyn (1982) points out how social class is maintained by a restrictive covenant which was established in 1893. The covenant prohibited owners from using Manor homes for anything other than private, single family dwellings. In 1960, New York City's Planning Commission also zoned Lefferts Manor "one-family only," thereby supporting the original covenant.

DeSena's research on Greenpoint, Brooklyn (1990), describes the informal strategies used by white ethnic residents in their attempt to resist the growth of minority dwellers. The major strategies used are: an informal housing network in which information about available housing is not advertised publicly, but by word of mouth; informal surveillance in which residents observe street life and often confront the intentions of strangers; formal surveillance in which a community organization was formed to serve as additional security to the police.

Suttles (1972) has developed the concept of a "defended neighborhood." The defended neighborhood is an attempt by a residential group to isolate itself. Suttles illustrates this concept by his study of the Addams area in Chicago. The Addams area is made up of Italians, Mexicans, Puerto Ricans, and blacks, who reside in segregated territories, and are separated by location and local institutional arrangements. Street corner gangs maintain the boundaries of each group's "turf."

Molotch's presentation of the South Shore of Chicago (1972) describes an attempt at "managed integration." A commission of residents developed strategies to maintain a balance between black and white residents, and to prevent white flight. Ultimately, these tactics did not work and South Shore became a black community.

The literature on urban neighborhoods seldom discusses community co-operation among various racial and ethnic groups. Studies by Rieder, and DeSena reviewed previously discuss how white ethnics organized both formally and informally to exclude racial and ethnic minorities from residing in these neighborhoods. Molotch's work shows how whites established a commission which attempted to engineer balanced integration.

This paper focuses on community co-operation between whites and blacks. It describes how whites and blacks worked together on neighborhood issues. They held common goals and shared interests.

Research Methods

This paper is part of a larger study on community power and activism in Greenpoint-Williamsburg, Brooklyn. It was carried out through the use of a variety of research methods. First, participant observation was employed. In 1979, I was elected to the Coalition's board of directors as an Area Vice President representing Central Williamsburg. There were three vice presidents elected from each sector of the community. I was viewed as a delegate from the Italian community. As a member of the board of directors, I had access to all Coalition meetings, the Coalition office, and organizing and support staff. Second, content analysis was used. I examined the following materials: newspaper accounts of Coalition events, progress reports sent by the Coalition's Executive Director to funding sources, grant proposals written by Coalition staff members and sent to funding sources, programs from the Coalition's annual conventions, and flyers which advertised Coalition meetings, local issues that the organization would undertake, and upcoming events. Finally, interviews were also utilized. During the summer of 1991, I contacted and interviewed 20 individuals who were Coalition leaders or organizers. These interviews were open ended and lasted between 1-2 hours each. In general, I asked each person to reflect on the Coalition and his/her experiences as a member of the organization, and to articulate current perceptions and thoughts about it. Most people welcomed the opportunity to discuss the Coalition, and viewed their involvement as a positive time in their lives, in which, they believe, that they accomplished something. Most people enjoyed the interview. Their names have been deleted or changed.

The Neighborhoods

The neighborhoods of Greenpoint and Williamsburg in northern Brooklyn make up Community Board 1. Greenpoint is a primarily white ethnic, working class area, while Williamsburg is comprised mostly of poor Hispanics and blacks. In 1990, Brooklyn's Community Board 1 had a total population of 155,972.[1] Of these individuals, 46 percent were white (non Hispanic), 7 percent were black (non Hispanic), 44 percent were Hispanic, and 3 percent were Asian and other non Hispanic groups.[2] As the GWCOCO was forming, it divided the Community Board into six areas to ensure that the interests of ethnic and racial groups were represented. These areas were: Greenpoint (white ethnic), Northside (Polish), Central Williamsburg (Italian and African Americans), East Williamsburg (African Americans and Hispanics), Southside (Hispanic), South Williamsburg (Hasidic Jews and Hispanics; however, the Hasidic community was not a regular participant of the Coalition). Each section elected three area vice presidents to represent it as well as voted for the Executive Board, namely President, Executive Vice President, Secretary, and Treasurer. Elections took place at an annual convention, and vacancies were filled at delegate assemblies, which were held four times a year. This paper will focus specifically on the community of Central Williamsburg. From this community, Italian and African Americans were elected to the Coalition's board of directors, and engaged in planning, arranging, and organizing around local issues.

Central Williamsburg

The Coalition identified Central Williamsburg as the area ranging from the Brooklyn Queens Expressway (Meeker Avenue) on the north to Grand Street on the south. It is bounded on the east by the Newtown Creek, and on the west by Union Avenue. In 1990, approximately 18,958 people resided in this area. Of these persons, 53 percent were white (non Hispanic), 9 percent were black (non-Hispanic), 35 percent were Hispanic, and 3 percent reported themselves as Asian and other non Hispanics.[3] Census tracts do not conform exactly to neighborhood boundaries. The largest, single, non Hispanic ethnic group reported was Italian.

In the Coalition's view, Central Williamsburg was made up of two major ethnic groups: Italian and African Americans. Hispanics were represented by other areas of the Coalition. In Central Williamsburg, Italian and African Americans had very distinct residential patterns. The Italian community were owners and renters of the many smaller, multiple dwelling housing structures, which are mostly wood framed. In contrast, the African American community resided primarily in a New York City Housing Project called Cooper Park Houses. Until the mid 1970s, there was little interaction between Cooper Park and the Italian community. The larger white community treated Cooper Park like an island and left it alone, while also warning their children not to enter its borders. Through the years, Cooper Park had developed an active Tenants Association, and Youth Recreation Center. With the emergence of the Coalition, a forum was available to bring together the white, ethnic community with people of color to work on local issues which affected both groups. In Central Williamsburg, it was Italians and blacks who, to an extent, learned to talk to each other, and to work together for a common goal: the preservation of neighborhood and community. A resident of the Italian community who was also a president of the Coalition expressed, "We could have built a wall to Cooper Park. The Coalition didn't. Whatever the issue was, we all went out and worked on it."

The Issues

The Coalition worked on a variety of local issues ranging from additional traffic and street lights, adequate sewers, and the demolition of dangerous buildings, to the maintenance of investment practices and essential city services. I will briefly describe some of the areas of neighborhood life which involved the Italian and African American communities of Central Williamsburg. They include: admission to a local high school, the activities of neighborhood women, and a youth Olympics.

Admission to High School

In 1979, New York City's Board of Education announced that the construction of Northeast Brooklyn High School was near completion. Parents in Greenpoint-Williamsburg looked forward to sending their children to a newly constructed building. However, the Board of Education had drawn the school's zone in such a way that "almost a third" (*Greenline*, March 15, 1980 p.1) of the students in Greenpoint-Williamsburg are not eligible to attend the new school. Students living east of Kingsland and Bushwick Avenues were "zoned out," which included parts of Greenpoint, Central Williamsburg (including Cooper Park and the St. Nick's area) and East Williamsburg. A student "will not be able to attend the new school, even though he will see it every morning from his kitchen window" (*Greenline*, March 15, 1980 p.1). A committee of the Coalition was formed to address this issue, and a series of community meetings was held. The sentiment expressed at these meetings was that residents wanted all students living in Community Board 1 to have access to the school. On March 26, 1980, the Coalition held a public meeting with officials of the Board of Education. At this meeting, the Board of Education agreed to admit all youths living in Community Board 1. And in discussions which followed, the Board of Education guaranteed that "all community youths could transfer to the new school as well" (*Program of the Fourth Annual Convention of the Greenpoint-Williamsburg Coalition of Community Organizations*, November 16, 1980 p. 42).

Neighborhood Women

The importance of women's activities in neighborhoods is presently being recognized by social scientists (DeSena 1990; Haywoode 1989). Local women are often involved in fostering positive race and ethnic relations. Women residing in Central Williamsburg were quicker to cross racial barriers than their male counterparts. This seems to be the case in other places as well (Kornblum 1974). With a common concern for the safety of children and the preservation of community, African and Italian American women in Central Williamsburg would band together to fight for city services. One example is a protest for a traffic light on a street corner where children were being hit by speeding cars. Neighborhood women of both races blocked traffic with baby carriages in order to get their message across to the Traffic Department.

African and Italian American women were also united in a college program sponsored by National Congress of Neighborhood Women, which has an office and program in Central Williamsburg (Haywoode 1991). According to a graduate of the program:

> A lot of people at the Congress came together to accomplish a lifelong goal because a lot of women quit school for a number of reasons. They weren't told they were smart enough. They got pregnant or married and were in traditional roles. You stayed home and raised the kids. You don't work and you don't go to school. [Through a community based college program] they had the opportunity to change and to do something better.

Many of the women leaders and activists of the Coalition were enrolled in this college program. Leadership training was a major component of the program, while women earned an Associate's Degree. These women were able to use their newly acquired skills for Coalition activities. They were found elected to the Board of Directors including the position of president. Neighborhood women chaired committees on a variety of issues, and debated with representatives of City government at public forums. These activities indicate the various levels of social organization in which women interacted, and the extent to which African and Italian American women worked together for common goals. Consequently, their focus was on their shared interests and similarities rather than on their differences.

Youth Olympics

There were also local events sponsored by the Coalition, which were thought of as community wide, and were organized to assemble people of different races and cultures in the spirit of unity. The Coalition's intention by these events was to begin to break down social barriers among residents of Greenpoint-Williamsburg. One such event was the Youth Olympics.

On May 21, 1978, the Coalition sponsored the first annual Youth Olympics, which was held in McCarren Park. The Olympics had a number of purposes. One was to link the communities of Greenpoint and Williamsburg in a positive way so that the Coalition could begin to carry out its mission. The notion of mixing people of different ethnic groups and races by this event was further illustrated by a group of students from Hunter College. A member of the Olympics Committee, who was a film major at Hunter College, organized a student film crew to record the day's events. They titled this film *The BQE is Closed*. The symbolic meaning behind this title was that the Brooklyn-Queens Expressway separated the neighborhoods of Greenpoint and Williamsburg. On the day of the Coalition's Youth Olympics, however, the BQE was closed suggesting that no divisions existed. Another purpose of the Youth Olympics was to hold an event for community youth. A third reason for sponsoring a Youth Olympics was to introduce the Coalition to a larger group of residents. The day's events included: a six mile run through the community, boys and girls 50, 100, 220, 440, and 880 yard dashes, and live music by local bands and soloists who volunteered to perform. Youth participants were organized through local youth programs, teams, block and tenants associations and schools. The event proved to be successful to the goals of the Coalition and as an event by itself. People congregated and expressed their willingness to work with each other on community issues. The Youth Olympics was held for the next four years. Each year it grew in attendance, sports events, and added an ethnic food festival.

The Coalition's Decline

In 1982 the Coalition closed its doors. The major reason was lack of funding. Reagan's cuts were fully instituted, and the Coalition's organizers were laid off. In fact, their last year was spent primarily in an unsuccessful attempt to raise funds. In addition, many of the community organizations that were members of the Coalition were also experiencing major budget cuts or loss of funding completely. The Coalition found itself in the awkward position of competing with its member organizations for funding. Divisiveness and competitiveness were not part of the Coalition's mission. The Coalition no longer exists, much to the regret of many of its leaders. According to one leader,

> A lot of things that the Coalition worked on are still in effect. But there's no one out there now to bring together ethnic, racial, and economic groups. There's no solid group out there fighting for any kind of funding, or fighting any of the budget issues.

Another leader remarked, "The Coalition could have been an asset and helped with the racial and ethnic conflict going on."

Conclusions

The existence of the Coalition and the impact it has had on the lives of people in Central Williamsburg raises a number of implications for social theory. First, this paper suggests that the political participation of working class and poor people can not be determined solely by voting behavior. They may not vote in large numbers, but they are certainly politically involved. They participate through their activism.

These findings also illustrate the notion of "social change from below." In an attempt to preserve the quality of life in the community, residents of Central Williamsburg in conjunction with the Coalition actively and literally fought government and corporations. Residents were unwilling to accept New York City's policy of fiscal austerity, which was implemented through cuts in services. They attempted to prevent its implementation or to change the policy, at least concerning Greenpoint-Williamsburg, and were successful on a number of issues.

This discussion also implies a high level of social organization that exists in this community. The Coalition was able to mobilize and mix the different ethnic groups toward action. In fact, Greenpoint-Williamsburg has a tradition of social activism which enabled the Coalition to develop.

Finally, this paper suggests a model for confronting urban problems, especially the promotion of ethnic and racial harmony. The Greenpoint-Williamsburg Coalition of Community Organizations unified residents of northern Brooklyn, who were of different colors and had different cultural backgrounds, to work on common interests and toward common goals. This organization created "a rainbow coalition," and "a gorgeous mosaic."[4] With all of the racial violence that has erupted in New York City recently such as the murders of Michael Griffith and Yusuf Hawkins, the attack on the Central Park jogger, the fire-bombing of real estate offices in Canarsie, the boycott of a Korean grocery, the killings and riots in Crown Heights, and the assaults on children and teenagers in the Bronx, the time is right to look to this model as a solution. Only in this way can the City of New York and American society move toward focusing on a common humanity.

ENDNOTES

1   This information was obtained from the *1990 Census, Total Population, Brooklyn Community District 1.*

2   This information was obtained from the *Population Change by Race and Hispanic Origin by Selected Ages; Housing Unit Change. Brooklyn Community District 1, 1980-1990.*

3   The source of these demographic data is *Total Population by Race and Ethnic Group by Census Tract, 1990, Brooklyn Community District 1.*

4   These phrases were created by Jesse Jackson and David Dinkins respectively.

REFERENCES

DeSena, J.N. 1990, *Protecting One's Turf: Social Strategies for Maintaining Urban Neighborhoods*, Lanham, MD: University Press of America.

Haywoode, T.L. 1989, "Working Class Women and Neighborhood Politics," *Contemporary Readings in Sociology*, J.N. DeSena, ed. Dubuque, IW: Kendall-Hunt Publishing Company.

Haywoode, T.L. 1991, *Working Class Feminism: Creating a Politics of Community Connection and Concern*, Unpublished Doctoral Dissertation, Graduate School and University Center, City University of New York.

Kornblum, W. 1974, *Blue Collar Community*, Chicago: University of Chicago Press.

Krase, J. 1982, *Self and Community in the City* Washington, D.C.: University Press of America.

"Local Parents Demand: We Want Our Kids in That School!" *Greenline* March 15, 1980.

Molotch, H. 1972, *Managed Integration*, Berkeley: University of California Press.

Program of the Fourth Annual Convention of the Greenpoint-Williamsburg Coalition of Community Organizations Sunday, November 16, 1980.

Rieder, J. 1985, *Canarsie: Jews and Italians of Brooklyn Against Liberalism*, Cambridge, MA: Harvard University Press.

Susser, I. 1982, *Norman Street*, New York: Oxford University Press.

Suttles, G. 1968, *The Social Order of the Slum*, Chicago: University of Chicago Press,

U.S. Bureau of the Census *Census of Population of 1990.*

13

AFRICAN AMERICAN STUDENT REACTION TO ITALIAN-AMERICAN CULTURE

Jerome Krase

Introduction

The goals of this paper are four-fold: First, to document a neglected aspect of the contemporary history of Italian American neighborhoods; that of intergroup relations and attitudes. Second, to provide an antidote to the simplistic media stereotype of the "character" of Italian American urban neighborhoods as universally hostile, indeed violent, toward strangers. Third, to introduce the notion of "Pure Phenomenology" as a useful theoretical and methodological perspective for the study of ethnic communities. And fourth, to emphasize the importance of documenting Italian American history as it unfolds around us as objectively as possible, and to archive these stories for future scholars to analyze.

A great deal of historical investigation takes place in libraries where researchers pore over newspapers and other mass media renditions of the past. The history of Italian Americans is being written in the popular media today. Therefore, it is likely that because of a series of highly publicized and politicized incidents of violence in Brooklyn, New York, in 1989, one hundred years from today scholars will conclude that the contemporary Italian American community was uniformly racist and intolerant.

A Media View of an Italian American Neighborhood

One need not wait a century to prove the foregoing hypothesis. It has

125

been already tested by Warren Strugatch who analyzed the coverage by four major New York City daily newspapers, *The New York Times*, *Newsday*, the *Daily News*, and the *Post*, of a "racially motivated" murder in late summer of 1989, and its aftermath. The community in which the homicide took place, and which undoubtedly will come to symbolize urban Italian American neighborhoods is Bensonhurst, Brooklyn (Strugatch, 1989).

Strugatch looked at Bensonhurst as it was portrayed by journalists who flocked to Brooklyn to write about a local incident which garnered national, and international notoriety. The incident drew such attention partly because it happened during a hotly contested New York City mayoralty campaign which itself had thinly veiled racial, ethnic and religious overtones. The Democratic Party primary election was a contest between Jewish incumbent Edward I. Koch and African American David Dinkins. The general election for mayor of New York City pitted an Italian American, Rudolph Giuliani, against Dinkins who had won the Democratic primary.

As Strugatch reiterated: "The story broke this way: A black youth was killed while walking down a Bensonhurst street by a young white man who mistook him for the new boyfriend of the girl he had formerly dated. Police said that Yusuf Hawkins, 17, was on his way to buy a second-hand car when he was shot twice in the chest, allegedly by Joseph Fama." (p. 27)

As rare as events like this are, this was not the first such incident. Regrettably similar violent acts had occurred in recent prior years in Howard Beach, Queens, and on Avenue X in Brooklyn. All these crimes were committed by variously marginalized youths, and took place on the fringes of predominantly white-working class neighborhoods. According to Strugatch: "In each case, a complex web of racial attitudes, physical violence, and community response became compacted into a handy geographic tag that also implicated a community in a terrible crime." (p.26)

Here is how Bensonhurst was depicted as summarized by Strugatch:

> In the southern underbelly of New York City, there is a community inhabited almost entirely by young men ranging in age from 18 to 22. They dress in tank tops and t-shirts, apparently do not work, and are preoccupied by race relations. They are proud to be white, and they don't like blacks.
>
> Middle-aged people — the generation that would include the parents of these young men and women — seem to be absent in this community.
>
> But the next older generation is represented in the community by elderly ladies who sell sausages at church-sponsored street fairs and retired gentlemen who linger outside the local members-only social club before entering to sip cappucino in the semi-darkness.
>
> Where were the verifiable community leaders, the

usual suspects invariably rounded up for community snap-
shots on the real estate beat? Where were the school principals, the chair of the school board, the chamber of commerce president, the zoning board chair, the local historian
—even the president of the Kiwanis Club?

Where were the people who could speak in complete
sentences?

Evidently, articulate community leaders were not on
street corners, and so they went uninterviewed. (p. 29)

Strugatch noted that one cannot cover a racially motivated homicide
without making a "connection between a neighborhood's character and
individual acts" (p. 28). However, this "reportorial instinct" should not be
followed simplistically. According to his analysis,

The coverage of Bensonhurst, like Howard Beach before it, mimicked the methodology and approach of mainstream sociology with none of its scientific rigor. And most
of the journalists purveying this pop sociology presumably failed to recognize the masquerade. (p. 26)

As to part of the reason why such a biased view of the community
emerged and was so widely broadcast, he opined that

Bensonhurst is not the kind of place most reporters
would pick to live. Few seemed to understand the rhythms
of the neighborhood. To them, one street corner source
seemed as good as the next, especially when one's presup-
positions were conformed so readily. (p. 28)

Although Strugatch considered most of the journalistic output to be
"amateurish sociology," he noted that, "Besides (Jimmy) Breslin, there were
other exceptions to the abundance of simplistic reporting. *The Times*, for
instance, gave some space to the perceptive comments made by a professor
who teaches sociology at Brooklyn College. (p. 28)

I was the "professor" he made reference to, having been quoted in *The
New York Times* saying that southern Italian culture in the neighborhood is

a very specialized culture that plays an important role
in this incident. It's very restricted. It's an attempt to
replicate the home-country village or the city neighborhood that's really a village ... There's a second order of
problem here which is the very negative stereotype of
blacks and other minorities ... They tend to see these
people as very threatening. That adds to the feeling that
they have to defend the family, the neighborhood, against

incursion. Of course, this is nothing that excuses killing someone. There is no excuse for murder, so now there you are seeing a schizophrenic reaction there.[1]

Why Phenomenologize?

Journalists who seek to sensationalize and/or romanticize stories are not the only people who create biased historical accounts of contemporary events. Filiopietistic, or otherwise biased "ethnic" chroniclers do similar damage to the accuracy of records. Even attempts to be "objective" can result in problems, as those who write history are biased toward the unusual rather than the mundane. Therefore, I suggest the much noted but little understood perspective of phenomenology as an antidote to the two extremes of filiopiety and simple minded stereotyping.

George Psathas succinctly describes the goals of phenomenological methods in this way:

> Thus for social scientists, the study of people must take them as they are — people who suspend doubt, live in the natural attitude, and live with the certainty that the social and the natural worlds exist. The serious and careful study of how people live with and renew their assumptions requires close and faithful description. It is to that undertaking that we urge our fellow social scientists to address themselves. The study of how the social order is produced by humans in their everyday activities is a study whose value may be as considerable as the more general theoretical study of how social order is possible at all. (1973, p. 16)

Although it might appear to some as an esoteric approach to historical understanding, phenomenological study, founded by the philosopher Edmund Husserl, is quite "conventional" in that it proceeds in the well known traditions of Max Weber, Georg Simmel, Karl Mannheim, William James, Charles H. Cooley, George H. Mead, W.I. Thomas, and Alfred Schutz.

The approach is most useful because the tests of a phenomenological explanation are found in the results of its inquiry. That is:

1. Would the subjects of the study recognize the description as true if translated back to them?

2 Would the reader of the account recognize it is real without prior experience with it?

3. Does the account provide a recipe to reproduce the event, e.g. can the reader become a player by following the rules?

In order to create a "close and faithful description" one must "bracket out" or suspend biased assumptions of the everyday world, and set aside preconceptions. The world must be described as an "achievement." As a chronicler, for example, the historian must accept his/her own and others' subjective experiences as true. However, one must realize the importance of the structure of language which gives order to both our experience and our accounts of it. Phenomenological training can help all social scientists to record what is and not merely what researchers want or believe there to be.

Student Views of An Italian American Neighborhood

What I wish to provide in the following pages are several examples of "naive" descriptions of Italian Americans and their community which contradict the characterologically negative stereotypes presented most frequently by the mass media, especially in regard to intergroup relations and interactions among Italian Americans. These descriptions have been selected from a group of twenty-four, three to four-page papers written by Black and Hispanic female students over two consecutive summer semesters at Brooklyn College (1990 and 1991) for my graduate sociology course "Sociology of the Urban Community." The materials excerpted here were part of their term writing assignment which was to describe a traditional urban community. To accomplish this, the students went on an unescorted field trip to observe the Feast of Saint Paulinus.

The celebration takes place every summer in an Italian American enclave which centers around the Roman Catholic Church of Our Lady of Mount Carmel. The area lies between the Williamsburgh and Greenpoint neighborhoods of Brooklyn, New York, and is nestled between the elevated Brooklyn-Queens Expressway and the deteriorating Brooklyn waterfront. The predominantly working-class neighborhood abuts a less affluent Hispanic area, and is one which most "outsiders" see as uninviting and therefore is avoided by outsiders.[2]

The minimally edited descriptions of my nonwhite students have been chosen for this paper because of their poignancy, and the contrast of their remarks to the "pop sociological" descriptions outlined previously by Strugatch. Most of these students had participated in a prior field trip to make observations of a modern urban community exemplified by the spectacular World Financial Center and the affluent Battery Park City residential complex in Lower Manhattan. Observations in this setting provide a comparison for some of their remarks. It must also be noted that their excursions took place during a time of heightened publicity surrounding the trials of the defendants in the Bensonhurst murder, and subsequent "interracial" incidents in Brooklyn. These students, being nonwhite, were especially wary of entering into what most people reading New York City newspapers would regard as "off limits" to them.

The students were instructed to merely observe and record what they saw. This caused them a great deal of anxiety, as students, like all objective researchers, usually go into the communities they study with a set of predetermined questions to answer, as well as specific expectations about what they will see and hear. Student A.:

> On the eve of July 15, I visited this festival. Initially my classmates and I were a bit disappointed. We expected to see people dancing in the streets and food galore, instead all we saw were various sheds and a few people wandering in the streets. This disappointment was merely temporary. We were simply too early, if there is such a thing as too early.
>
> The decorative lights were later turned on and one could easily recognize that a festive occasion was about to begin. The first thing that attracted me was a piece of architecture-like structure that resembled the Eiffel Tower in Paris. My classmates and I headed toward it. We noticed the shrine on top of the 7 story structure. Of course; it was Saint Paulinus.
>
> 'Would you like to know a bit about its history?' asked a young man who was beautifully decorated, referring to the statue. 'Very much so. Thank you very much.' I responded, reflecting for a moment on the difference in attitude of this young man as compared to those in the residential community of the World Financial Center.
>
> 'Saint Paulinus of Nola,' the young man said, 'was born in the year 353 at Bordeaux, France, to a wealthy family. He became governor of the province of Campania. He later married a Spanish Christian lady. His children were grown when he converted to the Catholic Church. After the death of his wife and children, he gave away his wealth and devoted himself totally to the religious life.
>
> 'In 394 he was ordained a priest and sent to Nola. In 409, he was raised to the holy office of Bishop. The town of Nola was raided by the Mediterranean conquerors but St. Paulinus escaped with the children. When the raid was over Saint Paulinus returned to Nola. There he found a widow whose only son was captured by the raiders. He traded himself in exchange for the widow's son. He was taken to North Africa. When a Turkish Sultan heard of the generosity of Saint Paulinus, he bartered for Saint Paulinus' freedom. When Saint Paulinus returned to Nola, he was met with a great welcome and celebration carrying lilies (gigilie) which is the flower that shows the purity of heart and love of mankind. The giglio (structure) was built in honor of Saint Paulinus and carried every year in his memory...'
>
> Within an hour and a half of our arrival the streets became entirely crowded. The number of people could be compared to what we encountered at the World Financial Center. However, the peoples' behavior and attitude was in sharp contrast. These people were friendly, volunteered information, and

were in no hurry. Everyone seemed to know each other. They appeared to be one happy family...

...The people's behavior was similar. For example, there was a group of young men playing what they called the "finger game."

They were gesticulating with their fingers, enjoying themselves and of course understanding each other. I stood in amazement, enjoying them enjoying themselves, making karate-like sounds, e.g., 'Chingo," one said, 'Arthro," another replied. Whatever that means, my God, I'm innocent. It seemed simple and innocent enough for me to write this.

I also had the opportunity to visit Our Lady of Mount Carmel Catholic Church. Here, me being a stranger to Catholicism witnessed the strangest and most beautiful scene. On either side of a section of the church, many candles were arranged, some of them burning. Several individuals walked in, knelt before the statue, handed money, e.g., a dollar bill to a lady and she pinned it to what they called a 'money tree' attached to the shrine. The lady explained what it symbolized. She explained that if you want any forgiveness or needed to make a wish, then you can give whatever you can afford and then make your prayers.

My best friend and classmate looked at me and teased, 'I guess you'll have to change your entire month's salary into single dollars. Please feel free to borrow mine also,' sarcastically, yet sweetly suggesting my multitude of sins.

It was now two and a half hours into the celebration. Bands were playing. 'Music is really a universal language,' I thought. I don't know a word of Italian, yet I fully understood and enjoyed the music (singing).

This experience made me think; people sincerely believe in tradition.

Student B: The streets were filled with people who came to participate in the celebration. There were many senior citizens, some who couldn't walk without assistance but nevertheless had to keep up the tradition. I was told by one person who I interviewed that many families who once lived in the community returned from other states to participate... In concluding, this "Turk Night" was dedicated to the memory of a former, deceased Turk, Angelo Tardalo. I saw great community participation. there was a feeling of belonging, and togetherness... This togetherness was shown when the entire crowd paused for one minute of silence, in remembrance of Angelo Tardalo. It was also traditional that male members of families continued the tradition of lifting the giglio... The atmosphere was one of peace, joy, and celebration... Also significant...was that people were not afraid to socialize, and to be interviewed by fellow students and myself.

Student C: As we strolled back and forth observing for two hours in search for an explanation to this madness, we ended up in the same place of utter confusion.

The light bulb then suddenly switched on in our little minds. We decided to interact with the people and ask them for explanations behind this gathering. Everyone that we approached was so warm and friendly. In their explanations of this fiesta you can hear the pride, faith, and joy overflowing in their voices, gestures and facial expressions.

...It was very obvious for many reasons that I was not a part of this community. But I was made to feel welcome by the warm friendly sincere smiles of the people in the community. I will definitely make it to their next gathering, Lord Willing.

Student D: No one seemed to mind when the homeless came around with their large supermarket carts collecting the cashable cans and bottles...

The men (Turks) who were to be in the boat were well-dressed with bright colors and large balloon pants. The younger men were dressed like pirates. They had on shorts of different colors and wore t-shirts that said 'Our Lady of Mount Carmel,' with red handkerchiefs around their necks, and caps. I even noticed three younger children dressed like the young men. At approximately 8:30 that night, the music became louder as the band played. The street light decorations lit up. There was hardly any room for walking around. People were anxious for the ceremony to begin. The Turks went inside the boat and they were to be carried by 250 men. They moved slowly down the street and people cheered.

I could not believe the reception that my classmates received from the people of the community. They welcomed us and shared information about the meaning of this event. They even provided us with literature from the church. It was amazing to see the interaction between the different ethnic groups as well as their attitude toward strangers. I enjoyed the food and the conversation I had with the people. There was definitely a certain warmth and friendliness that this community had expressed. Next year I intend to take my family, and perhaps I will join them in their traditional event occasionally.

Student E: I arrived at Havemeyer Street at approximately 6:00 P.M. There were decorations on the street light poles; most of the booths were empty and I wondered what was going on, — maybe I was in the wrong place. Am I lost? I started to get nervous because I didn't see my class colleagues or professor. I said to myself, 'How am I going to find out where this feast is going to be if this is not it?' I saw two police officers and I said, 'Excuse me sir, is this the Feast of Saint Paulinus?' They said, 'Yes, it is the Italian festival. You are in the right spot.'

I started walking down the block, then I looked up and saw this giant shrine with the saint mounted at the top, so I became more confident that this was the place... The aroma of the food stands had my salivary glands going wild, I didn't eat much that morning because I knew that food would be sold at a reasonable price, therefore my stomach was saying, 'Feed me, feed me.' There were Korean, Italian, American and Greek food stands. I tried something from each, but what had my taste buds popping was the thing the Italians call 'sweet bread.' I had two. I have never tasted anything like this. I wished I had brought some home. I told my friends at work about the sweet bread. It was very delicious.Around 7:00 p.m., the place became bustling with people of all nationalities. Everyone seemed very happy, laughing with each other. There people from all age groups; from babies to the elderly with canes and walkers enjoying the festive atmosphere. It seemed as if everyone knew each other. People passing by would give each other a smile, handshake, lots of hugging, or a 'Hello. How are you doing?' People talked very loudly and laughed loudly. Dressing was informal; t-shirts, jeans, slacks, sneakers, sandals, slippers, shorts, some men wore caps or hats, the older women all wore skirts and dresses.The vendors were all related to each other. For example, at one booth I spoke with an elderly man who said that he had been coming to the feast for over fifty years. He started with his father who passed the business over to him and he has been in the same spot for thirty years now and his two sons will be taking over when he passes away. He said that it was a family tradition going back many years...The elderly man I mentioned previously is John Tasullo, who said that he was the oldest of the feast businesses. He gave a little history behind the celebration. He said that the name Saint Paulinus is also called "Giglio-e-Paridiso" which means "Flower of Paradise." The celebration is in honor of Saint Paulinus because in 350 B.C. a woman's only son was captured by the conquerors and it was the Turks who rescued the woman's son and Saint Paulinus. This was the 104th anniversary celebration. This started in a small town outside Naples called S.S. Nola. The people cannot travel to this place every year so they have the shrine transported here and send it back to Italy after the celebration...

On the night of my visit the boat which the Turks used in the rescue was carried down the street by approximately 75 men who danced to the tune of a live band and sang Italian songs. Everyone was clapping, singing along and laughing. You could see the sparkle in their eyes. The lifting of the boat was a very dramatic scene. I wished I had a video camera to capture that moment. The boat weighed approximately four tons.

There was so much camaraderie among the people that I felt right at home. There were some elderly people looking out their apartment windows and some of them were sitting outside their doors on the sidewalk in chairs and chatting with each other and with people passing by. There was a tent set up near the church which had a shrine of Mount Carmel. People believe that the shrine had special powers. They would light a candle and say a prayer for whatever they desired; some even gave money which was attached to a large ribbon around the shrine's neck. They had a strong religious belief and strong family ties.

From observation, this community is homogeneous and its members have a strong sense of solidarity. The community is small and the people interact with each other in an informal atmosphere. They get to know each other well. There are no strangers. The relationships formed are long lasting and family and extended kinship are the building blocks for this community. Because of these closely knitted relationships, the community becomes stable and resistant to change. They do what was taught to them by their forefathers and believe that if anything was changed it would be a great dishonor to their ancestors...

This was one of the most memorable times in my life. I wasn't aware that such activities went on in Brooklyn. I will keep in touch with the committee for the next annual feast. Did I enjoy myself? Yes, most certainly I did. I also won a stuffed animal and a Chippendale photograph.

Student F: This observational field trip was quite interesting. This community was found to be quite structured and organized. The population was a mixed array of on-lookers and community residents involved in a sacred tradition. The atmosphere was one of dance and gay spirit. As on-lookers asked questions, it was interesting to hear the remarks given by the residents. I spoke with young and older residents, and somehow, I got more or less the same response. There was a sense of pride and dignity as they spoke of their patron saint. It was interesting to hear the young speak in Italian.

As I got close to the giglio and observed the fine work that went into the building of this monument, I could appreciate the meaning of a Gemeinschaft-like society. The spiritual richness and profound need for identity was evident. It was obvious that this community had no problems in identifying or relating with itself.

As I walked about the festival I could smell the delicious aromas which expressed culture. There was a mixed array of foods being sold. Interestingly, they were all cultural dishes.

This small community was found to have quite a large population. The houses were kept clean, which was indicative of pride. There could have been spatial competition, but it was not relevant. Throughout the festival there were community police patrols, however no trouble was ever noticed. The officers too joined in the festivities...

This community gathering was heterogeneous in its population, and yet they shared similarities as far as beliefs go. I observed a Haitian population within the crowd. When I asked them why they were at the feast, they easily informed me that there was another Saint who was also being honored. This Saint was Our Lady of Mount Carmel. She is the Saint of the Scapula. They too claimed a legend similar to that of Saint Paulinus. Ironically, it was interesting to see how Ferdinand Toennies' theory of Gemeinschaft could be observed at the international level. And more intriguing is observing how tradition brings people together for the good of a community. This community was found not to be self-indulgent. They openly allowed strangers in so that they too could share in the richness of tradition and the old folkways....

Summary

There are many insights which can be gathered from these naive descriptions of an Italian American neighborhood feast when they are analyzed phenomenologically. For example, the verstehen method of Max Weber is used extensively in all social sciences. Weber argued that the study of human society is different from all other disciplines because of the intersubjective nature of human experience. That is, social interaction (and therefore society) is possible because people can put themselves in the place of others with whom they interact. We are thereby able to anticipate how people will respond to our own actions and plan them accordingly.

Most social commentators today would not expect, given the context of intergroup relations in our troubled cities, that an African American could see herself so easily in the guise of an Italian American as did Student A as she contemplated going off her diet diet during the feast of Saint Paulinus:

Everyone seemed to be enjoying himself/herself. I particularly paid attention to an elderly Italian lady of stocky build. She was sitting in her lawn chair enjoying an Italian sausage. I enviously tried to read her mind; 'Today, I'm out here to eat and celebrate ... to Hell with dieting,' I thought she thought. I smiled and walked away. 'To Hell with dieting. This is a feast; today I weigh only 120 pounds,' I tried to fool myself.

There is also an historical irony in the Feast of Saint Paulinus which ordinarily would go unnoticed. African Americans tend to see themselves today as oppressed by the white working- and middle-classes. The villagers of towns like Nola were raided for centuries by North Africans (among many others) for booty and slaves. This is an almost stereotypical historical role reversal which few can appreciate. This missed irony demonstrates how both African Americans and Italian Americans have little idea of not only their own separate histories, but how their histories have been intertwined from at least the time of the Punic Wars through the recent large scale immigration of Africans to Italy.

Perhaps more important for organizations like the American Italian Historical Association and its members is how these observations and analyses point up the critical need to produce and collect records of the contemporary Italian American scene by a wide variety of interested as well as disinterested chroniclers. Scholars of the Italian experience in America have a responsibility to identify and gather local histories, oral histories, family histories, etc., and organize them in such a way that future researchers will have a view which is as panoramic as possible. Especially needed are the first person narratives of ordinary people as presented in these pages. Without this variety, and naive honesty, it is doubtful that the character of the Italian American community will be accurately portrayed by future historians who look back on this period of American urban history.

ENDNOTES

1   It should be noted that I attempted throughout the incident and its aftermath to provide journalists with objective information, and steer them toward responsible community spokespersons. These endeavors obviously had little impact on the initial coverage of the event. The frenzy to pursue the most sensational, and stereotypical story lines in the incident contributed to the likelihood that the historical version of the "Bensonhurst incident" which will be read by future scholars will be the most biased and least accurate one.

2   For the most recent work on the Greenpoint/Williamsburg community see: Judith N. Desena, *Protecting One's Turf: Social Strategies for Maintaining Urban Neighborhoods*, Lanham, Maryland: University Press of America, 1990.

For my own recent work on Italian American neighborhoods see: "America's Little Italies: Past, Present and Future," in D. Candeloro, *et al, Italian Ethnics: Their Languages, Literature and Life* Chicago: AIHA, 1990: 169-184, and "Bensonhurst, Brooklyn: Italian American Victimizers and Victims." Paper presented at the 22nd Annual Meetings of the American Italian Historical Association, San Francisco, 1989.

REFERENCES

Kifner, J., "Bensonhurst: A Tough Code in Defense of a Closed World," *The New York Times,* September 1, 1989, p.1.

Psathas, G., ed., *Phenomenological Sociology: Issues and Applications* New York: John Wiley and Sons, 1973.

Strugatch, W., "Bensonhurst: Cartoon Sociology Masquerades as Solid Reporting." *The Quill,* Number 27, November, 1989, Pp. 26-29.

14

THE ITALIAN AMERICAN THEATRE IN BOSTON, 1935-39

CHRIS NEWTON

As a brief example of the hyphenated experience of Italian-American Theatre I would like to relate the contents of two memoranda. The first was dated April 14, 1938, from John B. Mack, the Federal Theatre Director of New England. He sent an urgent notice to Italian clubs and press. The topic was the promotion of the upcoming premier of the FTP's play "Created Equal."

> [This] vivid story covers a period of one-hundred and fifty years... It is an epoch that represents the true psyche that has created America ... it shows the true spirit in the grand quest for nationhood.
> This Drama traces the birth of freedom in the United States from the time of Thomas Jefferson and 1776 down to the present day. It shows the passage of time through the early periods of expansion and the Revolutionary War, Slavery, the Dred Scott Decision of the Supreme Court, the Civil War, World War, Stock Market Heyday and Crash, and present-day government.
> ...the premier of "Created Equal" will include over 100 actors and artists...will be performed in English, but with the participation of Italian, Polish, French, and Negro groups as well as individual vaudeville, and radio performers. [I am] certain that "Created Equal" will be of utmost importance to Italians, and all those who struggle in the formation of this great republic. No Italian should miss it.[1]

Within the same theatre project, at roughly the same time an actor/director, Salvatore Tartaglia, wrote to headquarters with the details of a revision for his own production of "Juan Jose."

> I have had to postpone one or two scenes in the second and in the fourth acts, in order to obtain the desired effect of suspense during the fight between the two lovers; and evidently I have succeeded, because in whatever theatre I have played "Juan Jose," the audience at this point scarcely breathes in the spasmodic suspense of waiting to see which of the two men will win out; and when finally Juan Jose reappears, there is always a burst of applause from the audience, who recognizes the right of the lover betrayed. The play has always stirred a lively interest among our people; especially the meridians.[2]

I juxtapose these two items to suggest a few things:

1.   That a vital Italian Theatre was active in the Boston community, though little understood or recognized even by the government agency that supported it.

2.   That in the arts, good will and funding may not necessarily meet the needs of an ethnic community (in this case the Italian), but rather such programs are prone to supporting a self-serving political perspective. Credit is due John B. Mack and the WPA leadership for supporting ethnic theatre, but the agency's own records indicate that the Italian Unit presentations were far less important than the New Deal emphasizing material.

I do not mean to suggest that the Italian community could not have enjoyed both plays, but the evidence reveals that despite a great amount of publicity and an extravagant production "Created Equal" was poorly attended compared to the less publicized, low-budget, "Juan Jose."

My research concerns an aspect of the Italian American experience that highlights the tension between the expectations of an established cultural-political perspective and the needs of a separate and distinct ethnic community. The specific focus of my investigation is the New Deal Policy of Franklin Roosevelt and his sponsorship of a National Theatre. The Federal Theatre Project (which I shall refer to as the FTP) was a radical experiment in many ways. Combining relief work with a national arts program, the FTP presented many innovative forms of drama to a national audience. Many famous careers were launched by the FTP, including those of Orson Welles, Joseph Cotton, John Houseman, Burt Lancaster, and Arthur Miller. For many Americans, the free FTP shows were the first live performances they had ever seen.

An important element to the program was making theatre relevant to its audience. National Director Hallie Flanagan stated it this way,

> Our most urgent task is to make our theatre worthy of our audience. It is of no value whatever to stimulate theatre-going unless, once in our doors, our audience sees something which has some vital connection with their own lives and their own immediate problems.[3]

Indeed, the FTP leadership did extend theatre activity to groups in society usually overlooked by government — especially government art's policies. The Children's theatre effort was very successful and many companies outlived the WPA project. Small regional theatres were started by the FTP. Most important, for this presentation at least, was the encouragement and funding of ethnic theatres. Best known are the Negro and Yiddish projects, but besides these well-covered efforts were Spanish, French, German, Russian, and Italian federally funded theatres.

There are no records of how many Italian-Americans went to see "Created Equal." Reviews labeled it "propaganda" and even the internal review within the FTP was mixed. It was classified as "recommended with reservations."[4] "Juan Jose," on the other hand, played to packed houses in many neighborhoods. It was considered a gala event and suburban Italian-Americans took great pride in purchasing the most expensive seats possible. The production was an event that focused the community. "Juan Jose" was not the only Italian language play that emphasized the Mezzogiorno taste over obvious American content.

In the years 1936-1938, forty-nine Italian-language productions were opened in the Boston area under the sponsorship of the Federal Theatre Project.[5] Almost all of the plays focused on love, revenge, honor, and destiny within the framework of a Southern Italian context. Performers and directors were highly distinguished members of local Italian American society and the plays were attended by the entire spectrum of age and class within the Italian community. Small, makeshift theatres in school gymnasiums were consistently filled to capacity with up to one thousand audience members. But the Italian language theatre in Boston flourished for only a short period. Two rapid blows ended the FTP Italian language theatre activity. In 1939 the entire Federal Theatre Project was curtailed by funding cuts from Congress, and in 1941 the United States went to war against Italy. The cancellation was not for want of audience and the absence of Italian language theatre was lamented by older members of the Boston Community. The projects of the New Deal had failed to completely Americanize the theatrical tastes of Italian-Americans; ultimately it was loss of financial support, enactment of alien registration, and the outbreak of war against the homeland that halted a vital Italian-American theatre in Boston. Italian theatre efforts after the War are not insignificant, but habits of television viewing and the suburban lifestyle aspirations of second and third generation Italian-Americans changed the audience.

To its credit, the FTP did recognize some of the potential of the rich Italian theatre history in America. Yet it should be highlighted that a play like "Juan Jose" was a thin sampling of the Italian drama that was already in America. Recall that by 1805 Lorenzo Da Ponte had produced Italian plays at Columbia University. Throughout the 19th and early twentieth century, touring Italian opera stars were treated like royalty in America. During the period of great immigration around the turn of the century, ethnic theatres planted many seeds from Barre, Vermont, to the Napa Valley, in California.[6] Emelise Aleandri has done very important work to reveal the significant depth of Italian Theatre at this time.[6]

A rich variety of theatrical entertainment was available to Italian-Americans through the 1930s. At the most professional end of the spectrum touring performers such as Elenora Duse, Tommaso Salvini, and Antonietta Pisanelli could be seen by those who could afford the admission. "La Compagnia Comico-Dramatica Italiana A. Maiori e P. Rapone" brought Shakespeare, Dumas, Goethe, Suderman, Sardou, and Jules Verne to East Coast audiences up until 1914. Smaller scale vaudeville and Commedia performers toured with entertainment exclusively directed toward the Little Italy immigrants. A notable example is Eduardo Migliaccio's creation of a pick and shovel "greenhorno" character called "Farfariello." Touring operetta and marionette theatres were especially prolific just before the First World War. Some of the Italian-American theatre had an overtly political dimension. Anarchist, communist, and labor theatre groups had strong followings in large communities such as New York City, and Patterson, N.J. Especially significant was the political theatre in small Italian mining communities in Pennsylvania, West Virginia, and Vermont. Finally, the Catholic Church and related benevolent societies found frequent occasions to perform for benefits, saints' days, and the plethora of civic festivals. Suffice it to say that "Little Italies" throughout America did not want for entertainment.

Boston was no different, for it already had a lively Italian theatre scene when the FTP funding became available. Opera was very popular, and the San Carlo Company made many visits. Italian drama was presented regularly by touring groups such as Rocco DeRusso's "Arte Vera." DeRusso, with his wife Ria Sampieri, and occasional guest artists Dora Rinaldi and Itala Dea performed plays in Italian such as "The Irish Wife," "The Hero of the Italian-Ethiopian War" and "Civile Death."[7] High School gyms and community centers were more frequent venues than large downtown theatres for these performances, but Italian-American newspaper reviews were always enthusiastic no matter what the venue. Individual touring actors appeared frequently with local groups. One example is Alfredo Barchetta who regularly appeared with the North End Circolo Dramatico on Richmond street. Records also indicate that the famous "Farfariello" appeared in Boston in the late 30s.[8] The mix and example of the touring professionals frequently inspired local groups and audiences to carry on a dramatic tradition.

Though the touring artists were enthusiastically received, it was the local groups that made the Boston area such fertile ground for the FTP funded Italian theatre project. The most important professional theatre personality in Boston was the impresario, Tommaso Nazzaro. Tall and blonde, Nazzaro was known in the Italian-American community as being the consummate theatre producer, "...instrumental in introducing masterpieces of Italian Theatre to New England audiences."[9] Besides his association with Fortune Gallo and the San Carlo Opera Company, Nazzaro produced Elenora Duse, Tita Ruffo, Rosa Ponselle, Giovanni Martinellini, and Pasquale Amato in their Boston appearances. Nazzaro's Casino theatre still stands today on Hanover street in Boston's North End.

Within this rich theatrical atmosphere were many semi-professional and amateur groups. Government sponsorship and encouragement gave all of the organizations renewed vigor. Drama groups within the local churches were naturally very active presenting nativity plays around Christmas time, however, they also produced large scale productions as is evidenced by St Anthony's Parish in Somerville's production of an operetta titled "An old Spanish Custom."[10] Some clubs were set up by regional Italian affiliation, and the theatrical efforts of the groups reflected a regional flavor. Bel Canto groups frequently included large numbers of Neapolitans. Sicilian troupes promoted their own favorite son with the local Pirandello Society. The International Beacon and the YMCA sponsored a rich program of children's theatre including "Italian street scene(s), tumblers, tarantella dancing, songs, and Italian playlets in pantomimo."[11] Some efforts were centered around drama as a means to teach Italian American young women comportment. Mrs. Dina Malgeri had "an attractive program of practical Italian, diction, conversation, public speaking, drama, recitations, poetical compositions, discussions, and songs, etc...."[12] By 1940, a similar club headed by Emilia Ippolito included instruction in citizenship matters. Adults also could be part of the active Circolo Dopolavoro and the Circolo Letterario groups. There was a great amount of shared involvement as many individuals were members of more than one drama club. For a time the Dopolovoro and Letterario shared the same president, Gino Merluzzi.

From the core of the local theatre activity, four drama groups were created by the FTP Italian theatre branch. The groups needed to report through a chain of command of directors. At the neighborhood level was a prominent lawyer, Gabriel Piemonte, at state level was also a local Italian American, Tom Senna, but thereafter the aforementioned New England director, John B. Mack, and New York headquarters seem to have little knowledge of the needs of the Italian project. The FTP bureaucracy was extremely hampered by constant cutbacks, resignations, and restructurings. It is remarkable that given the frequent flux of the FTP management and occasional bias and ignorance of the leadership toward the Italian community, so many productions were successfully produced.

The first troupe was headed by the actor/director Salvatore Tartaglia who had been directing plays at the Circolo Letterario. Little was written about Tartaglia's directing and performance in the local papers, but he appears to be the most prolific leading man of the FTP Boston Italian stage.

The other group was directed by a high school teacher and son of a famous tenor. Gino Gallozzi had come with his father, Thomas Gallozzi, to America in 1920. After a career at La Scala, Thomas Gallozzi came to Boston to retire as a voice coach. Certainly Gino Gallozzi benefited from the performance atmosphere in his father's house. Throughout the short but active years of the FTP Italian theatre Gallozzi was made a spokesman for local culture and the FTP Italian language theatre effort. He was frequently interviewed by local newspapers and was much sought after as a guest speaker at banquets. Besides being a director, Gallozzi also served as translator and occasional playwright. His best known work was a parody of "Othello" titled "The Sword of Damocles." It was premiered by the FTP. He also appears to have been a proud stage father. His six-year old daughter, Elena, was dubbed the "Italian Shirley Temple" by the *Italian News*.

It is not clear how distinct Tartaglia and Gallozzi's groups were. They frequently joined forces to produce plays. A pattern seems to emerge that reveals Tartaglia most frequently in the program credits, but Gallozzi in newspaper accounts and interviews.

Two amateur youth groups were also sponsored by the FTP. The distinction between the professional FTP groups and the youth groups was:

1   Pay—everyone involved with Tartaglia and Gallozzi's theatre was supposed to be of professional status, and thereby they were paid relief as unemployed artists. The amateurs received free tuition in the program, but no pay.

2   The professional troupes performed exclusively in Italian and the amateurs only in English.

3   Whereas Tartaglia and Gallozzi were from the Boston Italian Community, the directors of the youth groups (Golda Orleans and Henri Roulliard) were social workers, not residents of the Italian Community. The plays the youth group performed were occasionally directed by Italian Americans from the community, but the acting and voice classes were taught by the social workers.

It is interesting to note the division of the Italian Immigrant generations in the FTP programs. The generation born in Italy was able to see plays written by Italians, directed by Italians, performed in Italian (frequently dialect), in an Italian performance style. By contrast, the second generation Italians, in America since infancy, performed international plays, in English, under the guidance of government workers. No documented evidence has come to light that proves a written policy of separation existed between first and second generation Italian immigrant, but *de facto* the FTP served to pull the younger generation into a mainstream outlined by FTP philosophy while reluctantly accommodating the parents who wished to preserve something of the old world.

A close examination of the plays performed helps to highlight the tastes and tensions within and without the Italian Community. A typical example of the material the professional group produced was "Juan Jose" by Joaquin Dicenta. It opened in Boston on December 9, 1937, and toured for a year to various venues — Brighton High School, Lynn Women's Clubhouse, The Roosevelt Theatre, East Weymouth, and St. Rose Hall in Chelsea.[14] Salvatore Tartaglia directed and took the title role. The play according to the newspaper *La Notizia*[15] centered around love, vendetta, and death. Juan Jose, a poor stone mason, marries Rose. "But Rose is not satisfied with love alone and she taunts him with his poverty"[16] Juan Jose becomes a thief to buy Rose jewels. He is caught and sentenced to prison. While Jose is in prison, an old witch named Isadora induces Rose to become the mistress of the young and wealthy Juan Paco. Juan Jose learns of the affair, he escapes from prison, and when he finds Rose with Juan Paco there is a fight that gets carried off-stage. Juan Paco can provide no effective defense and Juan Jose strangles Rose with his bare hands. If Tartaglia's account of his histrionic acting ability is to be believed, the final climax effectively brought down the house of six hundred or more patrons.

The setting was 19th century Madrid, and oral accounts suggest that a few professionals and many volunteers helped construct four elaborate interior sets. According to FTP accounts $89.76 was spent on the set.[17] This was quite a modest sum considering the set was built to be transported. In addition to the materials for the set, props and fabric were mostly supplied through donations. One example of the support provided by the community was the volunteer effort to produce the elaborate Spanish military uniforms and colorful peasant costumes.

The press reception did not address specific aesthetic merits or flaws of the play, but there was unanimous encouragement of this engaging type of entertainment. Prices for tickets for the suburban evening performances were listed as "popular" meaning cheap — 40, 30, and 25 cents. Daytime shows for those on relief were free. Even without the positive press reception and popular prices the word-of-mouth publicity and community level involvement would have certainly made the theatre a success.

"Juan Jose's" popularity with the exuberant audiences of the Boston

Italian Community was no guarantee that State and National project directors appreciated the activity. The production of Giacometti's "Civil Death" is a good example of how little the FTP leadership understood its audience. All play proposals had to be submitted to a screening committee in New York. Reader reports were generated and they included the play's vital information of title, playwright, number of characters, and genre. A synopsis was followed by a comment and designation of acceptance or rejection. A brief synopsis of "Civil Death" relates: "Having escaped from jail to look for his wife and child, Conrad finds that the latter is happy as an adopted child of Dr. Palmieri, [Conrad] renounces his claim and dies of grief."[18] To a modern critic the story may seem simple and saccharine, but for recent Italian immigrants, many of whom were separated from extended families, the issues and passions were extremely relevant. Local promotion by *La Notizia* promoted the play in the following manner: "Civil Death" is a play whose stirring and interesting plot will provide the audience with a high degree of artistic enjoyment until the curtain falls on the last act. There are many and varied scenes in the play, and the role of the hero is followed with keen interest. The action takes place in Calabria and Sicily about the year 1810. The members of the cast are the untiring actors of the Federal Theatre players.[19] To be sure, the play was a success with the local audience selling out its 300 opening night tickets. Yet the play was almost never produced. The two-person review committee gave the script one rejection and one recommendation with reservations. One critical comment reads as follows:

> "In style as well as in theme and treatment, this play definitely belongs to the dead past. There is absolutely nothing in it which would interest a modern audience. It is too plain, too obvious, too tearfully and passionately romantic to move anyone. And very boring too. As to the Sicilian passions which are spread abundantly over the whole five acts, I believe (don't you?) that they have gone the way of the horse and buggy a long time ago. So, why stir the dead? REJECTED.[20]

It is hard to imagine a more scathing assessment and inadvertent criticism of the audience that loved the play. The recommendation that came with reservations was patronizing, though it seems to have been somewhat more sympathetic to the needs of the audience. He wrote,

> …It has heart-rending and hair-raising scenes, so much so that the reader felt a lump in his throat. If we strip it of all these theatricals, we would still have a blood stirring drama, albeit not a very realistic one. The action is fairly well sustained and it holds one's interest. However much

of the story is anticipated before it actually happens, and this is another weak point...[21]

The difference between the reception from FTP headquarters and the Boston Italian Community once again highlights the schizophrenic nature of the government project. Indeed, other play reading reports were consistently dismissive even though many of the plays were eventually produced. The play "Rehabilitation" was savaged as "crude and banal," "The Blood Stain" deemed "...childishly emotional," and "I due Fratelli" was labeled an "infantile attempt at playwriting."[22] The readers apparently did not understand Hallie Flanagan's policy of making theatre vital to the lives of the distinct Italian American Community. Obviously local directors were able to override or circumvent the judgment of FTP headquarters. If Tartaglia and Gallozzi had not been able to eventually get permission to perform plays they knew the audience wanted, it is unlikely that the Italian Unit could have continued.

The amateur youth groups, on the other hand, had little trouble with having their material approved. Besides Shakespeare's "A Midsummer Night's Dream" and Chekhov's "The Boar," the two groups performed popular American melodramas, "Nemesis" and "Night of Terror." Like the Italian language professional group, the performers toured to different theatres, albeit on a much reduced schedule. The venues were generally small, but occasionally large crowds would be drawn in when the two groups would compete for theatrical honors. The approach to production was also quite different than the professional Italian language theatre of their parents. Lower budgets made for more spartan sets and costumes, but the style was effectively harmonious with the contemporary modern theatre of the thirties. Symbolic and suggestive scenery and costumes were both a necessity and a fashion. The acting approach was also more modern than the boiling-blood histrionic technique of the older generation. Accounts from participants relate that Golda Orleans instructed her actors to use the cutting edge (for the time) methods of emotional recall and psychological motivation.[23]

Besides the formal dramas, it should be mentioned that the WPA sponsored frequent talent nights, amateur vaudeville, marionette shows, and debates. The participants were young, second generation Italian Americans. The process of "Americanization" can be examined in the entertainment forms that the young people embraced. Within the talent night format, Italian songs were followed by swing bands, and traditional peasant dances made way for tap. Perhaps the greatest demonstration of the New Deal government's self-interest was the promotion of a debate in 1937 at the Michelangelo school titled "resolved the WPA be continued." Naturally the affirmative was victorious. Unfortunately little more than a year later congress exercised its veto at a much higher level and the entire FTP project was curtailed.

By the Spring of 1939 it was apparent that Roosevelt was going to sacrifice the relatively small theatre project to save the rest of the WPA. Congressional Hearings into the alleged communist activities of the FTP were well publicized. (The proceedings foreshadowed the excessive claims of the House Un-American Activities hearings after the war. At one point Shakespeare's contemporary Christopher Marlowe was suspected of being a communist by a Republican committee member.) Hallie Flanagan was not allowed to defend the project and members of the FTP began to look for new work. For the Boston Italian theatre, the timing was unfortunate because plays were being toured to packed houses. For a brief moment it appeared that the Italian project might be able to stand on its own.

Divisions within the Italian Community became stronger however, as many individuals questioned the prudence of identifying so strongly with "Italianness" and by association with Mussolini's Italy. This doubt, the cutback in funding, and the threat of alien registration stalled such a high profile activity as Italian language theatre. What did vigorously continue, however, were the youth programs. The FTP youth recreation was swallowed up by the Junior league and benefit performances became very common.

The adults in the professional theatre group made more substantial transitions. Tom Senna went to the American Federation of Actors to supervise performers at the New York World's Fair. Gabriel Piemonte continued with his law practice and become more involved in politics. Madame Ippolito, the choral director, headed her support group for citizenship and Americanization. Salvatore Tartaglia turned to radio, where he produced an Italian language program for many years. And Gino Gallozzi returned to teaching High School. Out of town touring shows appeared sporadically into the fifties, and local groups still do occasional shows, but the momentum of a consistent Italian language theatre had been lost forever.

There are other questions that need to be asked before we have a complete view of Boston's Italian theatre of the 30's. The political dimensions of the theatre activity needs to be further examined — Fascist, New Deal, and labor perspectives undoubtedly clashed backstage. Italian regional differences also could be further examined within the theatrical context. These issues are, however, material for future research.

In the final analysis, what can be said about the impact of the brief FTP project on Italian drama and the Boston ethnic community? On the one hand, it seems that the government effort and Italian Community were an excellent match, for the Southern Italian traditions of fraternal support organizations appeared to fit very easily into the government arts and relief organization. The WPA, and specifically FTP, used the multitude of existing clubs and organizations to great effect. It also appears that the members used the government money well, while it lasted. The production of at least forty-nine productions in less than four years is prolific by any theatre company's standards. Yet, as my first example of the two memoranda demonstrates, there did not exist a great amount of communication and understanding between government overseers and community directors. One cannot imagine that the split personality of the ethnic theatre could have continued for very long with "American History plays" being ignored by Italo-Americans and "Italian dramas of passion" disparaged by FTP leadership. Indeed, the FTP was such an easy target by its critics because it did have significant "foreign" elements. Especially during a war, a government is not likely to have a generous attitude to diverse ethnic needs. Whereas the professional theatre disintegrated, the youth programs flourished because there was more "American" example involvement. The social worker, to some degree, supplanted the example of the parents and instead of looking solely to their roots (as most first generation Italians did), the Italo-American youth looked quite naturally to the future. That view suggested success was achieved by assimilation and what could be more enjoyable than play acting parts of that new role.

In March of 1936, the "Italian News" published an extensive article comparing the 6 year old Italian language star, Elena Gallozzi (the "Italian Shirley Temple")[24], with a veteran Italian Actress of 75, Madame Matilda Fiorenza. Madame Fiorenza, after a career in Modena and Bologna and then as a character actress in Hollywood, was performing with young Gallozzi in the FTP group. Elena Gallozzi was one of the few members of the younger Italian-American generation who was carrying on within the tradition of her parents. The optimistic journalist was intimating that the torch of Italian craft and culture was being passed from one generation to another. The article suggested that Elena Gallozzi would become "the future Elenora Duse." Less than four years later the company was disbanded and the Italian language theatrical career of Elena was cut short. During the war years, Elena, like the rest of Italian Americans, had to adjust to new ideas of what being American meant. The failures and gaps of the Italian American Theatre tradition are easy to point out, but the hope for a continuation of traditions is important to note. The pressures and realities of belonging to American culture are real. But perhaps it is worthwhile recalling the admonition of Hallie Flanagan that theatre must be relevant to its audience — "have a vital connection with their own lives and their own immediate problems." By 1940, the "immediate problem" for many Italian Americans was not the obvious presentation of old country traditions, but rather the accommodation of the new host, America. Thus ended the most fertile years of Italian theatre in Boston.

In manner of an epilogue, a consideration of the post-war Italian theatre is revealing. Despite the dispersal of Italian neighborhoods and the aging of the first generation, Italian language performances continued periodically into the 1970s. Italian language radio broadcasts were (and are) especially important for keeping language and drama traditions alive. Within the past decade, a new development has refocused at least part of the mandate of the WPA "relevant" theatre. Cable Television reaches many scattered communities with Italian language dramas. Perhaps in a most fitting response to the disparaging FTP playreaders, the *Tele Italia* channel in Boston has been linked with *Bravo*, "A quality selection of cultural education...." Though it may be sacrilege to the live theatre to suggest this, one answer for today's Italian American audience's quest for ethnic identity may lie in the proliferation of Italian American cable television.

ENDNOTES

1   "Created Equal," *The Italian News*, 14 April 1938, p.4.
2   The National Archives, Washington, D.C., Production Bulletin *Juan Jose*.
3   "The People's Theatre Grows Stronger," *FTP Magazine*, 6 May 1936, p.6.
4   Library of Congress Federal Theatre Project Collection at George Mason University, Fairfax, Virginia. Play Reader Report. *Created Equal.*
5   *Ibid.* Federal Theatre Project Production Schedule.
6   Aleandri, Emelise, *A History of Italian-American Theatre: 1900 to 1905* Ph.D. Dissertation - City University of New York, 1983. This is a thorough background for the early Italian American Theatre.
7   Immigration History Research Center at the University of Minnesota, Minneapolis, MN. Files on Fortune Gallo and Rocco De Russo. These sources are especially helpful in understanding the nature of touring Italian American performers.
8   *Gazzetta Del Massachusettes* 5 December 1936,p. 3.
9   Carlevale, Joseph William, *Leading Americans of Italian Descent in Massachusettes* (Plymouth, MA: Memorial Press, 1946).
10   *Italian News*, 4 May 1936, p.4.
11   *International Beacon*, 15 March 1940, p. 2.
12   *Italian News*, 17 January 1936, p. 4.
13   *Ibid.*, 7 May 1936, p.4.
14   Library of Congress Federal Theatre Project Collection at George Mason University Library, Fairfax, Virginia "Juan Jose" File.
15   *Ibid.*
16   *Ibid.* Play Reader Report.
17   *Ibid.* "Juan Jose" File.
18   *Ibid.* "Civil Death" Play Reader Report.
19   *La Notizia*, May 1938, p. 2.
20   Library of Congress Federal Theatre Project Collection at George Mason University Library, Fairfax, Virginia "Civil Death" Play Reader Report.
21   *Ibid.*
22   *Ibid.*
23   Pietrina Maravigna, Oral Interview with Chris Newton, 17 October 1991.
24   *Italian News* 27 March 1936, p. 7.

15

THE BOTTO HOUSE NATIONAL HISTORIC LANDMARK

ROBERT B. IMMORDINO

You will not find the name of Pietro or Maria Botto in any biographical listing or *Who's Who* of famous persons, but of the millions of Italian immigrant working class families, theirs is the only home to have been declared a National Historic Landmark. Their home, in Haledon, New Jersey, earned this distinction because of its role in the Paterson silk workers strike of 1913.

The Bottos would be surprised to learn that their strong sense of justice would one day result in their home becoming the only active memorial to a landmark event in the annals of the American labor movement. Their granddaughter, Bunny Citro Kuiken, a curious and persistent Italian American woman, initiated a series of events that in 1973 would lead to this distinction.

Pietro Botto was born in 1864 in Biella, in the Piedmont region of Italy, then a center for the production of wool. His future wife, Maria, was born there six years later, in 1870. They were married in 1885, and in 1892, they and their young daughter, Albina, emigrated to America, settling in West Hoboken, New Jersey. Fourteen years later, in 1906, the Bottos bought a building lot in Haledon, a suburb of Paterson, where many fellow Biella townspeople had settled. Two years later, the Botto family, now numbering four daughters, occupied their newly constructed home.

The silk industry in Paterson has a two-hundred year history, earning the community the title of "Silk City." The golden age of Paterson's silk industry was the period between 1880 and World War I. By 1909, the silk mills were producing over 20 percent of the total silk manufactured in the United States.

Paterson's "golden age" coincided with the great wave of immigration of Italians, Poles, Jews, and other southern and eastern Europeans. Immigrant workers became easy prey for American employers, who were eagerly seeking strong, cheap, docile workers. These workers endured low pay, long working hours, unsafe working conditions, widespread child labor, and the demeaning epithets—i.e., wop, sheenie, etc.—of the manufacturers, American Federation of Labor leaders, and others.

Italians dominated in the new immigration to Paterson. Many who came in the 1880s were northern Italians who had worked as weavers in Piedmont or as dyers in Lombardy. These workers became skilled dyers and weavers in Paterson. After 1890 however, southern Italians with no experience in textiles began to arrive in Paterson in great numbers to work as dyer's helpers. By 1910 there were 7,000 to 8,000 Italians working in the manufacture of silk in Paterson, making them easily the largest nationality in the silk industry. While northern Italians were more skilled, and often professed a variety of radical ideas, southern Italians were thought to be more docile workers. Both groups, however, faced what was perhaps the most mistreatment and disrespect of any other ethnic group. When Italians fought back, they were treated brutally by police. Jews were the second largest group working in Paterson's silk mills, numbering from 3,000 to 5,000. The 1913 strike brought about a powerful alliance between Italians and Jews.

When the Henry Doherty plant, one of the newest and largest of Paterson's 250 silk mills, forced the "four loom" system on workers long accustomed to operating "two looms," 800 broad-silk weavers reacted on January 27, 1913, by going on strike. The striking silk workers were distrustful of the conservative A.F.L. craft-oriented leaders, and at the strong urging of Italian weavers, sought out the assistance of the Industrial Workers of the World (I.W.W.) A year earlier, in 1912, the I. W.W. had conducted a successful nine-week strike of immigrant workers in Lawrence, Massachusetts.

Within a month of the Doherty broad-silk weaver's walkout, the city of Paterson found itself in the throes of a general strike, as plant after plant sought to redress their grievances: a shorter work week, an end to child labor, better wages, and more respectful, humane treatment.

The unity and determination of the striking immigrant workers, most significantly between northern and southern Italians, confounded the local police and mill owners. They decided to employ drastic action in order to break up and prohibit strikers from meeting in Paterson halls. At one of these meetings, Pietro Botto and Haledon's mayor, William Brueckmann, invited the strikers to "Come to Haledon," and they did. On April 3, 1913, the first of a series of Sunday strike rallies was held at the Botto House.

The Bottos' twelve room house was perched on the side of a hill surrounded by open fields, and the second floor balcony overlooked the fields, providing a natural amphitheater. Each Sunday afternoon, speakers in Italian, Hebrew, French, German, and Swiss addressed a crowd of thousands. Among the Italian speakers were Carlo Tresca, Arturo Giovanetti, and Joe Ettor. These three Italians had also been involved in the successful Lawrence strike of 1912.

In the course of this six-month strike, two Italians lost their lives. One striker, Vincenzo Mandonna, a broad-silk weaver, was killed in a scuffle with a strikebreaker who was carrying a gun; a permit was issued by the anti-labor mayor. The second, Valentino Modestino, an innocent bystander, was shot in the back by one of the private detectives employed by the mill owners. Neither of the two killers of these men was prosecuted.

Communal and fraternal organizations helped the Paterson strikers during this time. The Sons of Italy membership was strong in the area with nearly 3,000 members, and held conventions in Paterson, one in 1911, and another in 1914. The Workmen's Circle, a Jewish organization, and the Purity Cooperative Bakery also aided strikers, and further cemented the alliance at this time between Italian and Jewish workers.

Silk mill owners and their governmental, community and professional allies tried to break the unity of the immigrant strikers. The A.F.L. United Textile Workers Union, under President John Golden, tried to draw the striking workers away from the I.W.W. but their efforts failed.

Six months of strike without any income took their toll. A New York reporter wrote, "They were starved — literally starved — back to work." An Italian striker was quoted as saying, "I think the reason we lost was we had no money. They drained us," he added, "and a lot of mutual aid societies paid two dollars a week for relief, but that was practically nothing if someone had children to feed and rent to pay." On August 2, 1913, the strike was officially called off. Both sides, however, lost something. Paterson's thriving silk industry never recovered.

Pietro Botto and his daughters lost their jobs. The silk mill owners blacklisted them, and one daughter was forced to change her name to find employment. Maria Botto died one year after the stike at the age of 44.

As a teenager, Mrs. Botto's granddaughter Bunny Citro, enjoyed looking through her family's photo album. Included among the photos was one of her grandparents' home. "Why are there so many people around our house?" she repeatedly inquired of her grandfather Botto and other family members. Her questions went unanswered. Her family's strike experiences had been so painful and so bitter, that they chose to try and forget. In 1973, on the 60th anniversary of the Paterson silk strike a local newspaper, the Bergen Record, featured a story on the six-month ill-fated event. Now for the first time, forty-three year old Bunny Citro Kuiken, who was living in the Botto house, began to realize the historic significance of her grandparent's home. She "vowed not to let people forget." She contacted local and state historical agencies and asked for their help in finding out more about her family's home. She also enlisted the sympathetic assistance of Sol Stetin, a local labor leader, who at one time was the National President of the Textile Workers Union of America, A.F.L.-C.I.O. Mr. Stetin was a Jewish immigrant from Poland and had worked in the Paterson dye shops. He persuaded his union to erect a historical marker at the Botto House, which was unveiled at a dedication ceremony on June 7, 1975. Four of Pietro and Maria Botto's daughters were in attendance, one of them Bunny Citro Kuiken's mothers, as was seventy-three year old Alfred Cappio, a local historian, who was 13 years old during the strike, and who delivered a personal account of it as seen through the eyes of a teenager.

The T.W.U.A, A.F.L.-C.I.O historical marker at Botto House reads as follows:

> On this property, which has been designated as a National Historical Site, Pietro Botto and his family provided a haven for free speech and assembly for thousands of Paterson textile workers during their historical struggle in 1913 for the eight hour day and an end to child labor.

In the years after, Mrs. Kuiken and her husband became increasingly concerned about the future of their family's historic home. Once more she sought the help of Sol Stetin, who had in 1980 become the President of the Board of Trustees of the American Labor Museum. In 1982, with a loan of $75,000 from the National Trust for Historical Preservation's Endangered Properties Revolving Fund, and $50,000 raised at a retirement dinner for Stetin, the Botto House was purchased by the American Labor Museum. At that time, John Herbst left his post at the New Jersey Historical Society and became the Labor Museum's first Executive Director. Also in that year, the Secretary of the Interior declared the Botto House a National Historic Landmark. The Museum officially opened on May 1, 1983.

The Botto House National Landmark, operated by the American Labor Museum, is a reality today because of the efforts of Bunny Citro Kuiken, a concerned third generation Italian American, the financial assistance of a Sol Stetin, a genuine trade unionist, and the abilities and talents of John Herbst, who when asked about his interest in the post of Executive Director of the new Museum, stated, "My mother is Italian."

By providing the initial spark in this worthy endeaver, Bunny Citro Kuiken has demonstrated what an interested, determined Italian American can do to proudly express his or her ethnic identity. She has helped to preserve and now to exhibit her family's immigrant past and their historic home with its herb garden and grape arbor, and mementos like their Italian trunk, handmade bocce balls, and clothing, including a pair of baby shoes now on display at the recently opened Ellis Island Museum. In so doing she has contributed to our knowledge of American history.

BIBLIOGRAPHY

American Labor Museum, *et al., Life and Times in Silk City,* Paterson, New Jersey. 1984.

American Labor Museum Newsletter, Fall, 1982.

Cahn, W., *Lawrence 1912 — The Bread and Roses Strike,* New York: The Pilgrim Press. 1954.

Cappio, A., *Paterson Silk Strike of 1913,* Unpublished paper, July, 1975.

Colin, S., *The Fragile Bridge, Paterson Silk Strike, 1913,* Temple University Press: 1988.

Kuiken, B. Personal interview "I vowed not to let people forget." *I'm a Preservationist,* January/February 1983.

Sheire, J., *National Register of Historic Places — Inventory Nomination Form,* Historical National Park Service, Division of History, 18 June 1982.

WPA Writers Project, *Stories of New Jersey The Silk Strike,* Bulletin No. 7 1941-42 Series.

PART V
TRANSITION

16

PUBLIC POLICY AND THE MEXICAN ITALIANS OF EL PASO, TEXAS (1880-1920)

VALENTINO J. BELFIGLIO

> "The rugged brow of careful Policy."
> Edmund Spenser, Dedicatory Sonnets.

Introduction

From the unification of Italy in 1861 until 1900, many Italians from *Alta Italia* (the northern regions), and the Tyrol, migrated to other lands. At that time, the Italian government placed very few restrictions on emigration. Nearly two-thirds of these people were from Piedmont, Lombardy, Liguria, Veneto and Emilia-Romagna. The prosperous countries of Europe, such as Germany, Switzerland, and France were their favored destinations. However, Northern Italians also emigrated to Latin America, and a number of them settled in Mexico.[1] Some of these Mexican Italians later settled in El Paso, Texas. The purpose of this paper is to examine the impact of the public policies of the Italian, Mexican and American governments on the ethnic hierarchy and assimilation of Italians living in Mexico, and El Paso County, Texas, between 1880 and 1920.

A Historical Overview

The earliest known Italian settlement in Mexico was founded at Texquitipan (Veracruz), near the Tecolutla River in 1856, during the administration of Mexican President, Ignacio Comonfort. Two hundred Italian immigrants cultivated vanilla vines, alongside Mexican laborers, in this isolated, tropical area. Malaria was endemic to the region.[2] Most of the Italians sought personal fortunes and were determined to return to their homelands. At this time the governments of the Italian peninsula could offer little advice to the emigrants. This was the period of the 19th century movement for Italian political unity (the *Risorgimento*).[3]

During the administration of President Sebastian Lerdo (1872-1876). Mexican leaders began an aggressive program designed to induce Europeans to populate the less developed areas of the country. They believed that European immigrants could help enliven agriculture, industry and the arts, and that they would be a counterbalance to growing American influence in Mexico. Mexican authorities gave preference to Spaniards, Italians and Frenchmen, because these Latin peoples could easily be assimilated into the Mexican society.[4]

Under the laws of May 31, 1875, and December 15, 1883, the Ministerio de Fomento, Colonizacion, Industria y Comercio de la Republica Mexicana, promoted immigration through contracts with private, European companies. The Mexican government either paid a subsidy to the companies for each immigrant, or covered the expenses of their transportation. Government contracts allowed private companies in Mexico to become owners of one-third of all vacant lands that they agreed to survey. These companies often were given the option of buying an additional one-third of the surveyed lands, in blocks no greater than 6,000 acres. Mexican law required purchasers to maintain at least one colonist for every 500 acres of acquired land. The law also exempted immigrants from military service and most taxes, and allowed them to easily become Mexican citizens. Companies could sell 10 to 20 hectares of land to the immigrants on long-term loans.[5]

To facilitate the emigration of Italians to Mexico, Mexican companies entered into agreements with firms in Northern Italy. Examples of these companies include Barbieri House in Genoa, Rovatti & Cia in Livorno, and Rizzo & Fulcheri of Rome.[6] Between 1881 and 1884 these companies entered into contracts to supply farm workers for six rural colonies on uncultivated lands within the states of Morelos, Puebla, Veracruz, San Luis Potosi; and the Federal District. All of the colonies were located in central or eastern Mexico. Contracts called for a mixture of European and Mexican workers so that the native population could benefit from European skills and techniques.[7]

Northern Italian *contadini* (peasant farmers) and *braccianti* (workmen) emigrated from mountainous areas where the soil was relatively unproductive. Most of the lands in *Alta Italia* were owned by wealthy proprietors, who leased them in large and small parcels. Farms in many localities were small, with short growing seasons, and stony soils. The average daily wage of agricultural workers in northern Italy in 1905 was thirty-seven cents.[8] This barely was enough to provide a minimum of food, shelter and other necessities for their families; and upward social mobility was extremely difficult.

Some northern Italian peasants looked upon Mexico as a land of opportunity. They believed that they could earn enough money to be able to retire comfortably in their homelands. Villagers from the provinces of Mantua, Venice, Treviso, Trent, Verona and other parts of *Alta Italia* and the Tyrol, sailed from Genoa or Livorno to Veracruz with high expectations.[9] Voyage by steamship took between 21 to 33 days, depending on the number and duration of ports of call. Possible stops included: Marseilles, Barcelona, Cadiz, Havana, Saint Thomas, and finally Veracruz.[10] Immigrants then traveled by railway,[11] and then by covered wagons or on foot to their final destinations — plantations near Huatusco (Veracruz), Cuautla (Morelos), Cholula (San Luis Potosi), Chipiloc (Puebla), Mezatepec and Teteles (Puebla), and the Federal District.[12]

When Italians arrived at these sites, they discovered that they were on high estates owned by wealthy landlords. This was a situation similar to the one in Italy that they had sought to escape. Some plantations specialized in one crop: others grew a variety of agricultural products. Two colonies produced dairy products and meat. Table I gives the population and major products of the Italian colonies in 1885. The accompanying map shows where these colonies were located. Italians worked from sunrise to sunset on the great plantations, with primitive tools such as shovels, hoes, machetes and axes.[13] They cleared and cultivated the lands,[14] helped by teams of oxen, mares and mules.[15] Workers earned between seventy-five cents and $1.50 a day. Italians eventually purchased small tracts of land, which provided

TABLE 1   FOREIGN-BORN LIVING IN MEXICAN COLONIES, 1885

Colony	Total Population	Number of Italians	Major Products
"Porfirio Diaz" (State of Morelos)	102	15	corn, beans, rice, bananas, melons & watermelons.
"Fernandez Leal" (State of Puebla)	359	334	cattle, hogs, milk, butter, cheese, ham & a flour mill.
"Carlos Pacheco" (State of Puebla)	150	70	corn, rice, panela, tobacco & coffee.
"Manuel Gonzalez" (State of Veracruz)	492	419	mainly coffee, with some bananas, pineapples & oranges.
"Diez Gutierrez" (State of San Luis Potosi)	95	65	corn, beans grapes & tobacco.
"Aldana" (Federal District)	18	13	corn, alfalfa, milk & butter.
TOTAL	1,216	916 (75%)	

Source: Compiled from data contained in Jose B. Zilli Mancia, *Italianos en Mexico* (Xalapa, Ver.: Ediciones San Jose, 1981), pp. 327-379; 386-388.

COLONIE AGRICOLE STRANIERE NEL MESSICO

(Da: PROBLEMAS AGRICOLAS E INDUSTRIALES DE MEXICO)

① Colonia Russa

② Colonia Mormone

③ ④ ⑦ ⑧ Colonie Mennonite

⑤ Colonia Flamminga

⑥ ⑨ ⑫ Colonie Statunitensi

⑩ ⑬ ⑮ ⑯ ⑰ ⑱ ㉒ Colonie Italiane

⑪ ⑭ ⑲ Colonie Francesi

⑳ Colonia Portoricana

㉑ Colonia Giapponese

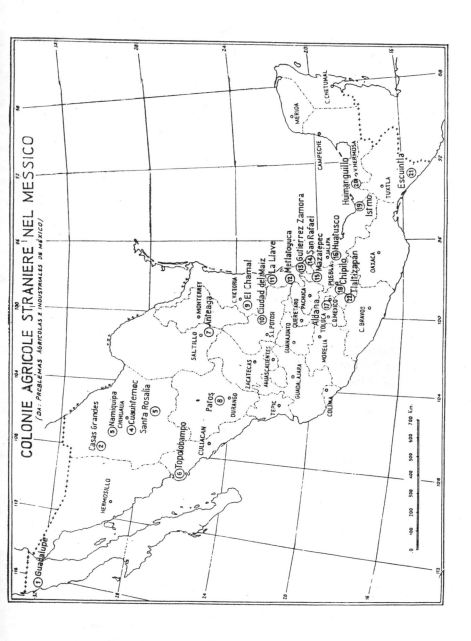

COLONIE AGRICOLE STRANIERE NEL MESSICO
(DA: PROBLEMAS AGRICOLAS E INDUSTRIALES DE MÉXICO)

① Guadalupe
② Casas Grandes
③ Namiquipa CHIHUAHUA
④ Cuauhtemoc
⑤ Santa Rosalía
⑥ Topolobampo
⑦ Aríteaga
⑧ Patos DURANGO
⑨ Ciudad del Maiz
⑩ S.L. POTOSI
⑪ La Llave
⑫ Mextlatoyuca
⑬ Gutierrez Zamora
⑭ San Rafael
⑮ Mazatepec
⑯ Huatusco
⑰ Aldana
⑱ Chipilo
⑲ Istmo
⑳ Huimanguillo
㉑ Escuintla
㉒ Tlaltizapan
El Chamal

them with little more than the minimum of food and shelter necessary to support their families.[16]

Italians lived along dusty, dirt roads in communities near the fields. Their houses were built of wattle or adobe, with flat or slanting roofs made of straw. Many of the homes were small, with only one room, a hard packed dirt floor, one door, and few if any windows. They slept on straw mats and ate out of clay bowls. Some Italians built cooking fires on the floor; although, they prepared much of their food outdoors. Staples included: corn, pork, chicken, peppers, beans and cheese. The immigrants grew onions, tomatoes, garlic, squash and fruits for home consumption. They drank milk, coffee, fruit drinks, and homemade wines.[17]

Each colony essentially was a self-contained community served by a variety of specialists, including an engineer-director and his assistants; a paymaster, interpreter, printer and steward; medical personnel and a preceptorial staff.[18] All of the settlements had schools for the children of immigrants, and many had businesses. There were 13 sugar mills at the colony of Carlos Pacheco (Puebla), and workers manufactured brandy there. Fernandez Leal (Puebla) had a flour mill; and Manuel Gonzalez (Veracruz) maintained a church, court of law, telegraph and telephone facilities, and rail service to Cameron.[19] Italians produced milk, butter and cheese at the dairy farm of Aldana (Federal District).

Italians contributed materially to the economic development of the colonies, but many of them never became Mexicans.[20] Most failed to see the attractions which the Mexican government had promised.[21] To make matters worse, all was not well in the colonies. The Chico River overflowed its banks and devastated homes and farmlands at Aldana. A drought destroyed the coffee crop at Diez Gutierrez (San Luis Potosi); and a measles epidemic plagued Manuel Gonzalez.[22] Meanwhile, settlers suffered from tropical diseases, such as malaria and yellow fever, and from parasitic insects at the colony of Porfirio Diaz (Morelos).[23] During the intervening time Italians lived in misery and extreme poverty at the unsuccessful colony at Chipiloc.[24]

Ethnic Hierarchy and Assimilation

The migration of Italians to Mexico was voluntary.[25] *Contadini* experienced peaceful coexistence and a rough economic and political equality with the *peones* (peasants) with whom they worked. However, they were subordinate to the wealthy *latifundistas* (large landowners), who owned 97 percent of the land.[26] There were three dominant social classes in Mexico at the turn of the century. About one percent of the total population belonged to the upper class; eight percent to the middle class; and 91 percent to the lower class.[27] Unlike aristocratic Italy, some upward social mobility was possible in Mexico for those who were able to save enough money to buy land, or move to the cities. The low status of Italians could be improved through internal migration, and assimilation into the Mexican society.[28]

There were cultural similarities that facilitated the adaptation of Italians to the norms of the rural, lower class society of Mexico. The *contadini* came from a similar rural, lower class society in Italy. Moreover, Italian and Spanish are both Romantic languages that developed from Latin. Therefore, Italians had little trouble learning to speak the language of *peones*. Religion provided another source of cultural understanding for the two groups. The Catholicism of Mexico was similar to that of Italy, with a general allegiance to the church and little active participation except by women and children.[29] Devotions to the Virgin of Guadalupe in Mexico, struck a familiar chord in Italians, who had celebrated feasts to the Madonna, Saint Anne, and Saint Agnes in their native villages.[30]

The family forms, norms and values of the *contadini* and *peones* also were similar. This similarity allowed Italians to penetrate cliques and associations of the *peone* society at the primary-group level, and led to significant intermarriage between the two groups. Italian and Mexican families of the lower class typically were extended, cohesive and large. Neither group was wealthy enough to afford servants. Italian and Mexican families customarily included: spouses, children, grandparents, aunts and uncles, cousins, and godparents (it. *compari*) (sp. *compadres*). Through an important custom known as godparenthood (it. *comparaggio*) (sp. *compadrazgo*), carefully selected outsiders became part of a kind of extended family.[31] In addition, very close friends (it. *amici di casa*) (sp. *cuates*) recognized mutual obligations not present between more casual friends.[32]

Italian and Mexican families were very cohesive. Family members expected from one another loyalty, material and spiritual assistance, emotional support, physical protection, and even flexibility in the enforcement of laws, norms, and regulations. Both family systems were patriarchal, with clearly defined roles for men and women. The Mexican concept of *virilidad* (manliness) was well understood by Italian males, who knew the term as *virilita`*. Both groups had large families: the average couple had six offspring.[33]

However, the assimilation of Italians did not include the development of a sense of identity linked to the core society: a value consensus still held the group together. They continued to speak Italian at home, demonstrate a preference for Italian foods and beverages, and to write letters to relatives in Italy. Many Italians dreamt of returning to their homeland, and some of them eventually did. They formed benevolent-fraternal organizations to perpetuate their culture and Italianism, such as the Societa` de Mutuo Soccorso.[34]

Like the *peones*, *contadini* occupied a subordinate position of prestige, privilege, and power in Mexico. However, it had not been their intent to migrate to a foreign land in order to replace the exploitation of wealthy

Italian landowners with wealthy Mexican landowners. Most Italians abandoned their agricultural pursuits. Some moved to Mexican cities and became assimilated into the life of the country. Others returned to Italy. Several migrated to the United States, where wages were higher, and opportunities for upward social mobility were greater.[35]

One means of getting to the United States was by working on Mexican railroads. Mexican President, Porfirio Diaz, granted major concessions to American companies in 1880, which allowed them to build railroads in Mexico. On September 8, Diaz awarded a contract to the Ferrocarril Central Mexicano (Mexican Central Railroad) for the construction of a line from Paso del Norte (Juarez), opposite El Paso, Texas, to Mexico City. Track-laying began on September 15, 1880; Italian and Mexican laborers worked together on the project. They completed the line on March 8, 1884.[36] Those Italians who migrated to El Paso in this manner were only partially, culturally and structurally assimilated into the *peone* society of Mexico.[37]

Italians Migrate to El Paso

El Paso, Texas, lies opposite Juarez, Mexico, beside the Rio Grande River: it is heavily influenced by Spanish history, culture and architecture. The Southern Pacific; Santa Fe; Galveston, Harrisburg, and San Antonio; and Texas and Pacific Railroads all entered El Paso between May and December 1881. The improved transportation facilities encouraged industries to settle there—smelting and refining, flour milling, cement manufacturing, cotton milling, oil refining, making of optical instruments, brewing, bottling, and meat packing.[38] The growing prosperity attracted Italians, Mexicans and other migrants. More than a third of the population of El Paso County between 1900 and 1920 were foreign-born Mexican.[39]

It is difficult to determine exactly when Italians began settling within El Paso County. It is known that a number of them were living there prior to the Spanish-American War. For example, Louis Cardis established a home in El Paso in 1864.[40] Cardis was born in Piedmont, in northwestern Italy in 1829. He was a captain in Giuseppe Garibaldi's army between 1848 and 1849; and, he came to America in 1854. Beginning in 1874, Cardis served two terms in the Texas State House of Representatives.[41] He spoke fluent Spanish, and was an acknowledged leader of the Mexican community of El Paso.[42]

Another Italian, Father Giuseppe Montenarelli, arrived at the ancient mission of Ysleta in 1881, to help minister to the needs of the Indian and Mexican population.[43] Ysleta is now part of the city of El Paso. Michele Rotunno moved to El Paso in 1884. He was born in Italy in 1856. When Rotunno was twelve years old, he served an apprenticeship as a marble cutter under a skillful master at Padule (Perugia) Umbria, in central Italy. He migrated to the United States about 1878. Rotunno established a marble and general stone-cutting business in El Paso.[44] Father Carlo M. Pinto went to El Paso in 1892. He was born in Salerno (Campania), in southern Italy. Father Pinto entered the College of the Jesuit Fathers, and sailed to the United States in 1870. He built five parish churches and three schools in El Paso, and a parish church in Juarez.[45]

The U.S. Census for 1880 lists no Italians living in El Paso County. However, the El Paso City Directory for 1885 mentions several persons with Italian surnames. Three examples are James Bono, a tinsmith, who lived on Franklin Street, John Cereghino, the proprietor of an Italian restaurant located at 28 South El Paso Street; and Charles Leoni, a barkeeper at the Vault Saloon, situated at 4 East San Antonio Street.[46] Table II gives the number of foreign-born Italians living in El Paso County between 1890 and 1920. The table shows that the number of Italian residents more than tripled between 1910 and 1920.

TABLE 2   FOREIGN-BORN ITALIANS LIVING IN EL PASO COUNTY, (1870-1920)

YEAR	TOTAL POPULATION	NUMBER OF ITALIANS
1870	2,601	none listed*
1880	3,845	none listed
1890	15,678	29
1900	24,886	30
1910	52,599	52
1920	101,877	182

* El Paso County was created from Bexar District in 1849 and organized in 1850. The U.S. Censuses for 1840-1860 also make no mention of Italians living within the County.

Sources: United States Census Office, Ninth Census of the United States (1870), Population, Volume I, Washington, D.C., 1872, p. 372.

United States Census Office, Tenth Census of the United States (1880), Population, Volume I, Washington, D.C., 1883, p. 529.

United States Census Office, Eleventh Census of the United States (1890), Population, Volume I, Part I, Washington, D.C., 1895, p. 661.

United States Census Office, Twelfth Census of the United States (1900), Population, Part I, Washington, D.C., 1901, p. 784.

United States Census Office, Thirteenth Census of the United States (1910), Population, Volume III, Washington, D.C., 1913, p. 816.

United States Census Office, Fourteenth Census of the United States (1920), Population, Volume III, Washington, D.C., 1920, p. 1022.

Ethnic Hierarchy and Assimilation

The migration of Italians to El Paso from Mexico and elsewhere was voluntary. When they arrived, the Anglo business and professional establishment was exercising a controlling influence over county politics. Initially, Italians were subordinate to the dominant southern, Anglo-American group. Italians labored for a dollar a day as sharecroppers, and for the railroads. Some grew fruits and vegetables.[47] Others attempted to adapt their farming skills to the urban milieu, and sold fruits and homemade candies and preserves.[48]

Eventually, Italians learned new trades. By 1920 some owned retail grocery stores, restaurants, confectionary and fruit stalls; as well as barber and shoe shops.[49] They became petit bourgeoisie — that small group of merchants who control their businesses and do most of the work without outside help.[50] Italians most often lived in the same buildings or within walking distances of their shops. Generally, a whole family took part in an enterprise.[51]

Centuries of foreign domination, exploitation, and poverty, had taught Italians many lessons. They know that they could survive and improve their life styles only through adaptation and hard work. Men, assisted by their older children, toiled 10-12 hours a day. Most juveniles dropped out of school to help in family businesses. Women stayed at home to care for young children and attend to household chores. Wives shopped, cleaned, cooked, and tended to the minor medical emergencies of their families. Employment outside the home for women was usually discouraged, unless absolutely necessary.[52]

Policies of local government officials worked in favor of the upward social mobility of Italians. Because the Anglo establishment understood the importance of the votes of minorities, a reciprocal relationship was developed, assigning minor city and county positions to certain safe, cooperative, and dependable minority leaders. They were expected to organize and deliver the vote in return for a certain degree of ethnic protection in order to ensure their continued loyalty.[53] These policies were directed at the Mexican-American population. But they also helped Italian residents, because Italians were closely associated with the Mexican community. Operating between producers and consumers, Italian businessmen traded with people inside and outside their ethnic community. Some made valuable contacts with important persons of the dominant group. Eventually, a few Italians, such as Tony Lama, became managers or capitalists.[54]

Anthony "Tony" Lama founded a multi-million dollar leather manufacturing company in El Paso. His boots became known around the world, and were custom made for movie stars, country-western singers, and American presidents. Lama was born of Italian immigrants in Syracuse, New York, on June 15, 1886. He moved to El Paso in 1911, and opened a boot and repair shop there. His business eventually grew into the Tony Lama Company, Inc. Lama married Esther Ojeda Hernandez, the daughter of

Mexican immigrants, in June 6, 1916, and the couple had six children. Tony Lama died in El Paso on January 11, 1974.[55]

Many other Italians prospered in El Paso, and the initial stratification system became replaced by rough equalitarianism, along cultural pluralism lines. By 1920, Italians were substantially assimilated into the political and economic life of the dominant culture. However, they continued to retain distinct cultural, and primary-group patterns. They spoke Italian and Spanish at home, remained loyal to the Catholic Church, and preferred the traditional social context in which Italian and Mexican cuisine was prepared, served and eaten. Sunday dinners featured several Italian courses, and were reserved for families and very close friends. These people worshiped at Sacred Heart Church, located at 602 South Oregon, or the Immaculate Conception Church, located at 118 North Campbell.[56]

In spite of the close relationship between Italians and Mexicans, many Italians maintained a separate ethnic identity. On June 28, 1936, fifty-seven Italian men founded a benevolent fraternal organization, known as The Italian American Club "Cristoforo Colombo." The names of its officers were Angelo N. Lombardi, President; Ugo Bonaguidi, Vice President; and Salvatore Tamburro, Treasurer. The constitution and bylaws of the society were written in the Italian language. According to Article 2 of the Constitution, membership was open to Italians, Italian Americans, and Italian Mexicans, living in the cities of El Paso or Juarez.[57] Article 3 states that the main objective of the organization was to bring together all Italians living in the area, in order to celebrate and perpetuate Italianism.[58]

What caused this assertion of ethnic identity in 1936? Specific policies of the Italian and United States governments fostered the development of Italianism among Italian Americans throughout the United States. Beginning in late 1922 there were intense efforts by the Fascist regime in Italy, to maintain the loyalty of emigrated Italians, through the use of diplomatic channels and the media.[59] Article 4 of the Constitution of the "Cristoforo Colombo" society states that the organization welcomed affiliations with the Italian government.[60] The American Immigration Acts of 1924 and 1929 were used to exclude most immigrants from southern and eastern Europe, including Italy. Italian Americans resented what they perceived to be blatant discrimination against their ethnic group. This shared resentment caused them to become more mentally and morally attached to one another.[61]

Conclusion

This paper has examined the relations of emigrant Italians with Mexicans and Americans between 1880 and 1920. There were cultural similarities that facilitated the adaptation of *contadini* to the norms of Mexican *campesinos* (peasants). Some Italians moved from Mexico and elsewhere to El Paso, Texas — an area strongly influenced by Hispanic culture. Most

Italians benefited socially and economically from their migration there. They adapted well to the social milieu of El Paso.

Upward social mobility for Italians living in El Paso County was possible for five reasons. First, most arrived at a time when urban jobs were available, when capitalism was expanding, and opportunities were relatively abundant. Second, almost all of them had spent years working in Mexico, or other parts of the United States, before moving to the area. Therefore, they had acquired language and technical skills, and a little capital, prior to their arrival. Third, they enjoyed wide acceptance among the Mexican residents. Fourth, most found housing reasonably near their places of employment. Fifth, local politicians catered to minority voters, in an attempt to get elected and reelected to public office. However, policies of the United States and the Italian governments fostered the development of Italianism.

Italians worked hard to succeed in their chosen homeland. As a result, they contributed much to the city of El Paso. Consequently, several streets and avenues have been named in honor of some of them. A few examples include Cardis Court, Tony Lama Street, and Pellicano Drive. Pellicano Drive was named after Dolores Pellicano, queen of the Sun Bowl.

ENDNOTES

1   Ministero Degli Affari Esteri, Commissariato Dell'Emigrazione, *Emigrazione e colonie, Raccolta di Rapporti dei R.R. Agenti diplomatici e consolari,* Vol. III, Parte III, (Roma: Coop. Tip. Manuzio, 1908), pp. 14-64.

2   Ministero Degli Affari Esteri, Direzione Gunerale Dell'Emigrazione, *Emigrazione Agricola Nell'America Latina, (Brasile, Uraguay, Peru, Bolivai, Ecuador, Venezuela, Messico).* Vol. II (Roma: Stabilimenti Tipolitografici Vallecchi, 1953), pp. 543-547.

3   U.S. Congress, Senate, Reports of the Immigration Commission, *Emigration Conditions in Europe: Italy,* Vol. 12, S. Doc. 748, 61st Cong., 3rd sess., 1911, pp. 147-150.

4   Coerver, D.M. *The Porfirian Interregnum: The Presidency of Manuel Gonzalez of Mexico, 1880-1884* (Fort Worth: Texas Christian University, 1979), pp. 210-213.

5   Manica, J.B.Z. *Italianos en Mexico* (Xalapa, Ver.: Ediciones San Jose, 1981), pp. 50-52, 167-168, 405-410.

6   Moriconi, U. *Da Genova ai Deserti dei Mayas* (Bergamo: Istituto Italiano d'Arti Grafiche, 1902), pp. 24-34.

7   Manica, *Italianos en Mexico,* op. cit., pp. 93-106, 128-132, 198-202.

8   Reports of the Immigration Commission, *Emigration Conditions in Europe: Italy,* Vol. 12, *op. cit.,* p. 158.

9   Moriconi, *Da Genova ai Deserti dei Mayas, op. cit.,* pp. 17-19.

10   Courtesy of the Steamship Historical Society, 1420 Maryland Avenue, Baltimore, Maryland.

11   British engineers helped to construct a line from Veracruz to Mexico City. It opened to traffic in 1873.

12   Manica, *Italianos en Mexico, op. cit.,* pp. 386-388.

13   *Ibid.*, p. 319.

14   *Ibid.*, pp. 327-329.

15   *Ibid.*, p. 199.

16   Ministero Degli Affari Esteri, Commissariato Dell'Emigrazione, *Emigrazione e Colonie: America*, Vol. III, Parte III, (Roma: Tipografia Dell'Unione. Editrice, 1909), pp. 296-297.

17   This information was obtained from interviewing several Mexican Italians, whose ancestors migrated to Texas. For example, Henry Guerra, private interview held at 1119 North St. Mary's Street, San Antonio, Texas, May 30, 1990.

18   Manica, *Italianos en Mexico, op. cit.*, pp. 172-173.

19   *Ibid.*, pp. 179, 386-388.

20   Cumberland, C.C. *Mexico: The Struggle for Modernity* (New York: Oxford University Press, 1968), p. 197.

21   Manica, *Italianos en Mexico, op. cit.*, p. 166.

22   *Ibid.*, p. 388.

23   *Ibid.*, pp. 208, 231-235.

24   Ministero Degli Affari Esteri, *Emigrazione Agricola Nell'America Latina*, Vol. II, *op. cit.*, p. 550.

25   Schermerhorn, R.A. *Comparative Ethnic Relations* (New York: Random House, 1970), p. 98.

26   Valdivia, G.G. "Agrarian Reform and the Ejido," *Mexican Forum*, Vol. III, No. 4, October 1983, pp. 26-30.

27   Cline, H.F. *Mexico: Revolution to Evolution, 1940-1960* (New York: Oxford University Press, 1962), pp. 113-125.

28   Long, L.H. and Hansen, K.A. "Reasons for Interstate Migration," *Current Population Reports P-23*, No. 81, 1979, p. 6.

29   Grebler, L. *et al.*, *The Mexican-American People* (New York: Free Press, 1970), pp. 543-545.

30   For a complete discussion of the role of the Catholic Church in the lives of Italians and Mexicans, consult Silvano Tomasi, *The Religious Experience of Italian Americans* (New York: American Italian Historical Assn., 1973); Alicia de Olivera Bonfil, "La Iglesia en Mexico, 1926-1970," in James W. Wilkie *et al.*, *Contemporary Mexico: Papers of the Fourth International Congress of Mexican History* (Mexico City: El Colegio de Mexico and Latin American Center, University of California, 1976), pp. 295-316.

31   For a discussion of the custom known as godparenthood, as it was practiced in Italy and Mexico during the nineteenth century, consult Richard Gambino, *Blood of My Blood* (New York: Anchor, 1975), pp. 3-41; Larissa Lomnitz, *Networks and Marginality: Life in a Mexican Shantytown* (New York: Academic Press, 1977), pp. 159-174.

32   For a discussion of family life in Italian and Mexican villages, consult A.L. Maraspini, *The Study of an Italian Village* (Paris: Mouton, 1968); George M. Foster, "The Dyadic Contract: A Model for the Social Structure of a Mexican Peasant Village," *American Anthropologist*, Vol. 63, No. 6, December 1961, pp. 1173-1192.

33   *Ibid.*

34   Manica, *Italianos en Mexico, op. cit.*, p. 166.

35   This information was obtained from interviewing several Mexican Italians

whose ancestors migrated to Texas. For example, Louis Pellicano, private interview held at 3304 Nairn, El Paso, Texas, May 31, 1987.

36   Powell, F.W. *The Railroads of Mexico* (Boston: The Stratford Company, 1921), pp. 128-129, 142.

37   This information was obtained from interviewing several Mexican Italians whose ancestors migrated to Texas. For example L. Casavantes, M.D., private interview held at 914 N. Stanton, El Paso, Texas, June 26, 1990.

38   Hammons, N.L. *A History of El Paso County, Texas to 1900* (M.A. Thesis, El Paso: The College of Mines and Metallurgy, 1942), pp. 113-116; Catherine B. O'Malley, *A History of El Paso Since 1860* (M.A. Thesis, University of Southern California, 1939), pp. 46-64.

39   United States Census Office, Twelfth Census of the United States (1900), Population, Part I, p. 787; Thirteenth Census of the United States (1910), Population, Volume III, p. 816; Fourteenth Census of the United States (1920), Population, Volume III, p. 1022.

40   Parrish, J. *Coffins Cactus and Cowboys: The Exciting Story of El Paso, 1536 to the Present* (El Paso: Superior, 1964), p. 44.

41   Mills, W.W. *Forty Years at El Paso: 1858-1898* (El Paso: Carl Hertzog, 1962), p. 175.

42   O'Malley, *A History of El Paso Since 1860, op. cit.*, p. 30; Hammons, *A History of El Paso County, Texas to 1900, op. cit.*, p. 108; Harriot H. Jones (ed.), *El Paso: A Centennial Portrait* (El Paso: Superior, 1973), p. 192.

43   The University of Texas at San Antonio, Institute of Texas Cultures, *The Italian Texans* (San Antonio, 1973), p. 20.

44   Johnson, F.W. *et al.*, *A History of Texas and Texans* Vol. IV, (Chicago: The American Historical Society, 1914), p. 2050.

45   Institute of Texan Cultures, *The Italian Texans, op. cit.*, p. 20.

46   El Paso, Texas and Paso del Norte, Mexico, *Business Directory for 1885* (Albuquerque, N.M.: Rackliff & Wainey, 1885), pp. 27-29, 42, 51.

47   "Italians Pleased with Valley Lands," *El Paso Daily Herald*, March 6, 1907, p. 1.

48   Victor R. Arditti, private interview held at 1014 N. Mesa, June 25, 1990.

49   *Hudspeth's El Paso City Directory 1920* (El Paso: Hudspeth, 1920).

50   Barrera, M. *Race and Class in the Southwest* (Notre Dame, Ind.: University of Notre Dame Press, 1979), pp. 214-217.

51   Arthur Cruz, private interview held at 4760 Harmony Drive, El Paso, Texas, June 5, 1987.

52   Frank Lucisano, private interview held at 9205 Shaver, El Paso, Texas, June 6, 1987.

53   Timmons, W.H. *El Paso: A Borderlands History* (El Paso: The University of Texas at El Paso, 1990), p. 175.

54   Bertha Lucio Cabellero, private interview held at 155 Sancti Spiritus, Brownsville, Texas, February 17, 1990.

55   *The National Cyclopedia of American Biography*, Vol. 62 (Clifton, N.J.: James T. White, 1984), pp. 259-260.

56   Louis Pellicano, private interview held at 3304 Nairn, El Paso, Texas, June 5, 1987.

57   Statuto e Regolamento dell'Italian American Club "Cristoforo Colombo" di El Paso, Texas, S.U.A., 28 Giugno 1936; courtesy of Louis Pellicano, p. 4.

58   *Ibid.*, p. 5.

59   Fiorello B. Ventresco, "Italian-Americans and the Ethiopian Crisis," *Italian Americana*, Vol. VI, No. 1, Fall/Winter 1980, pp. 4-5.

60   Statuto e Regolamento dell'Italian American Club "Cristoforo Colombo" *op. cit.*, p. 5.

61   Ventresco, "Italian-Americans and the Ethiopian Crisis," *op. cit.*, pp. 10-21.

17

MAYOR VINCENT IMPELLITTERI, ANTI-COMMUNIST CRUSADER

Salvatore J. LaGumina

Ethnic politics has been such an electioneering staple in campaigns for public office throughout the course of American history that it can be called an abiding truism. Simply put, ethnic politics involves considerations and manipulation of ethnic factors (a combination of race, and religion, national background) for the promotion of political objectives, in contradistinction to exclusive social class issues. That ethnic politics has functioned as integral to the political equation is evident through such nineteenth century historical examples as Andrew Jackson pursuing Irish American voters or Abraham Lincoln courting the German American electorate, to such current instances as President George Bush and Governor Bill Clinton deliberately extending themselves during the 1992 presidential campaign in behalf of the Catholic vote or New York City Mayor David Dinkins attempting to mend fences with alienated Hispanics, even while it results in estrangement with other ethnic groups. While for the most part concerned with intra-national issues, on a number of occasions ethnic politics has also taken a distinctive transcontinental colorization thereby propelling ethnic politicians into the vortex of momentous foreign affairs activities. Such was the case in the years following the conclusion of World War II that saw the Truman administration deliberately interacting with Italian Americans as it sought to influence the anti-Communist shape of the international political scene in western Europe as that region grappled with ravagement in the aftermath of the terrible war. Although victorious in war, western European nations such as France and Italy were so devastated that they appeared on the verge of succumbing to the allurements of Communism. Clearly, democratic forces in those nations would be taxed to the utmost; and the United States, as acknowledged leader of the free world, would also have to rise to the challenge. Under these threatening circumstances President Truman sought help from prominent Italian Americans to halt the Italian Communist tide.

For Vincent Impellitteri, a natural-born son of Italy, the anti-Communist crusade was a cause of supreme importance — one that he fully embraced, that elicited his total commitment and in which he was determined to play a major part. Born in the Sicilian mountain town of Isnello in 1900, Vincent was brought to this country as a one-year-old infant. After a sojourn in New York City the Impellitteri family moved to Ansonia, Connecticut, where his shoemaker father eked out a living for a large family. Vincent's early education and work endeavors were therefore experienced in the prosaic but stable setting of a small industrial New England town that housed a substantial mix of working class nationalities. With the completion of high school and the outbreak of the First World War, came a separation from the homestead as young Vincent joined the United States Navy and saw combat action in European waters. His military service would firm up a staunch patriotic resolve that was a feature of his outlook for the rest of his life. Then came enrollment at Fordham University Law School, from which he obtained his law degree in 1924, a position as Assistant District Attorney in New York, a stint in private law practice and a return to civil service as secretary to two New York State Supreme Court justices.[1]

Throughout the years he was active in ethnic political organizations such as the Rapallo Lawyers Association, which he served as president and which boasted of a membership that included virtually all the prominent Italian American lawyers and elected political figures in the state. His role in ethnic organizational affairs brought him to the attention of Tammany Hall leaders who repeatedly enlisted his assistance for the promotion of Italian American candidates. Indeed, even the national Democratic organization cultivated his support in the critical 1940 presidential election amidst the feeling that Franklin D. Roosevelt was vulnerable due to the president's intemperate remarks about Italy's invasion of France being equated with a "stab in the back." Whatever else was conveyed in the Roosevelt message, it was considered unusually offensive to New York's Italian community which had labored for years to shed a negative stereotype as "stiletto wielders." It was this background of loyalty to the Democratic party that led to Impellitteri's designation as Democratic candidate for City Council President in 1945, in a race that ended successfully as did his reelection contest in 1949 when he received the largest total vote of the entire city Democratic slate.

As council president, Impellitteri promptly demonstrated his abhorrence of Communism by denouncing the proportional representation system. Adopted ten years earlier as a vehicle to provide representation to the city's various political hues including Communism, by 1947 the political innovation had become a center of controversy as Democratic City Council members in particular, disparaged their extreme left-wing colleagues. The latter group's seeming affront of New York's newly-named Catholic Archbishop, Francis Spellman, served to exacerbate already strained relations between left and right-wing council members leading to demands to alter or eradicate the system.[2] Impellitteri joined in the chorus of condemnation by urging council members to approve a referendum to abolish the proportional representation system which he denounced as an "ignoble experiment which should be discarded and relegated to the ash-heap...."

Always harboring a tender place in his heart for the land of his birth, in 1947 Impellitteri played a prominent role as Italian American political leaders organized efforts to aid the war-torn country of their ancestors. By 1948 Impellitteri, along with other prominent Italian Americans like Generoso Pope, publisher of the influential Italian-language daily *Il Progresso Italo-American*, and Baltimore Mayor Thomas D'Alessandro, became very concerned over the turn of political events in Italy. With the largest Communist party in the free world, there seemed to be a serious possibility that Italy's left-wing forces might achieve electoral victory in free elections — a prospect that held deep foreboding for American officials and Italian American leaders like Impellitteri.

Impellitteri's deep commitment to the cause of democracy in the critical Italian elections of 1948 was reflected in his activity during the letter-writing campaign in which he took to the air waves to urge Italian Americans to convince their Italian relatives and friends to vote against the Communist party. For example, eleven days before the April 18, Italian elections, Impellitteri broadcast a stirring plea directly to Italy advising Italians to exercise the franchise in order to prevent "your beautiful land to become enslaved under the crushing heel of communism." He further noted the inevitable consequences of becoming a communist satellite nation which would perforce effectively preclude access to western friends. It is no wonder that this effort elicited the personal gratitude of President Truman. (It is understandable also that throughout his career Impellitteri saw this participation as a highlight of his public labor.) Accordingly at the 1951 Columbus Day Dinner Impellitteri reminded his audience of the Italian American response to the communist campaign to take over Italy.

> Can we ever forget that splendid letter-writing campaign? We sent thousands of communications to our friends and relatives in Italy, urging them to defeat the Communist menace in the forthcoming elections And who can ever forget what happened? The Communists were decisively, completely and thoroughly defeated.[3]

Throughout the remainder of his tenure as president of the city council he continued to defend Italy against the communist threat. Thus, during the 1949 mayoralty election in which one of Democratic incumbent William O'Dwyer's opponents was Vito Marcantonio of the left-wing American Labor party, Impellitteri engaged in a strident sally against his communist-leaning fellow Italian American.

> Vito Marcantonio says that he is not a Communist.
> You *know* and I *know*, that his record bears startling similarity to the regular Moscow line.
> If Mr. Marcantonio says that he is not a Communist, however, I am willing to accept his statement... Mr. Marcantonio has made the grave mistake of begging for votes on the ground that he is a friend of Italy and the Italian people.
> I say flatly of this statement ... that it is a lie.
> Every time he had the chance, he voted against the millions of Marshall Plan dollars which a generous America is sending abroad to help a proud Italy get back on her feet.[4]

As mayor of New York City, Impellitteri persisted even more so in his position as anti-communist crusader. The most visible reflection of this role occurred within the first year of his mayoralty, when once again he was summoned by the national administration to play an extraordinarily critical part in the United States effort to thwart the move by the Italian Communist Party to gain ascendancy in Italy. This was in effect, a realization that although the major Communist threat of 1948 had been thwarted, that left-wing party still posed a serious menace, thus Washington would be well advised to do its utmost to ensure its defeat anew.

By mid summer 1951 there were rumors that President Truman had sounded out Mayor Impellitteri regarding a trip to Italy which, ostensibly a goodwill journey, was in reality a maneuver designed to prevent the further spread of communism. In other words the proposed junket was in conformity with the government policy of "containment." Truman voiced deep concern that, "In Italy, a determined and aggressive effort is being made by a communist minority to take control of that country."[5] Impellitteri soon met with Truman to discuss the journey, which included a side trip to Israel. Predictably the announcement met with derision as critics carped loudly about the need for such a sojourn and the deleterious effects that a lengthy absence from City Hall would have on municipal government. The hostile *New York Post*, could not resist the temptation to comment that while the city floundered, the frequently-absent mayor was dallying in Rome.[6] However valid were the detractors' arguments, they overlooked the critically important fact that a decisive aspect of the developing Cold War was the maintenance of warm ties with Italy and Israel.

Thus, an extended process of bolstering Italy to prevent its Communist Party — the largest in the free world — from sharing governmental power, was consequential to the Truman administration and to the United States. Prominent anti-Communist Americans with Italian connections were enlisted in the cause with the mayor of New York City playing one of the most conspicuous roles. Not only did Truman recall Impellitteri's 1948 efforts, but the fact that the city housed more inhabitants of Italian and Jewish background outside of Italy and Israel was not lost on the President. To enlist an Italian-born American politician then holding a position of public esteem as prominent as any American of Italian descent, in the important task of promoting friendly relations between this country and Italy, was a major stepping stone in the construction of American foreign policy. That Impellitteri figured so significantly in this endeavor may have eluded the ken of many observers and critics, however, it did not escape the tenacious mind of Truman.

For his part Impellitteri saw this as an opportunity to cement relations with Italy by offering himself as an example to the Italian people of how high a poor immigrant could rise through the democratic process even to become mayor of the largest city in the world. Hence it was that on September 18, Mayor Impellitteri, his wife and a small entourage flew to Rome to begin a whirligig of hearty ceremonies, joyous greetings and generous receptions replete with medals, honors and plaques. The outpouring of public dignitaries, the honors and scrolls bestowed on him by municipal and regional governments as well as the national Italian government, the huge, friendly crowds of ordinary Italian citizens who ventured forth to greet him were visible testimonies of the depth of affection between the two countries. Because this occurred against a setting of difficulty and shame for a proud nation then suffering the devastating physical and psychological effects of war on the wrong side of the contest, the reception accorded Impellitteri also possessed a special meaning since in recognizing him Italians were acknowledging that prestige and honor could indeed originate from humble, but sturdy Italian roots. Few Americans of that era, LaGuardia not excepted, were embraced by Italians as warmly and as enthusiastically as Impellitteri as cities and towns vied with each other to provide the most memorable occasions of pomp and festivities. He was, after all, one of their own who had made good in America, one who had been born in Italy — a fact that even LaGuardia could not claim.

And thus it happened that Vincent Impellitteri stood at pinnacle of the lustiest reception Italy had accorded any celebrity since the conclusion of the war.[7] That Italians were elated and appreciative of the visit in which the Mayor acted as informal ambassador, was manifest in the importance they attached to it. A large Italian police force had to struggle to restrain tens of thousands who had waited for hours and lined the streets from Ciampino

Airport to the city of Rome to catch a glimpse of the man. The mayor of Rome spoke for Italians in general when he greeted Impellitteri with the observation that the Italian populace "followed with great interest and received with great joy the news of your meritorious election to the maximum civilian capacity to which you have honorably risen." Italian newspapers depicted him as a self-made man who, by force of his own strength and tenacity had climbed to a brilliant position. They likewise commented on his distinctive Sicilian physical features, the possession of a warm Southern Italian disposition and an abiding affection for the land of his ancestors. Revealingly, one newspaper welcomed the contrast between his poised, pensive and composed manner, with that of the frenetic, hand-waving, emotional LaGuardia.[8] In the course of his sojourn Impellitteri met with Pope Pius XII, the President and Premier of the Italian Republic, and countless other officials. However, the most poignant stop on his tour surely was the visit to Isnello, his birthplace. Still remote with its narrow, curvy roads clearly not designed for easy access for the long, sleek, borrowed Pontiac transporting its most famous guest, Isnello remained a sleepy village of 4,200 perched on the foot of grey precipice high in the Madonie mountains of Sicily. The village still employed a town crier who proclaimed the impending visit by blowing his trumpet and instructing residents that "all animals — donkeys, goats, sheep and pigs — are to be shut in the houses and are not to walk on the public road."[9] The poor town expended the comparatively considerable sum of $600.00 to greet Impellitteri with English-language "Welcome Impy" banners and fireworks, as the church bells of San Michele, where he had been baptized, pealed and as townsfolk shouted "bravo Vincenzo." Out of respect for his mother and in the inimitable Sicilian dialect, local women greeted him with the traditional proverb, "Bedduzzo De Mamma." He was swamped by dozens of relatives, real or imagined, who importuned him to enable them to emigrate to America. Townspeople were so affected that they ascribed magical, if not miraculous powers to Impellitteri and even the vehicle that brought him. Thus, to touch the car, it was felt, would bring them closer to their dream of going to America. The accomplished writer, Carlo Levi, present during the visit, provided a literate account of its meaning to Isnello's inhabitants.

> There was something mysterious about this man Impellitteri whom they were awaiting, and whom no one knew because he had been taken away as a baby of one year old, fifty years ago; and who was now returning, surrounded with glory like a saint from paradise, from America; and one who, though unknown to everybody, was nevertheless, one of them. There was something mysterious about his birth, as that of Homer, and of Christopher Columbus (or, to be more precise, of Jesus Christ): and

there was something miraculous about his return and his approaching epiphany.[10]

Vittorio Emmanuele Orlando, ninety-one year old former Italian premier and a fellow Sicilian, wrote and apologized to the mayor that infirmities kept him from personally greeting him. Communicating the hopes of most Italians, Orlando further expressed the wish that Impellitteri's visit become the opportunity to create an indissoluble link between the United States and Italy.

That Impellitteri delighted in being able to play a principal role in the anti-Communist drive is abundantly clear in the vigor of his drive throughout the Italian peninsula and in the way he subsequently recalled the participation. In October, 1952, for instance, he summoned people to recall recent developments.

> It wasn't so long ago, even at peace, when we saw the ugly specter of totalitarianism hovering over Italy. The Communists were waging an allout campaign to take over that country and to destroy its democratic and spiritual institutions. The response, in that instance, of the Italian Americans will go down in the annals of history as both unique and purposeful.[11]

It is of course impossible to ascertain precisely how importantly Impellitteri's visit was in affecting the Italian elections of that year. Undoubtedly for Italians important domestic factors rather than foreign influence were the decisive issues, although in a close election the latter might tip the scales. Without exaggerating, it seems a valid observation to maintain that if the outpouring of enormous numbers of people throughout the country, the warm greetings on the part of ordinary Italians, the extraordinarily extensive coverage of Italy's most important newspapers and the unusual attention accorded the visiting Impellitteri by the leading public figures of the nation, are indications, it can be concluded that the Sicilian-born mayor of New York played a major role in the anti-communist crusade of the post-war era. It is a clear example of the confluence of national interests and (the positive utilization of) ethnic politics in a successful pursuance of desirable foreign affairs goals. An occasion of unparalleled joy to Impellitteri, the Italian visit deserves to be recognized as an immensely successful step toward the implementation of American foreign policy.

ENDNOTES

1   For further information on Impellitteri's youth see *The Evening Sentinel,* Ansonia, December 18, 1950.

2   Press release, October 29, 1947, *Vincent Impellitteri Family Papers.*

3   Address by Acting Mayor Vincent R. Impellitteri, Columbus Day Dinner, October 12, 1950, *Vincent Impellitteri Family Papers.*

4   Radio Address, October, 1949, *Vincent Impellitteri Family Papers.*

5   Truman, H.S. Memoirs by Harry S Truman, *Years of Trial and Hope* (New York: Signet, 1965), 279.

6   *New York Post*, October 17, 1951.

7   For examples of Italian newspaper coverage see *Il Messagero di Roma,* September 21, 1951, *Il Tempo*, September 21, 1951 and *Giornale Di Sicilia,* September 30, 1951. It should also be pointed out that Impellitteri's three day trip to Israel also elicited such an enthusiastic response that it was referred to as "the warmest welcome ancient Jerusalem has extended to a visitor in recent years." *The Daily American*, September 27, 1951.

8   *Il Momento*, September 20, 1951.

9   Levi, C. *Words Are Stones*(New York: Farrar, Straus & Cudahy, 1958), 35-36.

10   Levi, C. *Words Are Stones* 37-38.

11   Address by Mayor Vincent R. Impellitteri at the Columbus Day Dinner of the Italian American Professional and Businessmen's Association, October 12, 1952, *Vincent Impellitteri Family Papers.*

18

MADONNA AND MAFIOSO: A VIEW OF MYTHOPOEIA IN PRACTICE

Anthony L. Laruffa

This is a paper about meanings and consequently, an exercise in the interpretation of perceptions. I begin with one of our sacred texts, *Webster's New World Dictionary*, which gives meaning, actually meanings, to the word myth. The text defines myth as follows: "a traditional story of unknown authority, ostensibly with a historical basis, but serving usually to explain some phenonmenon of nature, the origin of man (woman?) or the customs, institutions, religious, rites, etc. of a people: myths usually involve the exploits of gods (goddesses?); any fictitious story or unscientific account, theory, belief" (942). One theoretically inclined astrophysicist suggested recently that the universe began as an enormous explosion emanating from a force of energy compressed in an area the size of a fist. If we were to substitute a different metaphorical text — the hand of God — we would have left the world of science and entered the world of myth. Myth and science share a common belief: to make sense out of life.

William Doty states that myth "provides information about the structure of society or its custom in a narrative form; it is experienced at some point in its development as both true and crucial to those who believe in it" (*Mythography*: 8). The elements of information and belief are crucial. Past and present information are integral parts of the mythopoeia process — the interplay of old and new information comprises the myth maintenance dynamics. Meanings are generated by the informational context. Belief is the emotional source that flavors the meanings. Stereotyping, the cognitive process of categorizing and generalizing through the selective use of data, is a crucial information collecting activity. Archetyping, a psycho-social

180

modeling process where individuals tap into subconscious experiences to secure a safe and knowable world for themselves, has both a cognitive and a strong emotional component to it. Archetypes are primal nurturing figures, powerful gods, heroes and antiheroes, the principals in the struggle between good and evil. Archetypes are often reflections of opposing forces: spiritual-worldly; chaste-promiscuous; saint-sinner; giver-taker; etc. In my view, myth making is an ongoing exercise of archetyping and stereotyping played out in the different social and cultural contexts.

Madonna and mafioso are in part expressive of Italian-American female and male role imagery and convey different messages: Madonna with child, demure and comforting, a nurturer through love and compassion; Madonna, the spiritual incarnation of womanliness. There is another Madonna, "the material girl," provocative, uninhibited, a sensual and passionate nurturer, the earth goddess that the media portrays as a contemporary sex goddess. The mafioso, the complete man, the embodiment of honor and respect, clever in dealing with the world around him, stylishly groomed, scrupulously loyal, and uncompromising in exacting fidelity, is also represented as vicious, obtuse, coarse, and devious. These historically contoured forms — partially the result of a collective archetype genesis — are points of reference for the recreation of contemporary images of Italian-Americans.

Stereotyping effected through discourse, both written and spoken, and through visual imagery, provides a crucial dynamic in the myth-making process.

The Madonna

For many Italians and Italian-Americans, the Madonna is a principal religious figure, the quintessential mother, primal nurturer of us all. The role of nurturer is singularly hers in that as mother she can feed, protect, heal, and console her children. With the Christ Child in her arms, she is the embodiment of biological and emotional motherhood. Iconic representations also portray Mary standing alone with her arms outstretched ready to embrace the needy, the sick, the troubled, and any who seek her help.

Mary, the Blessed Virgin, Our Lady of Perpetual Help, Queen of Angels, Our Lady of Peace; the Virgin of Chartres, Fatima, Lourdes, and Guadeloupe; the Madonna of Medjugorje (Yugoslavia); Monte Carmelo, Monte Vergine, Madonna dell' Arco, and the Virgin of Flushing (NY), are some of the numerous images of the Madonna, the archetypical mother. Carl Jung has suggested that the Madonna is emblematic of the feminine site — the "anima" — of an exclusively male God. On an ontological level, according to Jung, each of us has a female (anima) and male (animus) site, and the religious imagery reflects a projection of those archetypes. Are these forms biologically determined and species specific?

Or are we dealing with a very basic and universal dyadic context — the mother/infant nurturing relationship? This relationship touches on such fundamental psychological, biological, and social needs as feeding, easing of discomfort, generating a sense of security through cuddling and other expressions of love. It is this primary care relationship that engenders a lifelong need for nurturing. And the icons, the narratives, the visions, and the miracles tell us that there is such a being, someone who cares, someone reaching out to help us. Belief in the Madonna is re-acclaimed through prayers, novenas, homilies, processions, and pilgrimages.

The perfect nurturer, the Madonna, also served as a role model for the Italian and Italian-American woman. Since a woman was socialized to embrace motherhood within a family context, she was expected to begin her married life as a virgin. Loss of virginity prior to marriage seriously compromised her chances of properly beginning a new family. The young woman petitioned the Madonna to guide her so that she too can fulfill her role expectations as the primary nurturer of her family.

The Other Madonna

The "material girl" Madonna suggests a very different imagery. Through the miracle of media, she appears to millions on television screens, in movie theaters, at concerts, and in newspapers and magazines. Her image is that of a Hollywood sex goddess, the Harlow and Monroe of our time. Her dyed hair fits the mythical script that blondes do indeed have more fun. But there is more to the "material girl" than a vigorously expressive body topped with tinted hair.

The Madonna imagery has been turned on its head: passion for compassion; the taking of pleasure for the giving of comfort; the momentary expression of physical love for an eternity of spiritual love. Materialism is the cornerstone of our society and commercially packaged sexuality brings fame and fortune. The Italian-American "material girl" has become the reincarnation of a mythical figure — a sex goddess — the most recent apparition of the American Blonde Goddess. Does Madonna represent the "dark" end or the flipside of the Jungian archetype? Is she the primal nurturer who gives pleasure to millions of viewers for a price?

Within the context of the primal nurturing relationship both pleasant and unpleasant sensations are experienced between mother and infant. Many of the pleasant experiences are often pleasurable and help to strengthen the bond between parent and offspring. Unpleasant sensations reinforce the need for pleasurable ones. Suckling, cuddling, stroking, are viewed as positive expressions of nurturing. Infants make demands and more often than not the nurturers respond. At times, a nurturer may withhold gratification. Now she becomes an ogress, an evil person who can arbitrarily exercise power to deprive one of immediate satisfaction. Perhaps the "dark side" of Jung's anima archetype is the nurturer turned ogress. Nonetheless, the nurturer remains the primary pleasure giver, and Madonna, the material girl, is demonstrating how she can give pleasure to herself and to others. In short, the most recent Blonde Goddess is the materialization of both archetyping and stereotyping.

Mafioso

The male template, the Jungian animus, is formed in the early stages of socialization. Male infants are treated differently than female infants, often catered to and singled out as being very special. Still the male infant is dependent on the primary nurturer for his physical and emotional needs and becomes strongly bonded to a female figure. In the very early stages of life both males and females identify with the mother. For the female, however, it is merely reinforcement of gender identity; but for the male, it generates something of an identity crisis. The manifestations of role behavioral characteristics, indeed their exaggeration, is the road to gender separation. Whatever a male is supposed to be will be dramatized in how well he acts out his role. It seems that males in general are involved in a lifelong demonstration of their uniqueness, their manliness.

Many Italian and Italian-American men are socialized to be caretakers of sorts — hard workers who provide for wife and children. In discharging their primary (i.e. male) responsibility, they must be free of any female responsibilities. A clear division of labor separates the gender lines and leaves the male in the enviable position of maintaining gender boundaries and demanding nurturing with little or no reciprocation. The role of provider is the key to gender separation, and acting it out will engender pride and the respect of others. In addition, males are also socialized to be protectors of the household. The integrity of the family is related to the behavior of its members, most especially the females of the household. Virtuous females and industrious males are the essential ingredients of an honorable family. Blemishes must be carefully covered over, for even pretense is preferable to a loss of honor and respect. The well-groomed male in the piazza or sitting in a cafe on Mulberry Street or Carmine Street in lower Manhattan is in his sartorial splendor, emblematic of the perfect role performer, the mafioso. He exudes perfection in that he is properly dressed, properly situated, and always prepared to engage in the proper social amenities. The male is the main public actor, a dissimulator, if need be, of the real drama played out in the home and in the workplace. Often he appears to be what he cannot be and tries desperately to simulate — the perfect model.

The mafioso, a projected male role paradigm, has become ladened with mythic imagery. It is not so much that the "mafioso animus" in its collective manifestation created a "historical" mafia. It is, rather, a situation of a "mythical mafia" giving credibility to the mafioso configuration in its most distorted form. Archetyping is operative in the myth-making process but in the case of the mafioso — collectively perceived as mafia — stereotyping has undoubtedly played the major part. I would like to use Biblical analogies in somewhat altered forms to tell my story (or stories) of the mythical mafia.

Let us begin with the Old Testament, that is, the Old World (Italy). However, unlike the Old Testament, there are a number of Genesis books. I am going to present a synoptic reading of the Mafia Genesis texts.

Book I

Its beginnings date back to the Arab occupation of Sicily during the eighth and ninth centuries. People took refuge in caves (referred to as "maha" or "maafer") to escape the oppression of the invaders (De Angelis: 1).

Book II

The Mafia began as an anti-French movement in 13th century Sicily. The rebellion was symbolized by the motto "Morte Alla Francia Italia Anela," literally meaning death to France Italy desires (acronym form: MAFIA).

Book III

Mafiosi were Robin Hood type bandits responding to the pervasive poverty and powerlessness of the masses. As a collectivity — a mafia structure — it evolved from urban guilds and various secret organizations causing unrest and confusion in 19th century Italy.

Book IV

Some social scientists single out the 19th century gabelloti as the consummate mafiosi. They served as caretakers for the large estate owners and managed to swindle the owner and gouge the poor rentor. The gabelloti were supported by a band of toughs who provided the muscle when needed. There are undoubtedly other Books yet to be opened, new beginnings to be discovered.

Exodus (migration) follows Genesis, and the New Testament (the New World) follows the Old.

New Testament (New World)

Seeded from the Old World, the New World, according to the sacred texts, produced its own crop of mafiosi: extortionists who bled their co-ethnics; loan sharks; gambling moguls; bootleggers; hijackers and fencers; scam artists; and in general, heads of collective enterprises where large sums of money were made quickly and illegally. In all these activities, an Italian surname assured a mafioso persona for individuals involved and a mafia label for the groups.

Who are the New World successors of the Old World gabelloti and heads of secret organizations, and scions of those kind and respected bandits of the past? Capone, Luciano, Costello, Gallo, Columbo, Gambino, Luchese, Genovese, Gotti. These icons and their devotees, mafia families, are mythologized through empowering testimonies: newspaper articles, novels, biographies, scholarly publications, movies, television presentations, and the many millions of conversational exchanges. Yes, the mafia is alive and well. It rates global coverage. Buddhists, Hindus, Catholics, Jews, Protestants, Muslims, and Atheists believe in the mafia. Its ecumenical appeal as a credible entity attests to the significance of stereotyping in the myth-making process. And it is the power of the myth that empowers the mafia.

Concluding Statement

Mythopoeia, myth making, is an ongoing creation and recreation of believable explanations for what is happening in our world. The narratives link together past and present through the interplay of archetyping and stereotyping. The former is a projection of the psyche configuration, the product of the primal nurturing and socialization experiences; the latter is the sorting, classification, and application of information. The information is collected from a wide variety of sources, ranging from the mass media to the most scholarly of scholarly discourses. The Madonna imagery is primarily an archetyping process; Madonna, the material girl, is somewhat of a blend of both archetyping and stereotyping. Mafioso imagery, on the other hand, is mainly an illustration of the role of stereotyping in myth making.

I should like to conclude with yet another story. Not very long ago, a group of dedicated women and men revealed to the world that they discovered the mother of us all, and they were prepared to prove it. Their information came from the application of methods developed by certain molecular biologists, who through DNA and RNA analysis calculated that mutations in the RNA of the body's cells occur at a predictable rate. They claim that you and I and the remaining global inhabitants — all 5.5 billion of us — are the offspring of one particular woman who lived in Africa 200,000 years ago. In their scientific quest for the Black Madonna, the molecular biologists have embarked on a journey that all humans find hard to resist, the search for the prima archetype. And they have systematically collected, organized, and applied their information to support their theory that we are all descendants of a single mother. Truly, the Kingdom of Myth has many doors, one for each of us.

REFERENCES

De Angelis, R., *Mafia?*, Unpublished Manuscript. NY: 1987.
Doty, W.G. *Mythography,* U of Alabama P, 1986.
Guralink, D.B., ed. *Webster's New World Dictionary,* NY: Simon and Shuster, 1982.
LaRuffa, A. *Monte Carmelo,* NY: Gordon and Breach Science Publishers, 1988.
Pope, B. *Immaculate and Powerful,* Boston, MA: Beacon, 1985.
Storr, A. *C. G. Jung,* NY: Viking P, 1973.
Warner, M. *Alone of All Her Sex,* NY: Alfred A. Knopf, 1976.

19

THE ITALIAN WOMAN IN FICTION: A JOURNEY FROM PRIVATE TO PUBLIC

ROSE DE ANGELIS

> "Audacity had liberated them."
> Mario Puzo, *The Fortunate Pilgrim*

Italy's long history of political turmoil and shameful social and economic conditions left Italians looking inward to the only institution which had proved effective throughout the years and shielded them from the intrusions of the state—the family. In America, the Italian immigrant continued to rely upon the family as the source of stability and support, as well as having it function as a buffer between two cultures, Italian and American. The dynamics of Italian familial relationships served as an organizing force for establishing the rules of conduct and power relations between the sexes not only within the particular family unit, but also within the broader societal context, for, according to Colleen L. Johnson's study of Italian and Italian-American Culture, "The family ... [is] the core of the social structure and the source of all-pervading influence" (235).

The Italian woman occupied a pivotal role in and functioned as the centripetal force of the family. She was a nurturer/lover to her husband and served as a role model for the female child, thus establishing the continuity of the Italian lifestyle for later generations. For the male child, she assimilated and reinforced the Italian male rhetoric of authority. Any power the woman possessed, however, remained within the confines of the family. Italian society emphasized the specificity and limits of the female's role in society by confining her to the private sphere of the home in the capacity of two specific categories: wife and mother, with obedience and silence as prerequisites, and in general, defined the woman as a private rather than a public being. The Italian woman's journey from Italy, therefore, became more than just a physical displacement. It began her gradual transition from the private sphere of the home to the public sphere of the male. America provided other options for the Italian woman, marriage being one among a number of options and not her only option for self-realization. In *The Fortunate Pilgrim*, the narrator says that in America "audacity had liberated them," the "them," of course, referring to women (Puzo 10).

Two twentieth century novels, Italo Svevo's *The Confessions of Zeno*, dealing with an Italian family living in Italy, and Mario Puzo's *The Fortunate Pilgrim*, tracing the events in the life of an immigrant family living in New York, dramatize the differing roles of the Italian female in Italian and American society. In *The Confessions of Zeno*, the Malfenti women conform to the mores governing female conduct in Italian society. They respect the male as the authoritative *capo famiglia*, obey his commands, and remain silent to his many moral indiscretions. In *The Fortunate Pilgrim*, Lucia Santa defies the rules and takes the first step out of the private sphere; and later, her daughter Ottavia makes the complete transition. Lucia dares to disobey and speak, and her actions do more than displace the male patriarchy; they obliterate it. Commenting on the fate of Lucia's husband, the narrator says, "The father's banishment had relieved them ... Their rule [was] now absolute" (Puzo 131). By metaphorically exiting the confines of the female world, the two women, Lucia Santa and Ottavia, undermine any essential understanding of a fixed female identity and the concomitant powerlessness generally associated with that identity within Italian society. Shattering the Old World view of the Italian woman, they propose new affective relationships and forms of social organization in the New World.

In *The Confessions of Zeno*, Zeno discusses marriage in terms of "adventure" (Svevo 58). He sees women as a commodity at the disposal of men. In fact, he does not marry his previous "love" interest because, as he says, "She would not have seemed enough of a novelty" (Svevo 64). The Malfenti household, therefore, serves as the perfect environment for Zeno. Mr. Malfenti assumes the role of *capo famiglia* and the patriarchal privilege of disposing daughters and becomes Zeno's role model. He informs his wife and family of Zeno's visit, for, according to Zeno, "[Mr. Malfenti] had evidently talked about me a lot to his daughters" (Svevo 69). While Mr. Malfenti leaves the handiwork to his wife, he makes the decisions for his family, following a tradition that associates decision-making with the male and public life, and consequently, disassociates it from the female, who controls the emotional sphere in the privacy of the home. Mr. Malfenti, like Zeno, sees women as a commodity, and he uses his daughters to perpetuate his wealth and power through an arranged marriage, for the marriage/merger with Zeno is good business.

The Malfenti's marital relationship serves as the paradigm Zeno and Augusta will later follow. Mrs. Malfenti accepts her husband's extramarital affairs as a predictable inconvenience of marriage. She laughs when Zeno comments on the miraculous reappearance of some papers her husband mysteriously misplaces. The missing papers were love letters from Mr. Malfenti's mistress; and Mrs. Malfenti, as the agent of restoration, restores both the letters and the illusion of fidelity in the Italian marriage. Later, Augusta, imitating her role model, fosters the same illusion in her marriage to Zeno.

Zeno's actual courtship of first Ada, which he calls a "stupid adventure" (Svevo 76), and then Augusta, underscores the chauvinistic discourse governing the male/female relationship in Italian society and, as Schachter suggests, "reflect[s] the prevalent male prejudices — in particular the stereotype of women as either 'madonna mother figure' or 'whore'" (134). Zeno idealizes Ada and creates an identity for her that suits his purposes and his needs. "I endowed her," he says, "with every ideal quality to make my life's prize more beautiful ... She was to become not only my wife but a second mother to me" (Svevo 75). Later, as Schachter notes, Augusta accepts the role of wife/mother when she metaphorically kisses Zeno's bruises and smiles in reassurance as his own mother had smiled (135-136).

After Zeno's marriage, Clara, his mistress, assumes the role of female as whore and allows him to actualize his sexual fantasies. Clara's position as mistress, moreover, reveals the price a woman pays for stepping out of her traditional role and hoping to shape her own identity outside of marriage. Clara, however, ends the illicit relationship with Zeno and returns to the confines of the home when she receives and accepts her singing instructor's proposal of marriage. The only other woman in the novel who wanders out of the private realm is Giovanna, the guard at the sanatorium. While Giovanna's occupation allows her financial independence and suggests the role of protector and, by implication, therefore, of an authority usually associated with the male, the description of her behavior in stereotypical male terms borders on the grotesque. As the smoking, drinking, and sexually aggressive woman, Giovanna becomes a monstrous deviant of the female form. Zeno, however, neutralizes Giovanna's guard with his amorous overtures; and her eagerness to submit reinforces the "masculine sexual fantasy that women want to be mastered and dominated by men," thus reinstating her figuratively within the private sphere (Schachter 141). The prospect of giving Giovanna an actual performance of his sexual prowess as payment for the forbidden cigarettes he receives forces Zeno to flee from the sanatorium, for Giovanna's characterization as the "monstrous" female categorizes her as undesirable. Zeno's flight underscores the female as an object of male desire, suggesting that, as Schachter notes, "only women attractive to men [have] a right to happiness" (134).

Zeno proposes to Ada, who refuses; he rationalizes her refusal by saying, "I had never made a mistake before … I approached her not in order to win her, but with the direct intention of marrying her … Love approached in this way lacks its chief characteristic: the subjection of the female" (Svevo 77). In explaining Ada's rejection of him as merely an error in judgment, Zeno does not acknowledge the possibility of his being undesirable and reinforces the view of women as mindless creatures swayed by emotions and created as objects of desire for men. He reasons that if he had wooed Ada "to win her" — as he had wooed the many women before her — she would have succumbed to his amorous advances and become his love slave. Zeno denies the primacy of Ada's mind and rejects her right to establish her own history by choosing for herself; unfortunately, even though Ada claims her right to choose her own husband, she follows the paradigm set by her parents and the role played by her mother, remaining always within the private sphere of the home. Ada goes from her father's house to her husband's house; and after her husband's death, she enters the final confinement in her father-in-law's home.

Zeno's proposal to three of the Malfenti sisters mocks the idea of marriage based on love and on moral and spiritual equality and qualifies it as a marriage of convenience for him, objectifying, as it does, the woman as an interchangeable component of the matrimonial dyad. Ada and Alberta refuse his proposals; Augusta, however, accepts him and her role as wife/ mother, saying, "You need a woman, Zeno, to live with you and look after you" (Svevo 126). Augusta's use of the words "a woman" acknowledges her functional role in the familial structure, her objectification as a woman/ wife/mother in Italian society, and her participation in the disassembling process of her individual identity composed of body, mind, and soul, which would make her "the woman" equal to "the man."

The musical evenings at the Malfenti home establish the basis for the relationship Zeno and Augusta will have during their own marriage. Zeno and Augusta both play musical instruments; and even though Zeno admits that he played badly and that "Augusta's technique was quite good" (Svevo 75), he must establish himself as her master. "I was dissatisfied with her playing and inwardly thought: If I could play as well as you I would certainly play better" (Svevo 75). Despite his inability to master any profession or situation, Zeno must establish himself as Augusta's superior if he is to assume his status as capo famiglia. Throughout the marriage, Augusta remains the patient and loyal wife, even faithful to the moral obligation of her marriage vows. Zeno, however, not only breaks his marriage vows, but justifies his adultery, saying, "It in no way damaged my relations with Augusta — rather the reverse. I not only spoke to her with my customary affection but lavished on her also expressions of tenderness which were springing up in my mind for that other woman" (Svevo 170). According to Zeno, a man's indiscretions improve the quality of the marital relationship, and a wife should be grateful.

During the marriage, Augusta discharges her duties as wife/nurturer, as she nurses Zeno's bouts with depression and goes as far as effacing herself to reassure him. "Where should I turn for my second husband? Don't you see how ugly I am?" (Svevo 153). Augusta, like the other women of the Malfenti household, conforms to the established rules of conduct and remains confined to the private sphere of the home in the respective categories of wife and mother. She nurtures Zeno, caters to his whims, bears his rage, and remains silent to his indiscretions. Augusta lives for others, not for herself, and uses her familial power to maintain the harmony and reinforce the stability of the familial-social structure that keeps the Italian woman at home and out of the public sphere.

If Zeno discusses marriage in terms of adventure, marriage for Lucia Santa in The Fortunate Pilgrim is truly an adventure. The lack of a dowry, considered as "shameful as a bride rising from an unbloodied nuptial bed" (Puzo 11), forces Lucia into the arms of a childhood acquaintance three thousand miles away in an unknown land. Lucia travels from her father's house to her husband's house via the traditional route of the arranged marriage. While Lucia conforms and makes the necesssary marriage as the only means of establishing an identity for herself, in America, she begins making her exit, albeit metaphorically, from the male surveillance of the home by "usurp[ing] his power" (Puzo 29). Her husband's accidental death leaves Lucia devoid of the authoritative capo famiglia, six thousand dollars richer, and free to make her own decisions. The money feeds her dreams for the future, and the orchestration and implementation of her plans undermine the idea of woman as all emotion and no intellect. Years later, the memory of her first husband brings a grim smile to her lips as she thinks: "He had given them [her family] more dead than alive" (Puzo 29).

The absent father/husband and the independence the money allows Lucia lets her shape her own destiny and claim the right to choose for herself. Her choice, moreover, of Frank Corbo as a second husband reconciles the dichotomy of the female as either divine or whore, for she and Frank share both an idealized and a physical love. In the Malfenti household, sexuality is in the province of men, but Lucia brings sexuality into the realm of the female world: "She — a grown woman — had for the first time in her life become passionate about a man, the man who was to become her second husband. [She was] in love. Not the spiritual love of young girls or priests; … No; love … for the hot flesh, the burning loins, feverish eyes and cheeks" (Puzo 30).

Lucia continues to subvert the norms of female conduct as she inverts the traditional rules of courting and assumes the male role of aggressor. Lucia "becomes impatient" (Puzo 31) with Frank's idealization of her as the Madonna component of the Madonna/whore syndrome. She takes the initiative, preparing a sumptuous meal, an extra glass of wine, and a "conveniently placed pillow" (Puzo 32), and seduces him: "And in that act of love she had been the master" (Puzo 32). Lucia defies the masculine taboo on female sexuality and establishes the Italian woman as a sexual being. Unlike the Malfenti women, with the posssible exception of Ada, Lucia places her will above a man's, inverts the male/female roles by using the male as a commodity, and writes herself into the public realm of the male world.

After her marriage, Lucia, unlike Ada and Augusta who remain contained in the private realm throughout their marriages, continues her journey towards the public sphere of the male. She literally and figuratively leaves the domestic realm and writes herself as the male protector of her family's honor. She engages in a battle of words with Le Cinglatas as she speaks for the man, assumes his authority to "possess," and claims her property — her son Larry. Although Larry does not accompany his mother home, Lucia still emerges the victor, for her confrontation with Le Cinglatas' so-called lawyer proves her to be a worthy "warrior." Lucia's daughter Ottavia confirms and validates the power of her authority: "Her mother, a simple peasant, thinking this man a dangerous criminal, had not quailed or shown any fear. In fact, at the beginning she had looked as if she were going after the 'Tackeril'" (Puzo 71). With her actions, Lucia rewrites the female's role; and her command of the phallic "tackeril," the long wooden spoon she uses as a weapon, places male potency in her control and undermines the image of the impotent female reinforced in Svevo's work.

As the years pass, Lucia assimilates the male rhetoric of Italian society and places valor and honor before love and affection in marriage; and as she grows older, she displaces sexual desire with ambition, an equally threatening trait in a woman. Since her gender role within the Italian family only validates female power in the private sphere, Lucia channels her ambition into her children. Nonetheless, Lucia does reverse the accepted power relations between men and women established in the dynamics of Italian familial relationships and capitalizes on her husband's weakness, taking control of him. The banishment of Frank Corbo to an eternity of darkness in a mental hospital becomes more than a question of survival for her family. Lucia's decision not to sign Frank's release papers becomes an act of rebellion for all the times he had misused and abused his authority. Lucia overthrows the public power symbol of capo famiglia and establishes herself in the dual role of protector as the public and private head of the household. The narrator's comment — "She was the protector of them all, she held their fate in her hands. From her would come the good and the evil, the joy and the travail. It was for this she had cast her husband into the pit" (Puzo 171) — emphasizes her ultimate challenge to the established mores in the familial-social structure; and such phrases as "stood guard," "had conquered," "defended" proclaim her victory. Lucia, unlike the Malfenti women, overwrites her female nature with words and actions, placing female courage on a par with male valor. She blurs the distinctions between the sexes and subversively reinscribes herself within the public sphere of the male world.

Following her mother as a role model, Ottavia continues the transition from private to public. Refusing to feed the male's sexual fantasies and his idea of women as sex objects, Ottavia wears man-tailored suits and metaphorically crossdresses to "redress" injustices — one of which is the welfare worker's exploitation of her family. Her coarse language and vehement threats, behavior stereotypically male, make clear the facade of Mr. La Fortezza's male courage, as he flees from the Corbo household. Ottavia assumes male authority, restores order to her home, and reinforces the role of "warrior" woman established by her mother. Her verbal prowess and her extensive reading subvert the traditonal association of mind/ intellect with the male and public life; Ottavia transcends the limitations of her situation and journeys out of the private sphere of the home. Her marriage does not follow the route of the arranged marriage or the prescribed rules of conduct and power relations between the sexes. Ottavia redefines the woman's role, both in the private and public sphere, and metaphorically exits the confines of the female world.

Although Lucia's and Ottavia's actions do not restructure the social order or provide a definitive resolution to the power relations between the sexes within Italian society, they attack masculinity as a charade and undermine any essential understanding of gendered authority. Their transgressions reflect an evolutionary process of change, slow and gradual, as manifested in their sporadic episodes of rebellion, private and public. Their acts, unlike those of the Malfenti women, who reinforce patriarchal authority, destabilize the order of Italian society, predicated on patriarchal authority, and propose new affective relationships and forms of social organization in the New World.

WORKS CITED

Johnson, C.L. "The Maternal Role in the Contemporary Italian-American Family." *The Italian Immigrant Woman in North America,* Eds. Betty Boyd Caroli, Robert F. Harney, and Lydio F. Tomasi, Toronto: The Multicultural History Society of Ontario, 1978, 234-246.

Puzo, M. *The Fortunate Pilgrim,* New York: Fawcett Cress, 1964.

Italian Americans and Their Public and Private Life

Schachter, E. "Schmitz, Svevo and Sexuality" *Moving in Measure,* Eds. Judith Bryce and Doug Thompson, North Yorkshire: Hull UP, 1989 133-152.

Svevo, I. *The Confessions of Zeno,* 1930 Trans. Beryl de Zoete, New York: Vintage, 1989.

20

SOUTHERN ITALIAN-AMERICAN COMEDY: THE CASES OF MATTEO CANNIZZARO, LOU MONTE, LOUIS PRIMA, AND DOM DELUISE

SALVATORE PRIMEGGIA,
FLOYD VIVINO,
JOSEPH A. VARACALLI

Introduction

This essay analyzes the range of expression that is to be found within the present stage in the evolution of the southern Italian-American comedic tradition.[1] The four personalities chosen to represent the diversity of Italian-American comedians of the contemporary era are Matteo "Matty" Cannizzaro, Lou Monte, Louie Prima, and Dom DeLuise. These individuals, all of whom have made an impact in America, represent varying degrees and types of adaptation to American society. They still can claim legitimate ties to the evolution of the cultural tradition of southern Italian entertainment.

The Evolution of Southern Italian Comedy: A Case of Increasing Range Across the Generations

The authors' concept of the evolution of southern Italian-American comedy has its foundation in the insights of Robert Bellah.[2] Applying Bellah's theory to our discussion, the authors argue that comedic evolution in the southern Italian-American heritage has gone through five stages: the peasant, the immigrant, the neighborhood ethnic, the modernized ethnic, and the modernized Italian-American. The present stage allows all previous prototypical comedic forms to coexist within it. Translated into the concern of this paper, the present stage in the evolution of southern Italian–American comedy offers a range of variations: from the modernized Italian–Americanicity of a Dom DeLuise, to the modernized ethnicity of a Louie Prima and a Lou Monte, to the combined neighborhood ethnicity and immigrant and peasant articulations of a Matteo Cannizzaro.

The first stage in the evolution of southern Italian comedy, the peasant stage, took place within the traditional setting of pre-twentieth century south Italy. Sociologically, comedy occurred within a "community" (as compared to "society") framework in which culture and all social institutions took on a "taken-for-granted" quality.[3] By this is meant that all institutions and cultural meaning systems — including comedy — were perceived to be immutable, inevitable, and part and parcel of the social landscape. In other words, it was inconceivable to the host population in such traditional community settings that things could possibly be other than what they were.

It is also important to point out that pre-twentieth century south Italy was actually composed of somewhat disparate and geographically and socially isolated communities. As such, pre-modern southern Italian comedy — including the *Commedia Dell' Arte* — took on a variety of regional and linguistic variations with each variation representing, practically speaking, the only option empirically available to the local community. Regarding the *Commedia Dell' Arte*, those in the region of Naples had either their Pulcinella or Scaramucia characters, while those in Sicily had their Pasquino. The only possible exceptions to the taken-for-granted nature of pre-modern southern Italian humor came as a result of occasional travel or through exposure to any periodic traveling troupe which crossed regional boundaries. Regarding comedy, it is fair to hypothesize that most Neopolitans who came to America at the turn of the century migrated with a stock of comedic knowledge which was regional in nature.

The situation for the southern Italian migrant to America was qualitatively different in the second or immigrant stage for two reasons. First, there was a far greater chance for the immigrant to encounter other regional comedic expressions in America. For instance, while first generation Sicilians no doubt favored Sicilian comedians like Giovanni De Rosalia and his famous Nofrio character, it is probable that they were exposed to comedians from other parts of south Italy, now living together in the same Little Italy areas. Second, a new form of comedy was emerging primarily along regional lines. This was a comedy that addressed the material and emotional needs of fellow immigrants as they tried to adjust to a different and decidedly prejudiced American society. The transformed comedy, then, of the Neopolitan Eduardo Migliaccio — commonly known as Farfariello — was substantially different from the transplanted humor of a Pasquale Rapone who re-enacted familiar popular shows from the old world, such as Pulcinella skits. As such, the first generation Italian-American immigrant confronted a pluralism in comedy unknown to the premodern southern Italian.

The third stage in southern Italian-American comedy is that of neighborhood ethnicity which developed along with the emergence of a second generation, working-class, Italian-American population. This form of comedy was represented by such figures as the American born Sandrino Giglio, who performed only in Italian and catered to the more "Italianized" segment of the second generation and by the Sicilian Nicola Paone, a transitional [4] comedian, who sang his comedic songs in alternating Sicilian, English, and Italglish and had an audience that was both Italian and Italian-American. It also includes another transitional comedian, Lou "Baccala" Cary, who performs his stand-up comedy mostly to the more "Americanized" segment of the second generation.[5] This third stage is more pluralistic than the second, given the carry-over of the comedic forms available in the peasant and immigrant stage.

Perhaps no southern Italian comedic figure better represents the movement to the fourth stage of southern Italian-American comedy, that of a modernized ethnicity, than Pat Cooper. In the 1950s and 1960s, Cooper's strongest appeal was to the now emerging middle-class segments of the Italian-American population who either moved to the suburbs or who had experienced upward social mobility while deciding to stay in their Italian ethnic communities. Cooper's audience consisted of these Italian-Americans who were quite Americanized, spoke English fluently, yet knew some Italian, and were attracted to a comedy that capitalized on nostalgic reminiscences of the immigrant and neighborhood stages of Italian-American life. Again, Cooper's Italian-American humor coexisted with other performers who were either more purely Italian or regionally Italian in orientation.

The present (or fifth) stage has ushered in some Italian-American comedians (e.g. Joy Behar, nee' Josephine Occhiuto) whose routines are more Americanized, audiences more national, technology more modern, and careers not dependent on the Italian-American circuit. (See Chart One) Unlike the previously mentioned characters, the frame of reference of the modernized Italian-American comedian is not that of the Italian-American subculture. While these comedians are not as rooted in the history and traditions of southern Italian comedy, they nonetheless incorporate significant reminiscences and vignettes of Italian-American culture into their humor. Representative modernized Italian-American comedians, of course, coexist with more traditional Italian-American comedians in the present stage.

CHART ONE   THE ITALIAN-AMERICAN CIRCUIT, 1930s-1990s

1930s (100% Italian Language)	1950s (50% Italian Language)	1970s (25% Italian Language)	1990s (10% Italian Language)
Primary theatricals touring cos. lodge/fraternal halls religious feasts phonograph records radio	Primary theatricals lodge/fraternal halls religious feasts phonograph records night clubs resorts	Primary lodge/fraternal halls religious feasts night clubs cultural dates/ celebrations	Primary lodge/fraternal halls religious feasts cultural dates/ celebrations resorts
Secondary resorts radio	Secondary touring companies	Secondary resorts radio touring companies phonograph records audio-cassette	Secondary radio touring companies phonograph records audio-casettes night clubs variety shows on college campuses

The Italian-American circuit was never as developed as the Jewish-American (Yiddish) or African-American ("Chittlin") circuits. As indicated in the chart above, the nature of the circuit changed over time, with different features predominating in different periods.

**A typical Italian-American circuit booking route for the 1990s for a musical, comic, or novelty act with a strong Italian-American flavor might include the following: 1) resorts that cater to an Italian-American clientele (e.g. Friar Tuck's and Villa Roma in New York State); 2) dinner dances for such fraternal organizations like the Order Sons of Italy in America; 3) religious feasts (e.g. Our Lady of Mount Carmel/Giglio feast in Brooklyn, New York and the Dell'Assunta Society feast in Westbury, New York); 4) Columbus Day and other Italian-American celebrations sponsored by business groups; 5) and other forums such as radio appearances, private parties, night clubs, and variety shows on college campuses.*

Matteo Cannizzaro

Matteo Cannizzaro[6] was born in July of 1913, on Prince Street in the Italian-American section of Greenwich Village in New York City. Shortly after his baptism at Our Lady of Pompeii Roman Catholic Church on Carmine Street, the family returned to Calatafimi, Sicily. At the age of fourteen, Matty saw his first movie (*La Spilla Nera — The Black Brooch*) which inspired him to undertake a career in entertainment. He began by singing at house parties, then he and his friends organized a tragicomedy group which performed in and around Sicilian towns. In 1930, he returned to America to escape the growing presence of Fascism in Italy.

At first he freelanced in the Italian variety theatre circuit (or *varieta`*), which featured vaudevillian dramatic sketches and comedies throughout Brooklyn, New York. Cannizzaro then involved himself in dramatic groups such as the *filo-drammatico Spartico*, of Greenpoint, Brooklyn. Soon after, he worked at theatres like Prospect Hall, where the bill consisted of an Italian singer and himself as comic. His entertainment circle soon widened to include other halls in Brooklyn and downtown Manhattan.

In the 1930s, the golden age of Italian-American theatre, Matteo Cannizzaro was a *capo-comico* ("top-banana"), playing to packed houses. Still, most Italian-American entertainers made very little money. Many performers had to seek supplemental employment.[7] Cannizzaro enrolled in night school to learn the English language and attended barber school to learn a craft upon which he could depend as a consistent source of income. Shortly after the Great Depression of 1929, he opened his first shop in Manhattan. To this day, he continues this second career on Staten Island to support his ongoing activities as an entertainer.

Cannizzaro stands in the tradition of the turn-of-the-century *macchiettista*,[8] exemplified by the famous Neopolitan performer, Eduardo Migliaccio (*Farfariello* — the little butterfly.[9] In the classic style of this standard bearer of Italian-American theatre, Cannizzaro makes fun of certain social types and situations in the Italian-American community, now one generation removed from the immigrant experience.

Cannizzaro's comedic presentation evolved as his biographical experience continually intersected with surrounding historical developments. He admits that he and others in Italian-American variety "borrowed" material from one another.[10] He has picked up pieces of routines here and there and modified them to reflect changes in the Italian-American subculture, as well as events in the American culture at large.

In terms of style, Matteo Cannizzaro has been influenced by the old world Sicilian comedians of Catania, by the aforementioned *macchiettista coloniale*,[11] Eduardo Migliaccio, and by his contemporaries Giuseppe de Laurentis and Gennaro Amato. Additionally, he has embraced the American vaudeville tradition in general; specifically, tones of Pinky Lee, Milton

Berle, and Red Skelton are in evidence. Songs and skits of later Italian-American comedians, such as Lou Monte ("Pepino U Soriciello" *Pepino the Little Mouse* is a Cannizzaro favorite) are also in his repertoire.

In terms of content, his comedy includes traditional Italian-American themes of food, marriage, family and inter-ethnic relations. (Matty on Thanksgiving: "After the antipasto, escarole soup, and macaroni, who has room for turkey?" Matty on marriage: "A man's wife is killed by his dog. 'Can I borrow that dog?' asks a funeral bystander. 'Sure, get in line behind those 75 guys,' replies the grieving husband." Matty asks directions to the rest room in a department store: "The man responds, 'escalator.' 'Ask-a-later?' I have to go now.") Humorous commentary on more current American subject matter such as feminism, urban redevelopment, crime, and pollution is offered also by Cannizzaro.

Exhibiting his allegiance to the *macchiettista* format, Cannizzaro makes great use of the double entendre.[12] Clutching the microphone stand, Matty looks impishly at the audience stating, "This thing goes up and down. It gets better if I hold it for a while."[13]

Cannizzaro's act alternates between song and stand-up comedy; ad-libbing at times, he banters with the master of ceremonies, band, and audience. His broad slapstick comedy is largely visual. Parts of his routine are choreographed. On stage, Matty's singing comes to a sudden halt. He begins to strut in a large circle, rolling his big saucer eyes and smirking mischievously. Then, at the clank of the drummer's cowbell, he comes to a skidding stop with exaggerated pelvic thrust and leg kick.

Cannizzaro opens his act dressed in the manner of a colorful clown, complete with loud jacket, oversized bow-tie, ostentatious handkerchief and constantly pummeled fedora. A straw hat, vest and huge theatrical mustache are employed also on certain occasions. In fact, Cannizzaro embodies the classic clown.[14] Cannizarro's comedy presentation involves many costume changes and sight gags and often features a scene in which he is dressed as a woman, a tradition which is deeply rooted in both Italian and American vaudeville. Indicating the seriousness and professionalism he imparts in his work, Cannizzaro always takes his final bow dressed in a black tuxedo.

The musical component of Cannizzaro's act figures importantly in our study. Favorite songs that he performs include: *"O Gallo E A Gallina" (The Rooster And The Hen)*, *"T'E' Piacuta?" (Did You Like It?)*, *"Puppolino" (Little Doll)* and *"Torna Pulcinella" (Pulcinella Returns)*.[15] During the Depression, on Brooklyn radio station WNBQ, Cannizzaro premiered his own bilingual rendition of Gennaro Amato's *"U Shoemaker,"* which is, to this day, a standard in his repertoire. In the 1970s, he recorded two singles on the Primavera label; *"'A Signora D' Sobue" (The Woman of the Subway)* and *"Margari' Famme Trasi" (Margarette, Let Me In)*.[16]

199

The language utilized in his comedy runs the gamut from Sicilian and Neopolitan dialect to "Italglish"[17] He is quite capable of switching the language medium as the needs of the audience and situation dictate. Not surprisingly, his greatest appeal is to the quickly disappearing, first generation of southern Italian immigrants and the more Italianized segment of the urban working-class second generation. Recently, he has generated interest on the part of middle-class Italian Americans who are involved in the present day renaissance of southern Italian culture.

The technology media that Cannizzaro has employed falls short of those used by more modern comedians. He has performed on the stage, at feasts, at concerts for neighborhood and church clubs, for private parties and most recently at colleges[18] — perhaps the new vehicle for Italian-American vaudeville. He has appeared on national television[19] and in professional videos, though not in the role of comedian. He has been an extra in over thirty major movies and has appeared in a long list of commercials.

Matteo Cannizzaro has built his reputation in the southern Italian-American comedic circuit. He is part of a traveling entertainment troupe that includes Pat Caiano, Sal "Tuddi" Ferrara, and Mimi Cecchini. Together they play to the southern Italian-American communities interspersed throughout the greater New York metropolitan area. Cannizzaro has appeared in such historic entertainment establishments as Brooklyn's Walker Theatre[20] and the Ideal Ballroom. Now almost eighty years of age and still performing, Matteo Cannizzaro represents one of the last remnants of the immigrant comedy era. As southern Italian actress and colleague Mimi Cecchini puts it, "When he's gone, no one's left."[21] Cannizzaro is a true clown who can make people laugh in three languages — Italian, English, and pantomime.

Lou Monte

Lou Monte, an Italian-American of Calabrian heritage, was born as Louis Scaglione on April 2, 1917 in Manhattan, New York. He played the guitar and started singing as a child[22] beginning his professional career as a singer, comedian, and musician as a young man just prior to World War II. "After a stretch in the military, Monte settled in Lyndhurst, New Jersey and his first real break came when he had a radio show in Newark, New Jersey."[23] Eventually, Monte was given a television program on that same popular station, WAAT.

As June Bundy notes, "although Lou had been singing professionally for fifteen years, it wasn't until he recorded an Italian-English version of 'Darktown Strutter's Ball' at the end of 1953, that he hit the big time."[24] After that, his records, both comedic and not, sold in the millions. He appeared regularly at many famous nightclubs and, unlike most Italian-American comedians of the era, he was seen frequently on national T.V. At the pinnacle of his popularity, he was promoted in various press releases as "The Godfather of Italian Humor" and "The King of Italian-American Music."[25] Lou Monte died in Pompano Beach, Florida in June of 1989.

The medium of most of Lou Monte's comedy is song, although his extensive and impressive night club act also contained a good deal of stand-up. Many of his songs were sung, and nightclub acts performed, in English with a liberal interspersing of Italian dialect (both Neopolitan and Calabrian). As one commentator has noted, "He translates American music into Italian and Italian music into English."[26] As was stated in a past nightclub review, Monte's "songalog is heavily laden with pizza pieces, including Italo verses of his American numbers with emphasis generally on comedy tunes."[27] Monte's appeal to the Italian-American audience can be understood in both emotional and social terms. Emotionally, his humor provided some Italian Americans with a sense of comfort, of one-upmanship, or the sense of being a part of an inside joke, and, socially, of having a slice of their world recognized by others. His appeal to other ethnic groups was based upon their perception that his humor related to their own experiences in assimilating to American society.

An important theme in Monte's Italian-American humor is his tendency to Italian-Americanize American history and life. Such a technique served this marginal ethnic group by making it feel a part of America's early historical development. It also served to heighten a sense of in-group solidarity by the ludicrous layering of Italianicity on things supposedly rock-solid Anglo-Saxon. In one song, he asks the question, "What did Washington say when crossing the Delaware?" The answer: "Fa un'fridd! (It's cold!)." This bit is a take-off on a joke which was popular in the Italian-American community, although Monte sanitized the coarser punchline.[28] In this way, he played to the Italian-American audience, knowing its members would enjoy and relate to the reference.[29] In another example, according to Monte, the name of Paul Revere's horse was Baccigallup.[30] The hit song, "Please Mr. Columbus" offers yet another of Monte's unique historical interpretations.

Lou Monte became famous for his so-called novelty songs such as *"Dominick The Donkey," "Pepino U Soriciello" (The Italian Mouse), "Italian Cowboy Song," "Italian Jingle Bells,"* and *"Lazy Mary" (C'Era Luna, Mezza Mare).*[31] Like most Italian-American comedians, Monte's humor dealt with the common themes of marriage, courtship, sexual relationships, and food. In his food song, "My Rosina — The Menu Song," the lyrics include: "She is so good looking when she is cooking, what a beautiful sight among the pots and pans." In collaboration with Ray Allen,[32] Monte wrote, "Who Stole My Provolone?"[33] (sung to the tune of "Hang Down Your Head Tom Dooley") a song parody, making use of the double entendre.

Lou Monte's strongest appeal was to a broad spectrum ranging from working-class to professional middle-class Italian Americans. Although Monte's audience was varied, for the most part it precluded the Italian immigrant, for whom the humor was too Americanized and the very modern, assimilated Italian-American for whom the humor was too greenhornish.

Lou Monte effectively utilized a wide spectrum of vehicles and technologies in his show business career. He performed his nightclub act in such major locations as Chicago, Las Vegas, and New York City.[34] In addition to his first significant radio show on station WAAT of Newark, New Jersey, Monte also performed on popular radio programs as a guest star.[35]

Unlike most Italian-American comedians of his time, Lou Monte received much national television exposure on such programs as the Perry Como Show and The Ernie Kovacs Show. Monte's records sold in the millions. As a matter of fact, Reprise records had its first smash hit with Monte's "Peppino The Italian Mouse" recording. Monte also made appearances at prominent feasts and festivals[36] and had a role in the comedy hit film, "Robin and the Seven Hoods" (1964).

Lou Monte's participation in the Italian-American comedic circuit diminished by the 1950s, as his career hit stride.[37] In our evolutionary schema, Monte stands, roughly, half-way between the immigrant comedic experience and the modernized entertainment world with its national television, cable T.V., home videos, national marketing strategies, and perhaps, international forms of communication.

Louie Prima

Prima was the first Italian-American musical clown to become popular in mainstream America.[38] He had two audiences: one generic American and one Americanizing Italian, with roots still planted in *Il Sud.* To the delight of the second, Louie Prima took southern Italian folk songs (eg. *C'Era Luna Mezza Mare* and *Mamma*) and popularized them in this country. This appealed to working-class and middle-class Italian-Americans, caught between the two worlds of the ethnic ghetto and mainstream American society. This was a segment searching for symbolic figures who did not repudiate the former yet received respect from the latter. Louie Prima fit this bill nicely.

Louis Prima was born on December 7, 1912, in New Orleans, Louisiana. He was the roughneck son of a truckdriver.[39] As a child, Prima studied music and, "influenced by the sound of King Oliver...he switched from playing the violin to the trumpet. He started playing with Red Nichols and his Pennies...."[40] Without a doubt, "Prima's childhood admiration of Louis Armstrong was one of the inspirations that set his pattern of trumpet playing and throaty vocalizing that became his trademark and sent him on the road to stardom."[41]

Prior to coming to New York City in 1934, Prima's reputation was made by performing at the Sanger Theatre and the Shim-Sham Club in New Orleans' Vieux Carre'.[42] Arriving in New York with his New Orleans Gang, he opened at the new Famous Door at number 66 West 52nd Street.[43] In the late 1940s, Prima found work, "as a singer and trumpet player in local Los Angeles theatres before forming his band...Louie Prima, Keely Smith, Sam Butera and the Witnesses put together a sound which rocked audiences and set nightclub records all over the country throughout the 1950s."[44] After a prolonged illness, the nationally known Italian-American comedian, singer and composer died on August 24, 1978, in New Orleans.

The main vehicle of Louie Prima's humor was song. He performed in English but seasoned his songs heavily with Italian language sections, phrases, and words. In addition, he created a unique "Italglish" which not only added vowels to make English words Italian sounding but included New Orleanian Cajun slang and Creole colloquialisms. Some of the songs popularized by Prima with a strong appeal to and flavor of Italian-American life are "Josefina Please No Leana On the Bell," "Mari Yooch, She Walka The Pooch," "Felicia No Capisca," "My Cuccuzza," "Please No Squeeza the Bananna,"[45] and "Baccigalup He Makes Love On the Stoop," as well as his own composition of "Angelina."

The Louie Prima style of humor involved active interaction with his fellow performers—singer Keely Smith (and later Gia Maione), bandleader Sam Butera and/or members of the band — as well as with a live nightclub audience. In teaming with Keely Smith in the 1950s she, "...provided a deadpan contrast to Prima's boundless exuberance."[46] Often a song would be interupted by a crazy dialogue, liberally sprinkled with Italian dialect and phrases. The banter was often sexually suggestive and the classic double entendre came into play.

Additionally, like many of the earlier southern Italian comedians, Prima slipped some downright vulgarity into his act. Bathroom humor, such as the song, "Tutti Vogliano Caca," was part and parcel of the Prima comedy package.

Louie Prima had an impressive recording career, working on such established labels as Majestic, R.C.A. Victor, Capitol, and Dot. By far his best known smash hit was his famous rendition of "Old Black Magic," which reached the top-ten list in 1958.

Additionally, Louie Prima was able to utilize a wide array of technology to deliver his comedic message to the public. He was a regular T.V. guest on the Ed Sullivan Show and on the Dean Martin Show, among others. He performed in big-time clubs in New York and Las Vegas. Prima also appeared in the movie,"Hey Boy, Hey Girl" (1958) and was the voice of the King of the Jungle in the Walt Disney movie, "Jungle Book."[47]

Dom DeLuise

Dominic DeLuise was born on August 1, 1933, and raised in the Bensonhurst section of Brooklyn, New York. His father was born in New York City to a family with roots in Spinoso (Province of Basilicata), Italy.[48] The DeLuise family established themselves in Bensonhurst in 1928. A graduate of Manhattan's High School of the Performing Arts, "he was pounding the pavement and doing auditions ... really paying his dues ... Against all advice and with lots of discouragement ... Dom made it about 15 years out of high school."[49] Dom's professional stage debut in New York was in the off-Broadway production, "Little Mary Sunshine," in 1962.

While a good portion of DeLuise's popularity is derived from a comedic presentation which is not specifically Italian-American, there is no doubt that a portion of his humor is inspired by his ethnic background. A fine example of this is his first national exposure on the now defunct Gary Moore Show where he regularly performed his "Dominick the Great" routine. The skit featured a bungling Italian-American magician (DeLuise) and his lovely assistant (Ruth Buzzi). In an interview with Dom's sister Antoinette, she revealed that the "Dominick" character was consciously played with an imitation of their father's Italian accent.[50] As DeLuise himself stated, "I'm so proud to be Italian that nobody can affect my feelings about how lucky I feel to have part of that culture being a contribution to my life."[51]

Italian-American subject matter runs throughout DeLuise's comedy. Language, neighborhood, familial relationships, and religion are among his favorite topics, but by far, the most important theme is food which serves as the conduit to all subjects, both serious and comedic.

Two jokes from DeLuise's popular comedy cookbook and follow up videocassette series, *Eat This: It'll Make You Feel Better*,[52] further spotlight the comedian's all encompassing involvement with food. As he states: "Eggplant is to an Italian what sex is to a nymphomaniac. You can exist, but without it, what is the use of living?"[53] He further warns, "You might be late picking up your girl because your Mom made *pasta e fagioli* for dinner. Can you imagine? Macaroni and beans coming between you and your future wife?"[54]

Although DeLuise performs in English, he likes to weave Italian words and dialect into his patter. He employs the double entendre form of humor, as is nicely illustrated in Volume II of the *Eat This* videos[55] when DeLuise and entertainer Dean Martin banter about the, "three sizes of *cuccuzza* — small, medium, and large." Dom DeLuise innocently asks of Martin, "Did you ever milk your cuccuzza? Did you ever pound your *cuccuzza*?" Martin answers in the affirmative but adds, "but not with a hammer."[56] Earlier, when DeLuise was a member of the Dean Martin Show (1964), they would often quip to each other, "You've got a nice *braciola*!" or "How's your *braciola*?"[57]

Dom DeLuise is not primarily a stand-up comedian (although he occassionally performs a nightclub act entitled an "Evening with Dom

DeLuise"), rather he is a comedic character actor, and in this sense, we come full circle to the *Commedia Dell'Arte* roots of Italian humor. In the Pulcinella tradition, DeLuise is at his best, when he has a loosely knit story or script within which he is free to improvise and ad-lib until the audience responds with laughter. His Italian-American barber, magician, and chef characters are the perfect comedic vehicles for unrehearsed spontaneity and continual development which mirrors the methodology of the early immigrant vaudeville comedians.

DeLuise was never involved in the Italian-American comedic circuit. For one thing, such a circuit was attenuated by the time that DeLuise was a young comedian. In addition, his frame-of-reference was wider than that of the old-time Italian-American comedians and his training less specifically Italian and more attuned to the general entertainment field.

Of the comedians analyzed, DeLuise has the greatest access to and has employed the widest range of technology to forward his comedic message. Most important are his frequent national T.V. appearances as a regular and guest on various variety shows such as *The Gary Moore Show* (1963), *The Entertainers* (1964), and *The Dom DeLuise Show* (1967). He later went on to guest host *The Tonight Show*. Additionally, he played the character, Stanley, on the NBC sit-com *Lots of Luck* (1969), and is in numerous T.V. commercials.

DeLuise has had major roles in numerous movies, including seven, with close friend Burt Reynolds. Additionally, he has his own production company, Bacchus Films. As an accomplished actor, he can effectively slip into a role which is not specifically Italian-American (such as the gay director in Blazing Saddles) and carry it off with impact and credibility. With equal finesse, he assumed his role in the serio-comic movie, Fatso, once described by DeLuise as "my Hamlet"[58] in which he portrayed an obese Italian-American struggling for acceptance in his ethnic community.

Of the four Italian-American comedians examined in this study, DeLuise has the most universal audience. First, his material is not purely Italian or Italian-American in its focus. Second is his almost unlimited national T.V. exposure. Third is his association with non-Italian stars, like Burt Reynolds, Bob Newhart, Jackie Gleason, and Mel Brooks. Finally, and most importantly, DeLuise has managed to develop and capitalize upon an "everyman" image (which greatly overshadows but does not deny the fact that he happens to be Italian-American), to which millions can relate.

In terms of his comedic style and content, audience appeal, technology employed, and lack of reliance on a specifically Italian-American comedic network, DeLuise clearly stands as the most modern of the authentically Italian-American comedians studied in this paper. However, the humor of a Dom DeLuise does not necessarily represent the only plausible example of a modern Italian-American comedian. There is the possibility that some Italian-American comedians can utilize the sophisticated technology of a

DeLuise but better incorporate the humor of past generations of southern Italian comedy. In fact, there are a number of young Italian-American comedians, relatively unknown, who are attempting to make it in the entertainment world as Italian-Americans doing Italian-American humor.

Thematic Comparison of Comedians

In comparing the comedians under analysis, five considerations have been taken into account. The first is the content and style of the comedy routines. The second is the sociological characteristics of the intended and actual audience. The third is the nature of the technology employed to carry the comedic message. The fourth is the participation of each career in the Italian-American comedic circuit. The fifth is the way in which each personality fits into the evolutionary model as presented by the authors.

The first consideration involves such issues as the language medium utilized in the comedic routine (whether informal Italian, dialect Italian, "Italglish," dialect English, or formal English); the comedic material (whether derived from southern Italy or America or, more specifically, from which province in South Italy and from either a "Little Italy," suburban or national American culture or some combination thereof); and the *form* of the comedic presentation (whether "stand-up," "ad-lib," through song or through formal script). The second consideration involves such issues as what are the background socio-economic characteristics of the audience and just how "Italianized" or "Americanized" it is. The third consideration entails the comedic technological medium employed (whether through stage, records, books, radio, national and cable T.V. or video). The fourth consideration deals with the degree to which the comedian participated in the informal network of southern Italian troupes, communities, and entertainment establishments created in America. The final consideration deals with the era that each comedic character represents in the present-day range of Italian-American comedic options. Given these five considerations, the authors argue that Matteo Cannizzaro, with roots straight back to the turn-of-the-century *macchiettista*, Farfariello, is representative of the least modernized endpoint of this range and Dom DeLuise exemplifies the most modernized. Louie Prima and Lou Monte are seen as intermediate cases.

Regarding the content and style of the comedic routines employed, a clear movement, in terms of primary emphasis, from Cannizzaro to Monte and Prima to DeLuise, is discernible on many fronts. In terms of language, the emphasis shifts from Italian to English and from southern Italian and ethnic dialects to more formal English. In terms of the material employed, the movement is from old to new worlds and from immigrant enclave to mainstream society. In terms of how the comedic material is presented, evidence of a move toward a more formal and pre-written script, in lieu of the ad-lib and extemporaneous style, is seen.

206

Concerning the issues surrounding the respective audiences of the four comedians under review, the direction is from traditional to modern and from peasant to upper middle class. The comedic technological medium employed suggests a movement towards greater rationalization[59] and technological sophistication. The more modern a southern Italian comedian becomes, the less dependent he or she is upon the Italian-American circuit established in the immigrant period.

Finally, the evolution of southern Italian comedy in the United States has seen the continual emergence of a modal type of comedian that quintessentially meets the emotional needs and the embedded structural situation of southern Italian Americans in time and space. However, again, the fact that a Dom DeLuise represents the modal comedian for a fully modern, American, and successful descendant of *i contadini del Sud* does not preclude the continued importance in the present stage of the peasant/ immigrant/neighborhood humor of a Matty Cannizzaro, or the modernized but still very ethnic humor of either a Lou Monte or Louie Prima.

Conclusion: Speculations on the Future

· The ultimate question of the future of the southern Italian-American comedic tradition is basically a reflection of the broader issue of southern Italian assimilation into American society. To argue, as do many, that authentic southern Italian-American community and identity attachments are now past their twilight is, at the same time, to argue that their attendant comedic tradition is fast approaching its evaporation. To argue, as the authors do, that southern Italian-American community and identity attachments are constantly being adapted creatively to a changing world is to suggest that the evolutionary process is far from over.[60] Therefore, the southern Italian-American comedic tradition is in the hands of its future practitioners.

ENDNOTES

1   In previous essays, two of the authors analyzed the evolution of the southern Italian comedic tradition. See Salvatore Primeggia and Joseph A. Varacalli, "Southern Italian Comedy: Old to New World," *Italian-Americans in Transition* (edited by Joseph V. Scelsa, Salvatore J. LaGumina, and Lydio Tomasi) (Staten Island, New York: American Italian Historical Association, 1990) and "Pulcinella to Farfariello to Paone to Cooper to Uncle Floyd: A Socio-Historical Perspective on Southern Italian and Italian-American Comedy," *ECCSSA Journal* (Volume 5, Number 1, Winter, 1990). Also see Salvatore Primeggia, Pamela R. Primeggia, and Joseph A. Varacalli, "Uncle Floyd Vivino: A Modern Italian-American Comic," *New Jersey History*, (Volume 107, Numbers 3 and 4, Fall/Winter, 1989). The authors wish to acknowledge the invaluable editorial assistance offered by Pamela R. Primeggia and the typing services provided by Lillian Varacalli.

2   Bellah, R., "Religious Evolution," *Beyond Belief: Essays on Religion in a Post-Traditional World* (New York: Harper and Row, 1970). In his essay, Bellah argues that religious developments have gone through five stages with each successive stage being marked by the increasing differentiation of religion from culture and by increasing individualism.

3   Berger, P.L. and Berger, B., *Sociology: A Biographical Approach* (New York: Basic Books, 1972).

4   The authors understand a transitional comedian to be one whose comedy bridges two distinct eras.

5   Lou "Baccala" Cary's audience is mainly working-class Italian who live in either inner-city enclaves or the more "Italianized" segments of the American suburbs.

6   Interviews of Matteo Cannizzaro were conducted on May 14, 1990, and March 1, 1991. In addition, our analysis is based upon viewing a number of videotapes of Cannizzaro's performances, as well as being present at six different performances.

7   Some of the Italian-American top performers were able to support themselves and their families strictly from revenues derived solely from entertainment avenues. Farfariello, Mignonette, Clemente Giglio, the Martinelli family, Ria Rosa, and Salmaggi earned money from radio, theatre, phonographic records, and investments.

8   According to Giuseppe Cautela, in "The Italian Theatre in New York" in *The American Mercury*, Volume XII, no. 45, September 1927, p. 110, "The *macchiettista* performed *macchiette* which were character sketches."

9   Estavan, Lawrence, editor, "The Italian Theatre in San Francisco" *Monogram XXI* from Theatre Research, W.P.A. Project 10677.

10   They borrowed from what was known as "stock material." In addition to the Italian-American vaudevillians, this practice was typical of American, Yiddish, and African-American theatricals as well. This use of stock material continued until the advent of television. In American vaudeville, for example, Abbot and Costello performed nearly all stock material "borrowed" from Weber and Fields.

11   "Farfariello was a *macchiettista*, a vaudeville comedian whose art derived from the *Commedia Dell'Arte*. He transposed that tradition to burlesque those of the Italian colony (hence *coloniale*)" in Sogliuzzo, A. Richard, "Notes From The History of The Italian-American Theatre," *Theatre Survey*, Volume XIV, no. 2, November, 1973, p. 68.

12   Cautela, *op. cit.*, p. 110, speaks of the *macchiettista* relying upon the spectator to catch a hidden pornographic meaning.

13   At other times, in referring to the microphone in phallic terms, he states in dialect: "a cosa ca e' mushada" (this thing is soft; it has gone down).

14   Wolfgang M. Zucker, "The Clown As The Lord Of Disorder," *Holy Laughter: Essays On Religion In The Comic Perspective*, Editor, M. Conrad Hyers (New York 1969), p. 78.

15 .   With this song, Cannizzaro maintains a direct line to his southern Italian comedic roots where references to Pulcinella, in any format were stock in trade for a macchiettista.

16   In this song, especially, Cannizzaro's use of double entendre is clearly illustrated.

17   For an excellent explanation of "Italglish" see Michael La Sorte in *La America: Images of Italian Greenhorn Experience* (Philadelphia: Temple University Press, 1985), pp. 159-188 as well as Arthur Livingstone, "La America Sonemagogna," *The Romantic Review*, Volume IX (1918), pp. 210-226.

18   As early as 1958, Matty Cannizzaro performed with Domenico Modugno at Staten Island's Wagner College. Modugno was at the height of his American fame at this time with his hit song, *Volare*. In 1959, Cannizzaro returned to Wagner College with singer Alan Dale.

19   According to an article, "Matty Cannizzaro: Artistic, Musical, and Funny," (*Staten Island Register*, July 14, 1977, p. 11) in 1974 "he came very close to starring in his own television show, 'Pappa D'Alessandro.' Produced by Norman Lear as a sort of Italian-style 'All in the Family,' the show was suddenly shelved when another network aired the ill-fated 'Montefuscos,' based on a similar format." Cannizzaro performed in a movie produced by Columbia University that won an award, "The Afterlife of Grandpa," 1988, P.J. Pesce, Gobbe A 'Dosta Productions, New York. See Ervell E. Menczes, "Grandpa's Afterlife Delights," *Indian Express*, Bombay, India, Monday, March 5, 1990, p. 4.

20   Cannizzaro performed with Claudio Villa at the Walker Theater in 1980.

21   Mimi Cecchini interviewed in Brooklyn, New York, August 4, 1988.

22   Norm N. Nite, *Rock On* (New York: Thomas Y. Crowell, (1974),p. 443.

23   *Billboard Music Week* (Vol. 74, December 22, 1962), p. 14.

24   June Bundy, Record Sleeve, "Lou Monte Sings For You," RCA Victor, 1958.

25   Press releases quoted by Monte's son, Ray, in an interview held on January 15, 1991.

26   *Italian Tribune News*, June 22, 1989, p. 25.

27   "Night Club Reviews," *Variety* (Volume 237, December 23, 1964, p. 46). Also mentioned in this review is that "there was a strong Calabrian air about the entire production."

28   In the community version, the punchline is: "Fa un cazza di'fridd!"

29   A second punchline is issued in the bit of Washington Crossing the Delaware: an Indian guide in the boat hearing Washington utter, "fa un'fridd, responds in Italian dialect: "Puro tu e' Italiano?" (You too are Italian?)

30   By Monte's taking a standard Italian-American name and attaching it to Revere's horse, he attempts to, once again, Italian-Americanize American history.

31   In the "Lazy Mary" song, part of the lyric states: "pesce fritte e baccala ... essa va, essa vien,' siempre la pompa mana tiene" (fried fish and cod ... he goes, he comes always the pump in his hand he holds). Monte's use of double entendre here sounds less offensive, as usual, in Italian.

32   Interview with Ray Allen, February 1, 1991.

33   In this song, Monte "plays" with the use of a provolone (an elongated cheese) as a phallic representation. This is borne out in the lyric that has the wife saying, "go find it (the provolone) or don't you dare come home..." "My wife doesn't want flowers..." "If I don't bring my big provolone back, she will want to fight." Once again, Monte is true to an Italian and Italian-American tradition that plays off the double meaning, but diminishes the coarseness by falling back upon the softer Italian expression.

34   Monte performed at some of the best known nightclubs of the 1940s, 1950s, and 1960s: The Town Casino in Buffalo, New York; The Town and Country in

Brooklyn, New York; The Boulevard in Rego Park, New York; and Sciolla's of Philadelphia, Pennsylvania.

35   For example, he performed on Burt Parks' NBC *Bandstand, The Veteran Administration Radio Shows,* and NBC *Monitor.*

36   *op. cit.,* interview, January 15, 1991.

37   *op. cit.,* interview, February 1, 1991.

38   Prima's popularity eclipsed that of Jimmy Savo. Jimmy Durante's fame, however, exceeded that of Prima's. Nevertheless Durante's theatrical Italianicity pales in comparison to Prima's.

39   David Rosenthal, "*New York Times* Supplementary Material from *New York Times* News Services and The Associated Press," August 26, 1978, p. 50.

40   Norm N. Nite, *op. cit.* p. 501.

41   "Obituary (L. Prima), *International Musician* (Volume 77, October, 1978, p. 16). The link to Armstrong is headlined in *Variety* (Volume 292, Wednesday, August 30, 1978, p. 73), which proclaims: "Bandleader Louis Prima dies at 67 in N.O.; Italo Satchmo." There were those (*op. cit.,* David Rosenthal, August 26, 1978) who equated his gravel-edged voice as a combination Louis Armstrong and Popeye.

42   Arnold Shaw, *The Street That Never Slept: New York's Fabled 52nd St.* (New York, Coward, McCann and Geoghegan, Inc.), p. 107.

43   "Final Bar," *Downbeat* (Volume 45, November 2, 1978, p. 14).

44   Gary Null and Carl Stone, *The Italian-Americans* (Harrisburg, Pennsylvania, Stackpole Books, 1976, p. 161.

45   According to *Life* (Volume 19, August 20, 1945, p. 114), when Prima sang such Italian dialect songs such as "Please No Squeeza The Banana" in the 1940s, they were not positively received (outside the Italian-American communities) until Italy joined the Allies.

46   *op. cit.,* David Rosenthal. See also "At Al Hirt's, N.O., *Variety* (Volume 259, June 3, 1970, p. 52), for a description of the Prima crew providing "a series of sights and sounds that assault the eyes and ears, tickle the ribs and delight the musical senses of the customers... The Witnesses sing along with Prima or yowl, kidding each other...."

47   Stated in an article in *International Musician, (op. cit.,* October, 1978, Prima received a gold record in 1969 for the music in the movie, *Jungle Book.*

48   Interview with Antoinette DeLuise Daurio, June 21, 1990.

49   John Stevens, "That Comedian is Nick DeLuise's Brother," *The Long-Islander,* Huntington, New York, December 24, 1981, p. 5.

50   *op. cit.,* interview, June 21, 1990.

51   Mary Ann Castronovo, "Cooking with Dom and Mom," *Attenzione,* May, 1984, pp. 30-32.

52   Dom DeLuise, *Eat This...It'll Make You Feel Better* (New York: Pocket Books, 1988), p. 218. Interwoven in and around the recipes are humorous vignettes about his Italian-American neighborhood, nostalgic memories of growing up and things Italian-American. For example, he refers to the Feast of St. Ant'eny (St. Anthony), the foods of the event, and uses of the dialect word marone (a derivation of Madonna).

53   *Ibid.* p. 86.

54   *Ibid.* p.14.

55   In this videotape, he can use more dialect words interspersed throughout,

have Italian music playing in the background, and employ body language and gestures typically associated with Italian-Americans.

56. As noted above, historically, in the southern Italian and Italian-American comedic performances, there were certain key Italian words, phrases, and expressions that were phallic symbols. *Cuccuzza* (long squash), thanks to its shape, was an oft-used substitute.

57   The Italian *braciola* (meat roll) is a standard bearer of the phallic symbol as is the *cetriolo* (cucumber).

58   According to *People's Weekly* (13: June, 16, 1980, p. 126) this work written by Anne Bancroft had DeLuise in mind from its inception.

59   Max Weber's theory of rationalization is discussed in Berger and Berger, *op. cit.*, 1972, pp. 194, 310-312.

60   Primeggia, S. and Varacalli, J.A., "Community and Identity in Italian-American Life," Michael W. Hughey and Arthur J. Vidich (eds) *The Ethnic Quest for Community: Searching for Roots in the Lonely Crowd* (Greenwich, Connecticut: JAI Press, forthcoming).

21

ITALIAN AMERICANS AND PROFESSIONAL BOXING IN CONNECTICUT, 1941-1951

RICHARD RENOFF

What are my reasons for studying Italian Americans in professional boxing in Connecticut during the 1940s?

The first concerns vertical mobility. Professional boxing has been considered a means of socio-economic mobility[1] — not only for a young man trying to get rich and retire, but also within boxing itself. In 1951 over 70 percent of the fight managers and promoters in Connecticut were Italian American.[2] This slightly surpassed the statistic for 1945 when the percentage was 67 percent[3] and probably was smaller than 1936 when a list of six promoters contained only one with an Italian surname.[4] A second reason is that since the great majority of Connecticut boxers were either African American or Italian American, I wanted to find out if there was a process of *ethnic succession* between these groups inside the sport. The third is sentimental. I attended my first professional bout in 1948 at Danbury's State Armory where the promoter was a popular war hero, Pete Montesi (1909-1969), whom my father knew fairly well. (By the way, children were permitted to attend fights in Connecticut, a practice then illegal in New York State.) Finally, Willie Pep was prominent during that era. Pep was an Italian American from Hartford who in 1948 was considered the second best boxer "pound for pound" in the world.

During the 1930s and earlier a number of Italian Americans gained national recognition as professional boxing champions and contenders, mostly but not exclusively in the lighter weight divisions. Connecticut itself had produced two world featherweight champions, one of whom, Chris (Bat) Battalino (1908-1977, born Crescenzcenzo Battagli), who reigned from 1927-1932, was an Italian American from Hartford.[5] In fact, Connecticut had been the site of several world featherweight championship bouts[6] and was considered to have a tradition of producing outstanding featherweights. In 1941 Connecticut's best known active boxers were heavyweight Nathan Mann (Natalino Menchetti, b. 1915 in New Haven),[7] who had suffered a technical knockout in three rounds from Joe Louis on February 22, 1938,[8] and featherweight Bobby "Poison" Ivy (Sebastian DeMauro, b. 1919 in Hartford), who ranked in the top ten of his division, having won several important bouts. In addition, Jimmy Leto (b. 1919 in Hartford) was a fading former welterweight contender; and the future welterweight champion, Marty Servo (1919-1969) of Schenectady, was sometimes listed as being adopted by Hartford. Willie Pep (Guglielmo Papaleo, b. 1922 in Middletown), state amateur flyweight champion in 1938 and state amateur bantamweight champion in 1939, began his professional career on July 3, 1940, at Hartford by decisioning James McGovern in four rounds.[10]

Prior to World War II, boxing in Connecticut was promoted not only in major population centers as Bridgeport, Hartford, and New Haven but matches also took place in smaller places as Ansonia, Danbury, Manchester, New Britain, Thompsonville, and Waterbury. Each of these towns had sizeable Italian settlements. As was the situation elsewhere, there were two boxing seasons, the indoor which ran from about late October to late April and the outdoor which commenced around Decoration Day and continued through late September. Professional boxers, whether "preliminary boys" or contenders, fought much more often than they do now; for example, Willie Pep fought twenty-two times during 1941 yet complained he wasn't getting enough work."11" Connecticut had two layers within the sport, "pro" and "semi-pro," the latter actually being state regulated amateur boxing for which the participants were openly paid about five dollars a bout for three two minute rounds.[12] This writer saw Chico Vejar ("Chico Avalos," b. 1931 in Stamford), who is half Italian[13] and later became a popular television fighter, box in Danbury as a "semi-pro" on December 28, 1948. Willie Pep remembered a semi-professional fight against Sugar Ray Robinson which took place in 1938,

> I was 105 pounds, amateur flyweight champion of Connecticut. I won the Connecticut state championship that year. And, at that time, Sugar Ray Robinson was boxing under the name of Ray Roberts. They used to come down from New York, the Salem Crescent A.C. was their club, and Ray was the Golden Gloves Open Champion of New York City, featherweight champ, at the time. He would come into Connecticut and box under the name of

Ray Roberts. So I boxed Ray a 3-round fight in Norwich. I lost the fight. I lost a 3-round decision to him, but I had no business being in the ring with him. He was a much better fighter than I was. I was a flyweight and he was a featherweight. [14]

For such contests Pep would earn about eight or nine dollars for three rounds.[15] This paper deals mostly with the professional level.

Professional and semi-professional boxing had been regulated since 1925 by one commissioner which replaced a looser system of eight commissioners and more autonomy for the various cities and towns which held boxing cards.[16] Thomas E. Donahue, Connecticut State Boxing Commissioner, claimed that during 1932 Connecticut had the highest *per capita* attendance at fights of any state.[17] Still, there were abuses, one egregious one was that there were occasionally great weight differences between even lighter division boxers.

This paper is divided thematically and chronologically. There are two main thematic divisions. The first, *The Ethnic Factor*, deals with the relationship between the Italian American and other ethnic groups within Connecticut boxing. The second, *Vertical Mobility*, examines the upward and downward mobility of Italian Americans within the sport. Each thematic division contains a study of four different years: First, the year 1941 representing a pre-war year; second, 1945 representing a war year, and 1949 and 1951 representing two post-war years. Finally, there is biographical information about three Italian American fighters, each of whom became a manager or referee and of two Italian American manager-promoters.

THE ETHNIC FACTOR
The Ethnic Distribution

The boxers were divided into three ethnic categories: Italian, black, and "other."[18] The 1941 percentage of Italian boxers (53 percent) is interesting because it differs considerably from national data reported by S. Kirson Weinberg and Henry Arond.[19] The data for 1941 Connecticut boxers are found in Table 1.

Weinberg and Arond, however, found Italians to be the numerically dominant group in 1936 and blacks in 1948. These writers maintained that Jews and Italians were never as dominant as the earlier Irish and later blacks were. They wrote, "The Irish were very much above others in 1909 and 1916 (about 40 percent of all boxers listed); in 1948 nearly half of all boxers listed were Negro. The Jews and Italians did not have so marked a predominance."[20]

The pattern of ethnic succession which Weinberg and Arond were to document some years later was occurring in Connecticut in 1941 but with a much greater proportion of Italians. Italians were probably displacing mainly Irish boxers although I found only scanty data on the 1930s and earlier.

By 1945 the percentage of Italian American boxers had declined to 31 percent while black boxers and those of other backgrounds had increased to 69 percent. These data are contained in Table 1. Data for 1951 showed a tiny increase over 1945 in the percentage of Italian American boxers. By then, they constituted 34 percent of the state's boxers. Table 1 contains a statistical comparison of the three groups for the year 1951.

TABLE 1 ETHNICITY OF CONNECTICUT BOXERS, 1941, 1945, 1951

	1941 N	1941 %	1945 N	1945 %	1951 N	1951 %
Italian	9	53	22	31	15	34
Black/ Other	8	47	49	69	29	66
Total	17	100	71	100	44	100

(Sources: Nat Fleischer, comp., Nat Fleisher's *All Time Ring Record Book* (New York: Ring Book Shop, 1942)and various reports in T*he Ring* and *Hartford Courant* for 1941. (Italian surnames were also an indicator.) Nat Fleischer, comp., *Ring Record Book* (New York: Ring Book Shop, 1945), pp. 15-470; *Hartford Courant*, 1945. Nat Fleischer, comp., *1952 Ring Record Book and Boxing Encyclopedia* (New York: Ring Book Shop, 1952), pp. 251-594.

Although one questionable indicator of being black — British surname was used — photographs and other sources show that seven of the fourteen men classed as black in 1951 were definitely African American. In any case, this indicates that the percentage of African American fighters was much smaller than the national data for 1948 compiled by Weinberg and Arond which showed nearly half of the boxers were Negro.[22] Furthermore, during the 1940s Connecticut probably had more Italian American boxers than Black boxers.

Connecticut's black population was proportionately small (2 percent in 1940) compared to the nation as a whole.[23] This could account for the small number of black boxers. Another hypothesis is that Italian American promoters preferred Italian participants because of their marketability or simply discriminated against blacks. There was a genre of Negro middle-weights who fought in Europe because they were too tough and not marketable enough to get lucrative matches in America. Boxing historian S. DeCristoforo has described a 1940s black middleweight from Pittsburgh,

Charley Burley, who competed with Jake LaMotta for the sobriquet "un-crowned champ," as being "too good for his own good."[24] LaMotta, who was not in favor with mob-dominated managers and promoters in New York, also had to seek work elsewhere. He related,

> Most of the guys that I fought then were colored and they weren't able to get many bouts. A colored fighter could starve in those days because if a manager had a white kid who seemed to have some potential he would baby him and try to build him up on stumblebums or used-up names who were just looking for a payday.
>
> In those early days, even though Louis and Robinson had broken through, just the fact that they were so great made everyone leery of colored fighters. And some of them were great, believe me. Many of those colored six-round fighters would have chased some high-priced top-notchers right out of the ring. A lot of them would have to fight with handcuffs on just to get a pay night here and there.
>
> Well, with me, there was nobody getting paid to fight with handcuffs on because my manager wasn't afraid of anybody. We'll fight them all, he used to say, and fight them all I did. When one of those bombers got a chance against a white kid on the square, they sure tried their best to show what they could do, because they all had the dream that maybe they'd get enough of an audience clamoring for them so that someday some promoter would give them the chance they deserved and they'd get a shot at the real money. And I mean they were hungry fighters. You would just about have to kill them before they'd give up. Well, I had something going for me, too, on that score — I was just as hungry as they were.[25]

The hypothesis that black boxers could not get steady work in Connecticut and settled elsewhere would be very difficult to investigate. Connecticut did have several excellent black fighters such as Lee Q. Murray and Eldridge Eatman of Norwalk, Ted Lowry of New Haven, and Georgie Dunn of Hartford. Jimmy Beau of South Norwalk, who became a "television fighter" during the early 1950s, was managed during the late 1940s by Pete Montesi of Danbury but later fought under the auspices of suspect men including Frankie Carbo, Truman Gibson, and James Norris.[26]

Why was there an even greater pecentage of Italian American boxers in Connecticut than in the nation as a whole? A simple explanation is the high percentage of Italian Americans in Connecticut's population. In 1930, Connecticut's "foreign stock" white population, from which contemporary boxers were in large part recruited, numbered 656,238. Of these, 140,139 or 21 percent were Italian Americans.[27] Still, this indicates that during the 1940s the proportion of Italian American boxers among other "white

216

ethnic" boxers was considerably greater than the Italian proportion of the Connecticut "foreign stock" population.

A second possibility is the presence of local role models who were successful boxers. Role emulation and cultural transmission theory can help explain the large number of Italian American professional baseball players who came from the San Francisco Bay area and the Italian American boxers from the Arthur Avenue, Tremont Avenue, and Gun Hill Road area of the Bronx. Detroit has long produced excellent African American boxers; for example Sugar Ray Robinson lived near and emulated future champion, Joe Louis.[28]

A related phenomenon is the presence of several family members in boxing. During the 1940s Connecticut produced the Compo brothers of New Haven, the Kogons of New Haven, the Holts of Danbury, the four Polowitzers of the Hartford area, and the Vendrillos of Manchester. Living in an environment where information about and techniques of boxing are discussed could provide an advantage for a younger brother wanting to succeed in the sport.[29] Also, a young man entering boxing is consistent with the thesis that Italian American young men left school or worked part-time in order to support their family's value placed upon home ownership.

The location of gyms and sports arenas could be significant. However, Waterbury historian of Italian Americans, Sando Bologna, informed me that Mara's Arena (owned by Rocco Mara) and Mulligan's Gym (owned by George Mulligan) were not in Italian neighborhoods nor[30] to my own recollection was a Danbury fight club, Seifert's Armory. Hartford's Charter Oak Gym was located on Main Street just outside Hartford's Italian "East Side" as was the Foot Guard Hall where many bouts were held in the early 1940s. The "East Side" was an institutionally complete Italian neighborhood.[31] The New Haven Arena was within walking distance of an Italian neighborhood.[32] There was no consistent pattern.

Neither the above hypotheses nor the speculations of Lawrence F. Pisani concerning the prestige of professional sports[33] nor Joseph Lopreato's contention that success in sports indicates an acceptance of Italian Americans on the part of the outer American society,[34] in my opinion, explain the *origin* of interest in boxing among Connecticut Italian Americans. Some speculations follow. One is that there were few successful Italian Americans in other sports in Connecticut. (Yet, there were Italian Americans on Yale's 1945 starting football team and Andy Robustelli (later a professional) starred for Arnold College.)[35] From 1938 to 1941 Connecticut's only professional baseball team was the Hartford Chiefs, (Class A) which in 1942 had one Italian American regular player.[36] Of course, the major league Braves, Dodgers, Giants, Red Sox, and Yankees did have several Italian American players. It should be stressed that Italian Americans entered boxing in great numbers about a decade *before* they entered professional baseball.[37]

217

A more plausible explanation is the geographic closeness of the major boxing centers of Boston, Holyoke, Providence, and New York, which produced several lightweight and featherweight champs and contenders, and stimulated an interest in boxing among Italian young men of the second generation. These boxers included: Mike Belloise, Chester Rico, Petey Scalzo and Phil Terranova of New York, and Sal Bartolo of Boston. "Bat" Battalino was a local role model because he retired in 1940 and then taught boxing in the Hartford area for many years.

Lawrence Pisani has correctly pointed out that "indigenous Italian games (*bocce, morra,* etc.) held little appeal for the second generation of Italians" and "most took quickly to American sports."[38] Boxing did not spread among Italian Americans from *Il Sud* to America; indeed almost all successful Italian European boxers have been from the North.[39] Success in boxing is an American phenomenon. It is consistent with Italian American individualism since it is not a team sport. As Glazer and Moynihan have stated,

> The set of qualities that seem to distinguish Italian Americans includes individuality, temperament, and ambition, all of which, however, are restricted by the culture and outlook of the family and neighborhood. This produces a tension, the most satisfying resolution of which is some form of worldly success that is admired by one's family and the friends of one's childhood.[40]

It is of interest that an Italian American golfer from Connecticut, Gene Sarazen, was U.S. Open winner in 1922 and 1932 during an era — well before Italian Americans were prominent in professional team sports.

Ethnic Rivalry

The ethnic background of a professional boxer can be an important advertising and promotional ploy. Such rivalries as Irish *vs* Italian, Italian *vs* Jewish, black *vs* white, Latin American *vs* North American, etc., have long been exploited. (However, during an earlier era, "mixed bouts" between a black and a white boxer were frequently discouraged.) For this reason the ethnic backgrounds were compiled of the principals in the feature bouts in Connecticut's two largest cities, Hartford and New Haven, during the years 1941, 1945, and 1949. These cities were thirteen and twenty-six percent Italian, respectively, according to 1930 U.S. Census data which enumerated both foreign born and second generation.[41] The different percentages of Italians afforded the opportunity to see if there were different patterns connected to the different sizes of the two Italian settlements. The ethnic background of each boxer was classified as either "Italian" (i.e., an American or foreign-born Italian) or "non-Italian." The bouts were then classified as to whether they involved two Italians, one Italian and one non-Italian, or two non-Italians. It was hypothesized that there would be proportionately more Italians utilized in New Haven due to the higher percentage of Italians there. Another hypothesis was that there might be different patterns of matching Italians with non-Italians in the two cities but what they would be I did not anticipate. (I am confident that I have a record of almost every feature bout held in these cities for those years.)

1941

The year 1941 was a good one for Connecticut Italian American boxers. Pep was working on his spectacular winning streak which Nat Fleischer was to call the greatest in the sport's recorded history.[42] Bobby Ivy fought for the featherweight title. Lou Viscusi, soon to become Pep's manager, promoted a card with three main events, one of which was won by former lightweight champion, Lou Ambers (Louis D'Ambrosio). The show, held on February 14 at Hartford's State Armory was a dismal economic failure.[43] Viscusi's own financial success was still to come.

TABLE 2 ETHNICITY OF OPPONENTS — NEW HAVEN AND HARTFORD, 1941

	New Haven		Hartford	
	N	%	N	%
Italian *vs* Italian	2	15	3	27
Italian *vs* non-Italian	8	62	8	73
Non-Italian *vs* non-Italian	3	23	0	0
Total	13	100	11	100

(Sources: *Hartford Courant* 1941; *The Ring* April 1941-March 1942)

During 1941, thirteen feature bouts were held in New Haven, all of them in the New Haven Arena. Of these, two (15 percent) involved two Italians, eight (62 percent) involved an Italian versus a non-Italian, and three (23 percent) involved two non-Italians. These statistics may be found in Table 2. Thus, of twenty-six participants, twelve (12) or 47 percent were Italian.

Eleven feature bouts were held at Hartford in either the State Armory, the Foot Guard Hall, or the Bulkeley Outdoor Stadium.[44] Of these, three (27 percent) involved two Italians, eight (73 percent) involved one Italian and one non-Italian and none (zero percent) involved two non-Italians. The data are contained in Table 2. Of 22 participants 14 or 64 percent were Italian.

1945

Willie Pep was inactive for about half of the year because he was drafted into the United States Army and began service on March 14.[45] He had served in the Navy but was given an honorable medical discharge in January, 1944. It seems that the draft authorities had received complaints about professional athletes who were deemed unfit for military service competing in contact sports. Perhaps, to quell these complaints and to set an example, Pep was the first professional athlete to be reinducted. Following his honorable discharge on October 2,[46] the champ resumed his boxing career on October 30 by outpointing Paulie Jackson in eight rounds at Hartford.

The only arena to operate regularly was the Hartford Auditorium. A jurisdictional dispute closed the New Haven Arena early in the year.[47] When boxing resumed, heavyweight Nate Mann was compiling a winning streak and high school student, featherweight Eddie Compo, who five years later would fight Willie Pep for the title in Waterbury, was boxing eight-rounders. As boxers were discharged from service, several clubs were resuming operations.

Fourteen main events were held at the New Haven Arena in 1945. Of these bouts three (21 percent) involved two Italians, nine (65 percent) involved an Italian and a non-Italian, and two (14 percent) were between two non-Italians. Thus, of 28 participants 15 (54 percent) were Italians. Table 3 shows the distribution of the ethnic backgrounds of the principals.

During the summer of 1945 the Hartford promoters introduced a policy of presenting three eight round co-features with no single main event. This policy ran from July 3 until August 21. For this reason three bouts on most cards were classified as main events. Sixty-nine main bouts were fought in Hartford. Of these none (zero percent) involved two Italians, 19 (28 percent) involved one Italian and one non-Italian and 50 (72 percent) involved two non-Italians. Thus, 19 or 13 percent of the 138 boxers were Italian. These statistics are presented in Table 3.

These data show a much smaller utilization of Italian boxers in Hartford than New Haven for 1945, as well as a much smaller utilization than for either city during 1941.

TABLE 3 ETHNICITY OF OPPONENTS — NEW HAVEN AND HARTFORD, 1945

	New Haven		Hartford	
	N	%	N	%
Italian *vs* Italian	3	21	0	0
Italian *vs* non-Italian	9	65	19	28
Non-Italian *vs* non-Italian	2	14	50	72
Total	14	100	69	100

(Sources: *Hartford Courant*, 1945; *The Ring*, April 1945-March 1946)

1949

Connecticut featherweights were again in the spotlight. Willie Pep regained the title with a masterful boxing exhibition against Sandy Saddler at Madison Square Garden on February 11. Pep then defended against New Haven's Eddie Compo on September 20 knocking him out in seven rounds at Waterbury's Municipal Stadium. Promoted by George Mulligan, the Waterbury program drew 10,722 spectators.[48]

Boxing's economics were changing. Future television attractions welterweights Sammy Giuliani and Chico Vejar of Stamford were starting their careers. Meanwhile, veteran New Haven heavyweight, Nate Mann, who had been knocked out by Joe Louis in 1938, retired during the previous year and was now a Connecticut referee.[49] Television would hurt the profits at the New Haven Arena where Mann had boxed so many times.

During 1949 there was a very different pattern in the utilization of Italian American boxers than in the earlier years. At the New Haven Arena of sixteen feature bouts none (zero percent) involved two Italians. Eight (50 percent) involved one Italian and one non-Italian while eight (50 percent) involved two non-Italians. These data are presented in Table 4. Thus, of thirty-two boxers eight or 25 percent were Italian.

Twenty-seven features took place in Hartford during 1949. Of these, two (7 percent) involved two Italians, nine (33 percent) involved an Italian *vs* a non-Italian and sixteen (59 percent) involved two non-Italians. These data are in Table 4. Thus, of 54 fighters, 24 percent were Italian.

TABLE 4 ETHNICITY OF OPPONENTS — NEW HAVEN AND HARTFORD, 1949

	New Haven		Hartford	
	N	%	N	%
Italian *vs* Italian	0	0	2	7
Italian *vs* non-Italian	8	50	9	33
Non-Italian *vs* non-Italian	8	50	16	59
Total	16	100	27	99*

*rounding error

(Sources: *Hartford Courant*, 1949; *The Ring*, April 1949-March 1950)

A steep decline in the percentage of Italian boxers used in New Haven took place from 1945 to 1949 as Table 5 indicates. This is due to an increase in Latin Americans, because of the 32 boxers used in New Haven during 1949 six or 19 percent percent were Hispanic. (Surprisingly, only one was Puerto Rican.) During 1945 only one Latin American had fought a New Haven main event. Ethnic succession was occurring again.

TABLE 5 PERCENTAGE OF ITALIAN BOXERS AMONG
ALL BOXERS, NEW HAVEN AND HARTFORD,
1941, 1945, 1949

	New Haven	Hartford
1941	47% (n=26)	65% (n=22)
1945	54% (n=28)	14% (n=138)
1949	25% (n=32)	24% (n=54)

A puzzle is the small number and percentage of Italian main event fighters used in Hartford in 1945 relative to New Haven. In my opinion, this was due to local favorites Bobby Ivy, Willie Pep, and Marty Servo being in military service while Eddie Compo and Nate Mann were active in New Haven. (Up and coming lightweight, Johnny Cesario of Hartford, did box four main events in Hartford and, while he was still in the army, welterweight Tony Falco of Middletown boxed two.)[50]

Most surprising was the somewhat higher participation of Italian boxers in Hartford during 1941 compared to New Haven although New Haven had a far higher percentage of Italian Americans within its population. Hartford's promoter was Lou Viscusi, an Italian American, while the bouts at the New Haven Arena were promoted by Nathan Podoloff, a Russian Jewish immigrant (and brother of famed, professional basketball entrepreneur, Maurice Podoloff). Viscusi managed several fighters at least three of whom, Bobby Ivy, Jimmy Leto, and Willie Papaleo were Italian American. While Viscusi probably did not discriminate in favor of Italian American boxers as Italians and there is no suggestion that Mr. Podoloff discriminated against them, I think Mr. Viscusi promoted the interests of his own proteges and several of them happened to be Italian American.

There was a large difference between New Haven and Hartford in the percentage of matches between Italians and non-Italians during 1945. The difference was thirty-seven percent greater for New Haven. Were ethnic rivalries unimportant to the Hartford promoter and fans? Was this difference due to the lack of availability of Italian American boxers from New York and other distant places due to wartime travel difficulties? The answers would be speculative.

VERTICAL MOBILITY
The Managers and Promoters

The *1952 Ring Record Book* listed nine Connecticut managers and five Connecticut promoters and matchmakers. Of the managers six or 67 percent were Italian American and of the promoters and matchmakers four or 80 percent were Italian Americans.[51] Combining the managers, promoters, and matchmakers produces a 71 percent figure.

In 1945, of six managers and promoters four (67 percent) were Italian American which is a similar figure.[52] However, in the *1937 Everlast Boxing Record* of 10 managers and promoters listed, only one (Al Mele) had an Italian surname although two others (Al Caroly and Al Blondey) had names that very possibly were originally Italian.[53] There was, therefore, by the mid-1940s a clear predominance of Italian Americans among the managers, matchmakers, and promoters. Whether most of these men were former boxers I could not determine, although two (Carmen Cook and Pete Montesi) definitely were and others likely were.

Why was there this predominance? I suggest that the Italian American value placed upon entrepreneurship helps explain it. Glazer and Moynihan have noted the entrepreneurial spirit among Italian Americans.[54] On the other hand the Irish Americans have been government workers.[55]

During the 1940s, Connecticut's State Boxing Commissioners were Frank Coskey (Irish) and Billy Prince (Italian). Irish names seemed to predominate among the referees, although popular Italian ex-boxers, Lou Bogash and Nate Mann, and the Jewish former featherweight champion, "Kid" Kaplan, were referees. The Irish dominance in these spheres is probably due to an earlier entry into boxing and Irish American political power.

I further suggest that the Italian American managers functioned as a middleman or a *padrone* for unsophisticated Italian American or African American young men, mediating with the promoters and even the larger society itself. Boxing, like the old *padrone* system, had its exploitive elements. Willie Pep has written that he signed a contract to give Viscusi one-half of his purses if he became champion.[56]

The Boxers

Not all boxers have become impoverished after their careers were over. "Bat" Battalino taught boxing and other aspects of physical education in a prep school.[57] Nathan Mann became a referee,[58] and Chico Vejar had earned enough by late in his career to contribute quite a sum to charities.[59] These men did attain respect and a degree of middle class respectability. Battalino did concede, however, that he squandered most of his ring earnings.[60] Political patronage would help a man become a referee. In Vejar's case, his manager was the well-known television and radio comentator, Steve Ellis, who financed the fighter's education at New York University's School of Drama.[61]

Pep did not have much of a career outside boxing. In 1948 his manager told a writer for *The Ring* that boxing was Pep's only job and his major interest.[62] Before hanging up his gloves, Pep was managing fighters. He later became a referee, a boxing inspector, sports columnist, and even received a political appointment as a tax collector.[63] Pep has admitted that he was a heavy gambler and that he spent his money freely on young ladies.[64] At present, he is active in the Veteran Boxers Association, helping former fighters like his friend and former foe, Sandy Saddler. He is also a big booster of The International Boxing Hall of Fame, located at Canastota, New York.[65] Needless to say, he has been inducted into it.

Summary

The proportion of Italian Americans among Connecticut's boxers during the 1940s exceeded the percentage for this group nationwide and exceeded the percentage for African Americans in Connecticut. This was not merely due to their numbers in the state's population. Some speculative reasons for this are the paucity of successful Italian Americans in team sports in Connecticut during the 1930s and Connecticut's geographic closeness to major boxing centers. The attraction of boxing for Italian American young men is consistent with Italian American individualism.

A majority of bouts held at the New Haven Arena involved an Italian versus a non-Italian (see tables above). This was not the case in Hartford. However, during 1941 Italian boxers were utilized there with the greatest frequency. Promoter Lou Viscusi also managed several Italian American boxers and seems to have used his own men in Hartford.

During the late 1940s and early 1950s Italian Americans dominated the managerial and promotional side of the sport in Connecticut. This is consistent with Italian American entrepreneurship and the manager's function as a type of padrone.

Unquestionably, the boxers were financially exploited. One Connecticut contender was said to be definitely controlled by organized criminals.[66] Nevertheless, the successful Italian American boxers gained respect and even political patronage generally unattainable to working class youth.

African Americans were to dominate the sport as boxers by the late 1950s. In 1958, only 15 percent of active fighters were Italian. Among promoters and managers Italian Americans were still the largest ethnic group (six of twelve).[67] Since only two were black, this group was not replacing Italians in this stratum, but ethnic succession had taken place among the boxers.

Social mobility of Italian American boxers might be studied by comparing their prestige to that of their parents. Pep's father could not read and write English, was a construction laborer, and both his mother and father were immigrants from the Syracuse,[68] Sicily, region. Vejar's non-Italian father was also an immigrant.[69] Boxing brought these men social honor their parents never attained.

During his middle age, Pep married the daughter of a college basketball coach,[70] Battalino bought a farm,[71] and Vejar, originally a high school dropout, went to college.[72] However, these are examples of very successful boxers.

ENDNOTES

1   S. Kirson Weinberg and Henry Arond, "The Occupational Culture of the Boxer," *American Journal of Sociology* 57 (1952): 460-69.

2   Nat Fleischer, comp., *1952 Ring Record Book and Boxing Encyclopedia* (New York: n.p. 1952) 782-89.

3   Nat Fleischer, comp., *Nat Fleischer's Ring Record Book*, 1946 (New York: The Ring Book Shop, 1946) 741-72.

4   Eddie Borden, ed., *Everlast Boxing Record* (New York: Borden, 1937) 168.

5   Battalino's given name is noted in Joseph William Carlevale, comp., *Who's Who Among Americans of Italian Descent* (New Haven: Carlevale, 1942) 36; for a boxing biography consult John D. McCallum, comp., *The Encyclopedia of World Boxing Champions Since 1882* (Radnor, Pa.: Chilton, 1975) 274-76; for an autobiographical statement read Peter Heller, comp., *In This Corner: Forty World Champions Tell Their Stories* (New York: Simon, 1973) 140-48. (The non-Italian champion was Louis "Kid" Kaplan who reigned from 1925 to 1927 and fought out of Meriden.

6   Terry McGovern vs. young Corbett, Hartford, 28 November 1901; "Bat" Battalino vs. Andre Routis, Hartford, 23 September 1929; Petey Scalzo *vs* Bobby Ivy, Hartford, 10 July 1940 for NBA title.

7   Carlevale 263.

8   *New York Times*, 23 February 1938: 24.

9   For Ivy's record see *Hartford Courant* 30, August 1942, part 4:4.

10   For Pep's record consult Burt Randolph Sugar, comp., *The Ring Record Book and Boxing Encyclopedia* (New York: Antheneum, 1981) 729-31.

11   *Hartford Courant*, 28 September 1941: 15.

12   Research notes compiled by Sando Bologna, September 1991.

13   Willie Pep with Robert Sacchi, *Willie Pep Remembers* (New York: Friday's Heroes, 1973) 126.

14   Heller 254.

15   Pep 4.

16   *New York Times*, 27 January 1925: *New York Times*, 28 May 1925: 16.

17   Thomas E. Donahue, "Connecticut," in John Romano, comp. *Everlast Boxing Record* (New York: n.p., 1932) 53.

18   Nat Fleischer (1887-1972), legendary boxing journalist and publisher of *The Ring* magazine and numerous books, attempted to compile complete records for every professional fighter in the world. His first record book was dated 1941. These books frequently but not consistently noted a boxer's ethnic background, using the popular term of the time, "nationality." The New York Public Library holds most annual editions, some frayed or mutilated, but others in reasonably good condition. Thus, I was able to study the 1941 edition which contains records which carry through the end of that year. Unfortunately, this edition was not as thoroughly compiled as the later ones so it listed only seventeen active Connecticut boxers, most of them main event fighters. Other sources of data on a boxer's ethnic background were newspaper accounts and photographs and those in *The Ring* magazine which sometimes described a man as "Greek," "Hebrew," "Negro," "Pole," etc.

19   Weinberg 460-69.

20   Weinberg 460.

21   Many Connecticut boxers had French surnames indicating French Cana-

dian ancestry. An example was light-heavyweight champion, Jack Delaney (1900-1948, reigned 1926-1927) who was born Ovila Chapdelaine in Saint Francois, Quebec, Delancy attended Bridgeport schools, married a Danbury woman, and had business interests in Waterbury. For his biography see McCallum 96-97.

22   Weinberg 460.

23   *Historical Statistics of the United States Colonial Times to 1970*, part 1 (Washington: GPO, 1975) 25.

24   S. DeCristofaro, *Boxing's Greatest Middleweights* (Rochester: DeCristofaro, 1982) 106.

25   Jake LaMotta with Joseph Carter and Peter Savage, *Raging Bull: My Story* (Englewood-Cliffs: Prentice, 1970) 87.

26   During 1951 and 1952 Beau boxed in televised matches sponsored by the International Boxing Club which these men administered. It was ruled a monopoly in 1957 by a U.S. District Court; see Jeffrey T. Sammons, *Beyond The Ring: The Role of Boxing in American Society* (Urbana: U of Illinois Press, 1988) 164.

27   U.S. Department of Commerce, Bureau of the Census, *Fifteenth Census of the United States: 1930 Population*, III, part 1 (Washington: GPO, 1932) 360.

28   Sugar Ray Robinson with Dave Anderson, *Sugar Ray* (New York: Viking, 1970) 14. Robert Carolla, who commented on this paper, noted the communal nature of the local support given to successful boxers.

29   On a similar theme see David N. Laband and Bernard F. Lente, "The Natural Choice," *Psychology Today*, August 1985: 37-38.

30   Bologna, telephone interview, September 1991.

31   See the description of the area as it was during the 1920s in the novel Armund T. Peretta, *Take a Number* (New York: Morrow, 1957) 9.

32   The New Haven Arena was a large building at 10-40 Grove Street "designed, built and managed" by the Podoloff brothers, Nathan, Maurice, and Jacob, impressarios who promoted basketball, boxing, hockey, and other events. It was constructed during the 1920s and closed in the early 1970s; Mary Stokes Ahern, "The Old Arena: Many Memories," *New Haven Register* 13 March 1990: 19-20. The Arena was located in the central business area within walking distance of the Italian "Wooster Square" neighborhood.

33   Lawrence F. Pisani, *The Italian in America* (New York: Exposition, 1957) 173-74. (Willie Pep emphasized that his father was an avid sports fan; Pep 5).

34   Joseph Lopreato, *Italian Americans* (New York: Random House 1970) 146-147.

35   *Hartford Courant* 23 July 1945, part 4:2. For Robustelli's biography, see Ronald L. Mendell and Timothy B. Prares, comp., (New Rochelle: Arlington, 1974) 293.

36   Tim Rogers, letter and enclosure to the author, 19 October 1991, National Baseball Library, Cooperstown. The player was Ray LaManno who was promoted to the Cincinnati Reds that summer.

37   See statistics compiled by Richard Renoff and Joseph A. Varacalli, "Italian Americans and Professional Baseball," *Nassau Review* 6.1 (1990):107-09.

38   Pisani 174.

39   An Italian boxer from Milan, Aldo Spoldi, boxed in New Haven on 21

January 1941; *Hartford Courant* 22 January 1941:11. His biography is *L'ultimo K.O.* (Milan:Duca, 1960) 170 pp.

40   Nathan Glazer and Daniel Patrick Moynihan, *Beyond the Melting Pot: The Negroes, Puerto Ricans, Jews, Italians and Irish of New York City* (Cambridge: MITP and Harvard UP, 1963) 194.

41   U.S. Department of Commerce, Bureau of the Census 360.

42   Quoted in David L. Porter, ed., *Biographical Dictionary of American Sports: Basketball and other Indoor Sports* (Westport, CT: Greenwood, 1989) 450.

43   *Hartford Courant* 15 February 1941:9.

44   The Armory was located in Bushnell Park. The Foot Guard Hall was an armory with an auditorium on 160 High Street. Bulkeley Stadium, home of the professional "Chiefs," class "A" affiliate of the Boston Bees [Braves] was named for Morgan G. Bulkeley (1837-1922), former Hartford mayor, Connecticut governor, and U.S. Senator.

45   *Danbury News-Times,* 17 January 1945:12.

46   *Hartford Courant,* 3 October 1945:13.

47   Jack Kane, "Connecticut Ring News," *The Ring,* July 1945: 44.

48   *New York Times,* 21 September 1949:43.

49   Don Hamill, "Connecticut Ring News," *The Ring,* November 1949:43.

50   Various issues of *Hartford Courant,* summer and autumn 1945.

51   Fleischer, 1952, 782-89.

52   Fleischer, 1946, 471-72.

53   *Everlast Boxing Record,* 1937, 168-188.

54   Glazer and Moynihan, 206-07.

55   Glazer and Moynihan, 260.

56   Pep 9; Pep states Viscusi was a good manager.

57   Carlevale, 36.

58   Hamill, 1949: 43.

59   Pep 2; 130-31.

60   See his obituary in *New York Times,* 27 July 1977 B2.

61   Pep, 127-29.

62   Daniel M. Daniel, "No Business for Pep After Fight Career," *The Ring,* June 1949:38; 47.

63   Porter, 450.

64   Pep, 181-82.

65   International Boxing Hall of Fame Museum, 1 Hall of Fame Drive, P.O. Box 425, Canastota, NY 13032.

66   Barney Nagler, *James Norris and the Decline of Boxing* (Indianapolis:Bobbs, 1964), 100.

67   Nat Fleischer's *Ring Record Book and Boxing Encyclopedia* (New York: Ring Book Shop, 1959) 477-801; 903-19.

68   Pep, 4.

69   Pep, 126-27.

70   Pep, 3.

71   *New York Times,* 27 July 1977: II, 2.

72   Pep, 127.

APPENDIX A

CONTRIBUTORS

Mario Aste, Chairman and Professor of Italian at Lowell University, received degrees from the Universities of Cagliari and Turin. His Masters and Ph.D. were attained at The Catholic University of America. He is a member of the Executive Council of the American Italian Historical Association and has published numerous articles and reviews on Sardinian and Italian literature, cultures and folkways. His published books include: La narrativa di Luigi Pirandello; Two Novels of Pirandello: An Essay; and Grazia Deledda: Ethnic Novelist.

Valentino J. Belfiglio, Professor of Government at Texas Women's University, and winner of the Guido Dorso Prize in Literature for The Italian Experience in Texas, has written four other books and hundreds of articles. He has been awarded the title of Cavaliere dell' Ordine al Merito della Repubblica Italiana for his extensive work in promoting Italian culture in the United States.

Flora Breidenbach is Assistant Professor of Spanish, Italian and Portuguese at College of DuPage, Glen Ellyn, Illinois. She received a master's degree from Middlebury College and a doctorate from the University of Illinois.

Mary Elizabeth Brown, who teaches history at Kutztown University in Pennsylvania, received the doctorate in United States history from Columbia University in 1987. She is the author of From Italian Villages to Greenwich Village: Our Lady of Pompei, 1892-1992 as well as several articles on Italian American Catholicism in New York City.

Fr. Secondo Casarotto, a Scalabrinian, was born and educated in Italy. He has attended Boston College, Northeastern University and McGill University while working with migrant communities in various countries. He has published several articles on migration and ethnicity including "Italian Protestants and the Catholic Church in Buffalo, New York," (1991); "100th Anniversary of St. Anthony's Church, Buffalo: Memories," Ed; "The Contribution of Italian Missionaries to the Evangelization and Civilization of North America'" (1992). He is currently writing a history of St. Anthony of Padua Church.

Frank J. Cavaioli, a former president of the American Italian Historical Association, now serves on its Executive Council. He is Professor Emeritus at State University of New York, College of Technology at Farmingdale, New York. He is a co-author of <u>The Ethnic Dimension in American Society</u> (1974) and <u>The Peripheral Americans</u> (1984). He has also authored many articles on aspects of the Italian American experience.

Rose DeAngelis is a doctoral candidate at Fordham University. She received her B.A. from Lehman College (CUNY) and her M.A. from Columbia University. She is currently teaching at Fordham College while writing her dissertation. Her research interests include modern British fiction, gender studies, and Italian and Italian-American fiction.

Mary Russo Demetrick, a poet, is Assistant Director of Publications of Syracuse University Library, Syracuse, New York. She has given public readings of her poetry and fiction, much of which focuses on the Italian ethnic experience and some of which has been published in the <u>Plainswoman;</u> <u>Lake Effect; la bella figura; Voices in Italian Americana; il viaggio della donne; Footwork:Paterson Literary Review</u>. She also received honorable mention in the 1992 Allen Ginsberg Poetry Awards for her poem "Ways of the Past."

Judith DeSena, who holds a doctorate from the Graduate Center of the City University of New York, is an Assistant Professor of Sociology at St. John's University in New York City. She is the author of <u>Protecting One's Turf: Social Strategies for Maintaining Urban Neighborhoods</u>, (1990). Her area of specialization is community studies with a particular interest in the activities of working class women in ethnic neighborhoods.

Cindy Hahamovitch received her Ph.D. from the University of North Carolina in 1992 and is currently assistant professor of United States history at York University in Toronto, Canada. Her dissertation topic dealt with migrant farm workers on the East Coast.

Robert B. Immordino is an Ethnic Consultant with extensive roots in the New Jersey labor movement. He was co-founder and served as president of the Central New Jersey Chapter of the American Italian Historical Association and has been instrumental in bringing to fruition the publication of a number of works dealing with Italian American life in New Jersey.

Louis E. Keefer, who received his MA from West Virginia University, spent thirty-five years as a transportation planner. He took up writing as a retirement hobby. His second book, <u>Italian Prisoners of War in America,</u>

1942-46: Captives Allies?, was published in 1992. He is currently at work on a book on the United States Army Ashford Hospital in World War II.

Jerome Krase, is Professor of Sociology at Brooklyn College of the City University of New York where he has served as Director of the Center For Italian American Studies. Currently Vice-President of the American Italian Historical Association, he authored Self and Community in the City, co-edited The Melting Pot and Beyond: Italian Americans in the Year 2,000, and recently co-authored Ethnicity and Machine Politics. He has written and lectured widely in ethnic and urban affairs and is pursuing photographic research into ethnic vernacular architecture.

Suzanne Krase is currently administrator at Brooklyn Hospital Center where she directs a community health outreach project. She received her R.N. diploma from Kings County Hospital Center School of Nursing, B.S. from St. Francis College, M.S. from Hunter College of the City University of New York, and her Ed. D. from Columbia University Teachers College. She has held academic positions at St. Joseph"s College School of General Studies and at Empire State College of the State University of New York. Her recent reports include "Breast Cancer in New York City," and "North Central Brooklyn: A Community Profile."

Salvatore J. LaGumina, a former president of the American Italian Historical Association, is Professor of History and Political Science at Nassau Community College, State University of New York. He is currently a member of the Executive Council of the AIHA. His most recent books are The Immigrants Speak: Italians Tell Their Story, (1979), From Steerage To Suburb: Long Island Italians, (1988), New York At Mid-Century: The Impellitteri Years, (1992). He has co-edited Italian Americans in Transition, (1990). He has authored a number of articles on aspects of the Italian American experience and lectured widely on the subject. His current interest is on Italian American politics.

Anthony L. LaRuffa is a Professor of Anthropology and Director of Italian American studies at Lehman College. He is editor of The Library of Anthropology and Co-Editor of Ethnic Groups, an international periodical of ethnic studies. His research interests include social and cultural anthropology, epistemology and ethnic studies. His most recent publications are Monte Carmelo: An Italian American Community in the Bronx and "Conflict and the Development of an Italian American enclave in the Bronx."

Chris Newton is a graduate of Tufts University currently writing his dissertation on the Italian American theater of Boston during the 1930's. He has a forthcoming article entitled "Commedia at Coney Island: Farfariello's Development of an American Form."

Salvatore Primeggia, of Adelphi University, received his Ph. D. from the New School for Social Research. As a sociologist, he has focused his research interests on various aspects of the Italian American experience. He co-authored with Pamela Primeggia, "Every Year, the Feast," and with Joseph A. Varacalli, "Southern Italian Comedy: Old World to the New." He has authored a chapter entitled "Community and Identity in Italian American Life," in a forthcoming volume on ethnic identity and is planning research on Italian Americans and religion.

Jon E. Purmont, Associate Professor of History at Southern Connecticut State University, received a B.S. degree from Georgetown University and an Ed. D. from Columbia University. He served as personal assistant to Governor Ella Grasso. He also has published reviews in History Teacher and articles in Social Studies and other historical publications. His current research interest is Ella Grasso and her impact on American politics.

Richard Renoff is Professor of Sociology at Nassau Community College, Garden City, State University of New York. He is co-author of "Baseball and Socioeconomic Mobility: An Irish-Italian Comparison," AIHA Proceedings, Vol. XVI. He has also co-written articles on Italian-Albanians in the AIHA Proceedings, Volumes XVIII and XIX and has an entry on Italian Albanians in the Dictionary of American Immigration History.

Joseph Salituro is the president of the Friends of Italian Culture in Kenosha, Wisconsin.

Joseph A. Varacalli, who received his Ph.D. from Rutgers University in 1980, is currently Associate Professor and Acting Chair of the Sociology Department of Nassau Community College, State University of New York. He has written extensively in the area of Italian American and American Catholic studies. A former member of the Executive Council of the AIH A, his published works include "Italian American Catholic: How Compatible?," Social Justice Review and "The Changing Nature of the 'Italian Problem' in the Catholic Church of the United States," in Faith and Reason.

Floyd Vivino is an Italian-American comic. He is the creator of the "Uncle Floyd Show" and the "Italian American Serenade."

APPENDIX B

AMERICAN ITALIAN HISTORICAL ASSOCIATION PROCEEDINGS SERIES

Vol. 1   ETHNICITY IN AMERICAN POLITICAL LIFE. Edited by Salvatore J. LaGumina. 1968. Pp. 36. Out of Print.

Vol. 2   THE ITALIAN AMERICAN NOVEL. Edited by John M. Cammet. 1969. Pp. 35.

Vol. 3   AN INQUIRY INTO ORGANIZED CRIME. Edited by Luciano Iorizzo. 1970. Pp. 87. Out of Print.

Vol. 4   POWER AND CLASS. Edited by Francis X. Femminella. 1971. Pp. 58.

Vol. 5   ITALIAN AMERICAN RADICALISM. Edited by Rudolph J. Vecoli. 1972. Pp. 80.

Vol. 6   THE RELIGIOUS EXPERIENCE OF ITALIAN AMERICANS. Edited by Silvano Tomasi. 1973. Pp. 133.

Vol. 7   THE INTERACTION OF ITALIANS AND JEWS IN AMERICA. Edited by Jean Scarpaci. 1974. Pp. 117.

Vol. 8   THE URBAN EXPERIENCE OF ITALIAN AMERICANS. Edited by Pat Gallo. 1975. Pp. 177.

Vol. 9   THE UNITED STATES AND ITALY: THE FIRST HUNDRED YEARS. Edited by Humbert Nelli. 1976. Pp. 242. Out of Print.

Vol. 10 THE ITALIAN AMERICAN WOMAN IN NORTH AMERICA. Edited by Betty Boyd Caroli, Robert F. Harney and Lydio F. Tomasi. 1977. Pp. 386.

Vol. 11 PANE E LAVORO: THE ITALIAN AMERICAN WORKING CLASS. Edited by George E. Pozzetta. 1978. Pp. 176.

Vol. 12 ITALIAN AMERICANS IN THE PROFESSIONS. Edited by Remigio U. Pane with an Introduction by Giovanni Schiavo. 1983. Pp. 290.

Vol. 13 THE FAMILY AND COMMUNITY LIFE OF ITALIAN AMERI-CANS. Edited by Richard N. Juliani. 1983. Pp. 191.

Vol. 14 ITALIAN IMMIGRANTS IN RURAL AND SMALL TOWN AMERICA. Edited by Rudolph J. Vecoli. 1987. Pp. 204.

Vol. 15 THE ITALIAN AMERICANS THROUGH THE GENERATIONS. Edited by Rocco Caporale. 1986. Pp. 263.

Vol. 16 THE INTERACTION OF ITALIANS AND IRISH IN THE UNITED STATES. Edited by Francis X. Femminella with an Introduction by Geno Baroni. 1985. Pp. 308.

Vol. 17 ITALIAN AMERICANS: SUPPORT AND STRUGGLE. Edited by Joseph L. Tropea, James E. Miller and Cheryl Beattie Repetti. 1986. Pp. 312.

Vol. 18 THE MELTING POT AND BEYOND: ITALIAN AMERICANS IN THE YEAR 2000. Edited by Jerome Krase and William Egelman. 1987. Pp. 318.

Vol. 19 ITALIAN AMERICANS: THE SEARCH FOR A USABLE PAST. Edited by Richard N. Juliani and Philip V. Cannistraro. 1989. Pp. 304.

Vol. 20 ITALIAN ETHNICS: THEIR LANGUAGES, LITERATURE AND LIFE. Edited by Dominic Candeloro, Fred Gardaphe and Paolo Giordano. 1990. Pp. 478.

Vol. 21 ITALIAN AMERICANS IN TRANSITION. Edited by Joseph Scelsa, Salvatore LaGumina and Lydio F. Tomasi. 1990. Pp. 283.

Vol. 22 ITALIAN AMERICANS CELEBRATE LIFE. Edited by Paola A. Sensi Isolani and Anthony J. Tamburri. 1990. Pp. 180.

Vol. 23 A CENTURY OF ITALIAN IMMIGRATION 1890-1990. Edited by Harral Landry. 1994. Pp. 250.

Vol. 24 ITALIAN AMERICANS AND THEIR PUBLIC AND PRIVATE LIFE. Edited by Frank J. Cavaioli, Angela Danzi and Salvatore J. LaGumina. 1993. Pp. 240.

To order copies or for information write to:
AMERICAN ITALIAN HISTORICAL ASSOCIATION
209 Flagg Place
Staten Island, New York 10304

INDEX